Adolescent Literacy in the Era of the Common Core

Adolescent Literacy in the Era of the Common Core

●　●　●　●　●　●　●

From Research into Practice

EDITED BY

JACY IPPOLITO, JOSHUA FAHEY LAWRENCE,
AND COLLEEN ZALLER

Harvard Education Press

Cambridge, Massachusetts

Library of Congress Control Number 2013941192

Paperback ISBN 978-1-61250-604-3
Library Edition ISBN 978-1-61250-605-0

Published by Harvard Education Press,
an imprint of the Harvard Education Publishing Group

Harvard Education Press
8 Story Street
Cambridge, MA 02138

Cover Design: Deborah Hodgdon
Cover Photo: © Larry Washburn/fstop/Corbis

The typefaces used in this book are Minion Pro for text and Castle for display.

To Victoria, Milo, Emily, Jim, and Elaine—for your
constant love, support, and humor.

JI

To Quanah—for keeping me current and humble.

JFL

To Nick—for being there.

CZ

In memory of Margaret Metzger,
beloved teacher, mentor, and friend.

Contents

CONTENTS

1

Bridging Content and Literacy Knowledge and Instruction

A Framework for Supporting Secondary Teachers and Students

JACY IPPOLITO AND JOSHUA FAHEY LAWRENCE

Educators and researchers in the United States have been concerned about middle and high school students' reading and writing skills for over one hundred years.[1] However, with the implementation of large-scale accountability policies focused on literacy achievement at the outset of the twenty-first century (e.g., No Child Left Behind), policymakers, researchers, and secondary teachers have renewed their efforts to meet adolescents' specific literacy needs. Adolescent literacy research has been bolstered by targeted federal grants over the past decade, and new areas of study have blossomed: studies of disciplinary literacy; students' in- and out-of-school literacies and use of technology; and the tailoring of strategy instruction to fit more specific disciplinary purposes.[2] Many of the lessons learned from this work are reflected in the Common Core State Standards for English Language Arts and Literacy in History/Social Studies, Science, and Technical Subjects, which emphasize that literacy instruction must be shared across content areas to promote college and career readiness.[3]

Historical Context

In order to understand what the new Common Core standards mean for literacy in math, science, social studies, and English classes in the second decade of the twenty-first century, we need to briefly consider how we arrived here. Until recently, U.S. educators and policymakers focused far more on how young children learned to read and write than on the challenges faced by older students. Forty years ago, literacy educators and researchers were embroiled in debates about how best to teach reading and writing in the earliest grades. The "reading wars" were rife with debate about the amount of explicit phonics and spelling instruction young students needed, versus

1

whole language methods centering around meaning, comprehension, and authentic literature. These debates resolved in the late 1980s and early 1990s with the complicated answer from researchers and teachers that young students flourish with a balanced approach including explicit instruction about words and word parts *as well as* instruction focused on comprehension with rich, authentic, engaging texts.[4] Having established a consensus that balanced literacy worked for young readers, researchers, educators, and policy makers shifted their attention to the literacy skills of older students.

A range of factors contributed to the increased attention on adolescent literacy outcomes in the United States, including (1) the relatively poor achievement scores of middle and high school students on international assessments, (2) wider acknowledgement of the high-level literacy and content skills needed in the twenty-first-century job market, and (3) the lackluster literacy skills of middle and high school students as evidenced by the *Nation's Report Card*, otherwise known as the National Assessment of Educational Progress.[5] These factors motivated organizations such as the Carnegie Corporation of New York and RAND to commission research and policy reviews detailing challenges faced by struggling adolescent readers.[6] The influence of these reports can be seen across the Common Core standards, which explicitly highlight the reading, writing, discussion, and presentation skills secondary students must learn in content-area classes in order to be successful in college and the workplace. These reports, changing standards, and aligned state and federal initiatives have spurred teachers, teacher educators, and educational leaders to seek information about how to support adolescents' literacy achievement. The questions du jour have become: Why is success with reading and writing in the earliest grades not translating to improved academic achievement at secondary levels? How can we improve literacy for content-area learning in middle and high schools?

In response, the field of adolescent literacy has expanded rapidly over the past two decades, growing from a once-marginal area of research and practice to one of the hottest topics in research and publishing sectors. A quick search on Amazon.com, using the keyword search string "adolescent literacy," reveals less than a handful of books published on the topic before 1990, as compared to more than a hundred published over the next dozen years. Such rapid growth in the field is exciting, but also a bit daunting for teachers looking for ways to meet their students' needs. Where does one start?

Finding a Signal in the Noise: Why This Book and Why Now?

Given all of the attention being paid to adolescent literacy, how might one more book on the topic make a difference? This book is designed to be a signal in the noise, a stand-alone resource for at least two primary audiences: (1) the next generation of content-area teachers and their university-level instructors and (2) current teachers and leaders adopting and adapting the Common Core standards. Each of these groups, but particularly future secondary teachers, may be overwhelmed rather than comforted by the abundance of adolescent literacy resources currently available. This volume balances both a practical overview of the field of adolescent literacy (for readers new to the field, perhaps in a teacher preparation program) and a targeted investigation of the highest-leverage practices and frameworks available (for current teachers seeking to meet the demands of the Common Core standards).

As literacy researchers who prepare future teachers and work alongside current teachers, we have found that the sudden glut of information about adolescent literacy (not all of it research-based or practical) can be confusing and overwhelming for teachers. Thus, this book has been designed to introduce and review six domains that we have found to have the most leverage in shifting the thinking and practices of the teachers and teacher-candidates in schools we support. The bulk of this book is divided into six pairs of chapters, with each domain first introduced and discussed by researchers who present results from recent studies and provide useful frameworks for thinking about classroom implications. Then teachers, teacher educators, and instructional coaches illustrate each domain with examples and narratives of instructional strategies and approaches from their own experience working in schools and districts. The six essential domains include:

- Disciplinary literacy
- Vocabulary
- Discussion
- Digital literacy
- Multiple texts
- Writing-to-learn

We are well aware that there are many more domains that influence the success of all adolescent learners. However, this book is intended to provide a targeted look at powerful instructional approaches that make sense to secondary content-area teachers and leaders. If all content-area teachers were to carefully consider and apply the ideas within these six domains, they would increase their students' access to and use of sophisticated content-area texts. We have taken the recommendations of the Common Core standards seriously and have responded by narrowing our own focus and goals to those that we have seen make the biggest difference both immediately and over time in middle and high schools. Before describing these six domains further, however, we would like to explain how we have come to think about our own work in the field of adolescent literacy and why we believe these domains are critical.

Who Are We, and How Do We Think About Our Work with Teachers and Students?

Over the past decade, we have worked with hundreds of middle and high school educators across the United States. While there have been many differences between teachers' and administrators' beliefs and practices, one idea has been widely shared— the myth that "every teacher is a teacher of reading." This simple phrase has cropped up time and time again across conversations, and while at first it felt comforting and indicative of teachers' and administrators' interest in helping students become proficient readers and writers, over time this sentiment became worrisome. To explain, let us share a quick story about our own growing unease with the idea.

Dispelling the Myth That "Every Teacher Is a Teacher of Reading"

When we began our teaching careers (in the various roles of reading specialist, drama teacher, technology teacher, and ultimately literacy coach), it was clear to both of us that we were indeed *reading teachers*—we had been explicitly hired to increase the reading achievement of struggling readers in our respective middle schools. We tackled that task with passion and with what we saw as a necessary focus on classic young adult literature, short stories, poems, and the other genres typically associated with English language arts. After all, we thought at the time, *If we are going to help our teens become better readers, shouldn't we help them get better at reading books like* The Outsiders, Holes, The Giver, The Old Man and the Sea, To Kill a Mockingbird, *and all the classic texts that will be gateways to high school and college-level reading?* We went about our work diligently, and while our students did improve in specific ELA-related reading and writing tasks, we did not examine the reading, writing, and literacy tasks of our students beyond our own classrooms.

It was not until we were asked by our respective school leaders to adopt coaching roles focused on working with adult colleagues across content areas that we began talking with history, math, and science teachers about the reading, writing, and communication demands of their content areas in a serious way. In retrospect, it is not surprising that while our colleagues greatly appreciated our efforts, they were skeptical about our abilities to help them improve content learning in their disciplines. Our colleagues liked us a great deal and were very kind as they politely pointed out that our efforts to coach them to be better reading teachers simply missed the mark. They didn't want to be become better *reading* teachers; they wanted to become better teachers of historical, mathematical, or scientific ways of seeing, interpreting, and interacting with the world. For example, in Josh's school, even though Juan, a struggling eighth-grader, was able to finish reading *Maniac McGee* with additional comprehension and vocabulary support (it was the first book he admitted to actually reading and completing since second grade), this accomplishment did not naturally or completely translate into success in his other content-area classes.[7] In fact, Juan's math and science teachers saw little to no change in Juan's skills and achievement in their classes.

After engaging in several well-intentioned, flawed initiatives where we attempted to coach content-area teachers on how to adopt reading and writing workshop structures that mimicked traditional ELA structures and genres, we realized that there were multiple interpretations of the notion that "every teacher is a teacher of reading." Some of these interpretations seemed to be doing more harm than good. One of the key confusions was what we meant by "reading." As literacy researchers focused on learning outcomes for older learners, we now think about reading as building conceptual knowledge in the disciplines; making inferences, building content-general and content-specific vocabulary; and interpreting tables, graphs, and maps. Content-area teachers with whom we work are often happy to be "reading teachers" when this larger meaning is adopted. However, when we started this work, we were much more likely to think about reading as comparing and contrasting, predicting, and even decoding words. General reading skills are certainly important, but often less aligned to the core commitments of our content-area colleagues.

Jacy remembers one conversation with an eighth-grade math colleague (who had reluctantly agreed to take on "literacy" work in his classes) that influenced his thinking about these issues. In a moment of exasperation during a grade-level team meeting, the beleaguered teacher asked Jacy, "What exactly are these *genres* that you keep talking about? I don't know what that means, and I really have no idea why I would want to teach poetry, memoirs, etc. How is that going to help our students get better at *math*?" Such honest questions and comments were jolting and necessary. How *would* asking a math teacher to adopt writing workshop structures and teach about memoirs help students get better at math? Put simply, it won't. The myth that every teacher would willingly and easily become a teacher of reading was failing, but admittedly, we did not know how to replace it. We knew that the reading and writing demands of each content area would continue to be a challenge for our students unless explicitly addressed, but how might we successfully connect literacy and content goals?

Learning the Language of Disciplinary Literacy

As reading teachers and coaches, we had been following the nation down a misleading path, preaching to our content-area colleagues that if we all spent more time teaching reading and writing, our students' achievement would increase across the board. Unfortunately, lackluster student-achievement data, after decades of efforts to stitch together literacy and content instruction in secondary classrooms, has revealed a much more complicated picture. Many of the efforts to merge content and literacy instruction have had little success for a variety of reasons—well-intentioned but misguided attempts to export ELA strategies wholesale into history, math, and science classrooms; the fragmented departmental structure of middle and high schools that impedes cross-content collaboration; secondary teacher preparation privileging content knowledge over literacy or pedagogical knowledge, to name just a few.[8] Yet discouraging trends on national and international literacy, history, math, and science assessments fueled what researchers had already begun to talk about as an adolescent literacy "crisis."[9] The language of crisis acknowledged that while the United States had seen increased student achievement in elementary school students' reading skills, our teenagers were not achieving at similar levels. It was time for a frame shift, for conceiving of and responding to adolescents' academic needs in a more complex way.

Another conversation that changed the way Jacy thought about his work came in the middle of his second year working as an eighth-grade literacy coach. He began the year by talking with content-area colleagues about their goals, the big ideas of their disciplines, and the ways they wanted students to think about the content of their classes. Jacy's content-area colleagues were frustrated that their students didn't seem to comprehend their textbooks as well as expected, and they had a hard time synthesizing and remembering essential concepts. These teachers noted that student writing often did not reflect the teaching and learning that seemed evident in class discussions. Academic and content-specific vocabulary seemed to be lacking. While quite aware of the deficits, the content-area teachers were equally adamant that adopting ELA practices across their disciplines was not the answer.

At last, a patient and savvy colleague (a history teacher) sat down with Jacy and read aloud a chapter in a world history textbook to help them both better understand the challenges the students were facing. As they read the text together, the teacher talked about what he saw as important in the text and what he saw as extraneous, confusing, or distracting. He talked about the importance of understanding causal chains of events, noting important political figures and their differing perspectives, creating a mental time line and placing events on that time line, and connecting major historical events with current events. From this conversation, the pair began to collaboratively design reading guides to help students navigate more effectively through the textbook.

This initial work quickly expanded to include structured and differentiated homework assignments focused on how to read, interpret, and synthesize information like a historian. They developed structured note-taking guides that first focused students' attention on big ideas and causal connections and then pushed students to draw larger connections across time and to make informed arguments using textual evidence. Over the year, they expanded their efforts, bringing multiple primary and secondary sources into the classroom during specific units to push students to consider the intertextuality that historians constantly manage. They taught short lists of general academic words (e.g., *however* and *interpret*) found across all content-area texts, and discipline-specific words (e.g., *insurgency* and *oligarchy*) that historians would deem particularly important. Students were taught to make observations and inferences from political cartoons and political media events, then incorporate various media into their own PowerPoint presentations about major political figures and events. A few critical discussion structures were taught (e.g., team debates, four-corner opinion-building sessions) that helped students clarify their thinking and practice argumentation before writing.

At the end of the year, Jacy and the history teacher believed that the way they had adopted and adapted core literacy skills and strategies (i.e., focusing on comprehension, vocabulary, discussion, writing, multiple texts, nontraditional texts, and digital media) resulted in improved achievement in history coursework. They agreed that this success was due to the fact that they started and ended with history goals in mind. The literacy tools and strategies were carefully adapted to always serve content-area goals, and if a particular tool or strategy detracted from better historical reading, writing, or thinking, it was abandoned. As a result, both students and teachers learned a great deal about how to read, write, and think like historians—the fundamental goal of history classes at the secondary level. This experience radically changed the way that Jacy and his colleagues thought about connecting content and literacy instructional goals.

Little did Jacy realize at the time that his collaborations fit neatly into the *disciplinary literacy* framework that was gaining nationwide attention. Shanahan and Shanahan had popularized the notion of disciplinary literacy by clearly describing a three-tier framework for considering the development of adolescents' high-level literacy skills.[10] The framework starts with *basic literacy*—supporting students in the earliest grades in acquiring the fundamentals of reading processes (e.g., decoding words, recognizing high-frequency words, achieving basic comprehension, etc.). As students enter late elementary and middle school, a focus on *intermediate literacy* becomes important, with increased attention to comprehension, fluency, and expanding vocabularies. Finally, in middle and high school, attention needs to shift to *disciplinary literacy*, where teachers and students must explicitly uncover and focus on the literacy skills particular to each content area, or *discipline*, in order for students to successfully navigate the reading, writing, and communication demands needed to learn and flexibly use the content embedded in chemistry, physics, world history, or calculus classes. As Shanahan and Shanahan write, "A high school student who can do a reasonably good job of reading a story in an English class might not be able to make much sense of biology or algebra books, and vice versa."[11] Just as Jacy had determined through trial and error, collaboration, and frustration, if we wanted to effectively address the literacy demands of the different content areas, we needed to shift our frame of reference from *every teacher being a reading teacher* to every teacher *focusing on the disciplinary literacy demands of his or her content area*.

Working together in university and professional development settings, we consistently find that our content-area colleagues share our concerns about students' abilities to access information in their texts and effectively communicate the significant ideas of each discipline both orally and in writing. Now, we do not address these concerns by pressuring teachers across content areas to adopt ELA practices. Instead, we begin with interviews and group discussions of content-area goals, habits of mind, and ways of working. Following some of the methods used in Shanahan and Shanahan's study of connections between ways that professional scientists, mathematicians, and historians read and ways that high school teachers and literacy specialists read, we ask teachers to take note of and then model for students how they attend to, read, and respond to discipline-specific texts. After years of doing this work with groups of teachers across many schools and districts, we have found that there seem to be a handful of literacy-related domains of instructional planning and practice that make sense for content-area teachers to consider as they strive to make these content-area goals, habits of mind, and ways of working salient for students.

Forming a Bridge Between Content and Literacy Knowledge and Instruction

We see the six domains at the heart of this book as forming a bridge between content and literacy knowledge and instruction as well as between teacher practice and student learning of discipline-specific skills. The six domains could be (and have been, across various research- and practice-based books and articles) connected to a host of student skills in secondary classrooms. Without providing an exhaustive list, we emphasize a few of these connections below (see figure 1.1).

- Teachers' focus on *disciplinary literacy* encourages students' awareness of the different demands of discipline-specific texts, adoption of critical thinking skills within and across domains, and adoption of habits of mind and ways of working within and across disciplines.
- Teachers' focus on *vocabulary* encourages students' awareness of and fluency with academic and workplace language, strengthens reading comprehension within and across disciplines, and builds oral language proficiency.
- Teachers' focus on *discussion* encourages students' oral language skills, promotes evidence-based argumentation and rhetorical skills, supports vocabulary growth, and serves as a bridge between reading and writing.
- Teachers' focus on *digital literacy* encourages students' abilities to code-switch within and across content areas and domains, fluency with online and offline texts,

FIGURE 1.1

Bridging content and literacy knowledge and instruction

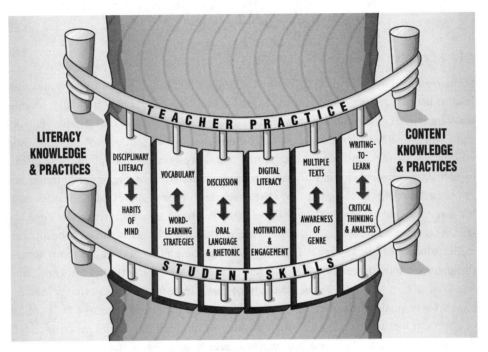

and understanding and use of the connections between formal academic and informal ways of talking about and understanding the world.

- Teachers' focus on *multiple texts* encourages students' awareness of and facility with content across a wide range of genres and promotes the adoption and practice of complex synthesis and analysis skills.
- Teachers' focus on *writing-to-learn* encourages students' adoption of workplace writing skills, use of writing to clarify thinking and make sense of complex texts, and ability to make evidence-based arguments when translating language/thinking into writing.

The pairs of chapters presented in this book introduce and illustrate these domains—presenting research- and then practice-based evidence for why secondary teachers must attend to these areas. We believe that these pairs of chapters make a convincing case that secondary content-area teachers who focus on these six domains will not only meet the demands of the Common Core standards, but they will also further content-area goals and increase students' literacy achievement. While some of the connections between teacher practices and resulting student skills in these domains are more clearly documented by rigorous research than others, we believe the examples presented in this book present new evidence, build on existing compelling data and cases, and offer new directions for research and practice for further exploration.

A Few Caveats

Some readers may be reading this book seeking a silver bullet—a solution to the adolescent literacy crisis never before seen or explored. Other readers may look in this book for laundry lists of just-discovered strategies, tips, and tricks that if delivered just right will boost achievement across all content areas for all students. Alas, this book will deliver neither, and while readers may wisely respond, "Well, of course I didn't expect simple answers or lists of brand-new strategies!" it is our experience that even in the savviest of schools and among the shrewdest of teaching teams, there lurks the hidden hope that somehow there will be a single, simple answer. We acknowledge up front that from our research and experience working in schools we believe the answer to the adolescent literacy crisis is not something completely new or different, something completely unheard of that will leave readers scratching their heads and saying, "*Discussion*—by Jove, I never thought of that!" Instead, we believe that achieving content-area goals while attending to adolescents' literacy needs means a redoubling of efforts to focus attention on a small number of research-based and practice-tested domains (such as the six we have selected) and then incrementally, systematically, and efficiently introducing and refining practices in those areas. There are dozens of books that present lists of classroom strategies, as well as books that compile the latest and most rigorous research on adolescent literacy achievement (we reference the best from both categories throughout this volume); however, in this book our specific aim is to help readers focus on a small set of domains that have the possibility to be quickly adopted and easily adapted by cross-content-area teams of teachers.

A second caveat is about adaptation. In our work with teachers, both future and current, we have noticed a deep hunger for *strategies* and *programs*. While there can be great confusion about what teachers, researchers, and students mean when they use these terms, we often hear requests for "something I can use in my classroom tomorrow."[12] We completely understand this desire, and we have felt it numerous times ourselves in our own classes. This book does showcase particular strategies and programs—examples, protocols, descriptions, and suggestions for teacher practice that might be implemented immediately. However (and here is the caveat), we present strategies and programs in this book not as infallible tactics that will work across all content areas, for all purposes, for all students. They must be understood as tools for particular content-area purposes and for particular groups of students. Ultimately, we pair research- and practice-focused chapters because we believe that the best strategies and programs are those designed by well-informed teachers who have a deep understanding of their content-area concepts and goals and the literacy demands required in their disciplines. We try to balance the desire for lists and recommendations with the need to provide larger frameworks for thinking about the ways literacy practices can serve content-area goals. Everything in this book should be read with an eye toward how, why, and when particular ideas should be adopted and adapted, always in service of content goals.

A third and final caveat—while the core of this book focuses on the six domains introduced above, we acknowledge that success with these domains also requires some attention to larger issues of adult learning and professional development in schools. Without attention to departmental structures, how teams learn together, and how leaders shape reform efforts, readers may have little influence on instructional practices beyond their own classroom. We have learned from working in and consulting with schools that when teachers adopt and adapt practices in isolation, larger gains in student achievement do not occur. *Collective efficacy*, or a group of teachers' collective belief in their own and their colleagues' abilities to effectively teach students, has been strongly linked to actual increases in student achievement.[13] It makes sense that teachers who believe their colleagues can improve student learning might also be working closely with those same colleagues, learning from them and reflecting on shared practices. Those schools that invest in collaborative, reflective teacher teams seem more able to shift instructional tactics as standards and student populations change.

This is why we have chosen to conclude this book with two chapters aimed at helping readers consider how they might effectively study and experiment with the six domains as part of professional learning communities focused on meeting Common Core standards. These chapters are only small windows into much broader disciplines focused on professional learning, yet we believe it is important to end the book by intentionally discussing how literacy-related work might be best undertaken as part of collaborative, reflective, intentional professional communities.

An End and a Beginning

Ultimately, we agree with, and continually refer colleagues to, the RAND Reading Study Group's 2002 definition of reading comprehension as the interaction of a particular reader with a particular text and activity within a larger sociocultural context.[14] Given this definition, we encourage readers to consider their own particular purposes as they read and use this book to support teaching and learning in individual classrooms and schools. Although we feel there is coherence and logic to the order of the chapters as we have presented them, they do not need to be read sequentially.

Readers might dive into the topic they are most interested in, and start with either the research or practice chapters. Also, many online resources referenced throughout the book can be easily accessed through our support website: www.adlitpd.org/book; these include links, templates, protocols, webinars, and presentations created by and suggested by our authors. We are proud of the expert researchers and practitioners whose work we have brought together in this volume, and while their views are often aligned, we also acknowledge that reasonable experts sometimes differ in their interpretations of research, policy, and practice. Similarly, we encourage readers of this volume to always evaluate the research and suggestions presented here (and beyond) using professional experience and judgment. Test and reflect on suggestions with trusted colleagues in schools. Many teachers in our extended network have done so, and we thank them for their collaboration, feedback, and encouragement as we work together to support adolescent reading, content learning, and disciplinary literacy.

Additional Resources

Buehl, Doug. *Developing Readers in the Academic Disciplines*. Newark, DE: International Reading Association, 2011.

Christenbury, Leila, Randy Bomer, and Peter Smagorinsky. *Handbook of Adolescent Literacy Research*. New York: Guilford Press, 2009.

Snow, Catherine E., Peg Griffin, and M. Susan Burns. *Knowledge to Support the Teaching of Reading: Preparing Teaching for a Changing World*. San Francisco: Jossey-Bass, 2005.

❷

Research in Disciplinary Literacy

Challenges and Instructional Opportunities
in Teaching Disciplinary Texts

**EMILY PHILLIPS GALLOWAY, JOSHUA FAHEY LAWRENCE,
AND ELIZABETH BIRR MOJE**

> Some things are due to nature; for others there are other causes. Of the former
> sort are animals and their parts, plants, and simple bodies like earth, fire, air,
> and water—for we say that these and things like them are due to nature.
> —Aristotle, *Physics*

We open this chapter with a quote from Aristotle to remind ourselves of the kinds of challenges that face any reader approaching a text that is bound in disciplinary assumptions.[1] In trying to understand this quote, readers are challenged on many levels. First, words such as *nature* and *causes* have particular meanings within the discipline of Aristotelian science that some readers may not fully grasp. Similarly, some readers may recall that Aristotle developed a theory about the relationships between the four elements (earth, fire, air, and water), but they may not remember how this theory explained basic physical processes such as chemical change. Thus, while in some sense these readers may comprehend this quote, in another sense it is incomprehensible.

Fundamentally, most readers don't understand the purpose of this text, the alternatives that Aristotle was arguing against, or how someone might have applied these principles to make sense of the world (all results of the socio-political-historical context in which Aristotle was writing). In sum, disciplinary texts, as tangible manifestations of how knowledge is constructed and how language is used by disciplinary "insiders," present challenges to readers who are often "outsiders."[2]

Of course, the specialized langauge found in the writing of every discipline evolved not for the purpose of excluding novices, but rather to support concise and precise communication between members of each discipline.[3] In addition to shared language, members of a discipline also share knowledge of an existing network of theories and ideas (background knowledge) to which all new ideas must be linked.[4] However, while the norms of disciplinary writing provide a shorthand for members, they pose challenges to newcomers. In particular, adolescent students face the daily difficulty of traversing disciplinary boundaries as they read in math, science, English, and social studies.

So, what can be done to support students in better comprehending disciplinary texts? In this chapter, we suggest the use of *disciplinary literacy pedagogy*, which makes use of texts written for both expert and novice audiences, as one method of bringing outsiders into the language of the disciplines. Our intention is not to suggest that teaching language is the end goal of disciplinary instruction. Rather, as specified in the Common Core State Standards, the goal is to begin to apprentice students into understanding disciplinary approaches to knowledge by making transparent the practices and habits of mind (realized through language) that underlie the writing and construction of content-area texts.[5] The goal is not necessarily to produce disciplinary experts, but rather to develop the capacities of young people so that they are ready to engage in college-level work in the disciplines. Further, we believe that as the language of each content area is demystified, students are provided with the resources to express their opinions, ideas, and understandings as well as master disciplinary content when reading in the content-area classroom.[6]

In this chapter, we first highlight the importance of disciplinary literacy instruction and explore both the unique and shared challenges that disciplinary texts present for novice readers. Next, we discuss in greater detail our vision for using expert texts with novice readers and, by examining texts written by experts across the disciplines, illustrate how disciplinary habits of mind are realized through language. Finally, we connect these recommendations to the classroom by identifying instructional opportunities for this brand of disciplinary instruction in one middle school.

Teaching Disciplinary Texts: Common and Unique Challenges

While teaching disciplinary literacy requires a multifaceted pedagogy that engages students in text-based discussion, hands-on inquiry activities, and disciplinary writing, this chapter seeks to highlight the centrality of using challenging, disciplinary texts with adolescent readers. For educators to effectively teach complex texts, they must anticipate the challenges that these texts present. Below, we highlight both common and unique aspects of disciplinary texts that pose particular difficulty to novices.

Disciplinary Language: Common and Unique Challenges

Common Challenges Across Content Areas. In this chapter, we define written language broadly to refer not only to words and phrases, but also to ways of organizing and structuring texts. Even though this chapter illuminates the instructional value of teaching linguistic elements that are unique to each content area or applied differently across content areas, we also believe that there are some common challenges posed by the language used in all academic texts. In fact, recent research suggests that there is a core set of written language features that are used to communicate in all disciplines that appear to contribute to text comprehension difficulty for adolescent readers.[7] For example, phrases that connect ideas in all academic texts (however, as a result, first, then) are important to teach because they often are key to understanding how ideas in a text relate.[8] Unlike discipline-specific language, which is often explicitly taught to students and highlighted in textbooks, cross-disciplinary features receive little instructional attention.[9] Given this, we suggest that disciplinary literacy instruction should focus on teaching both discipline-specific and general academic language because both differ from the spoken language that is used to communicate orally with friends and family and present significant barriers to text comprehension for students.[10] In fact, even students who communicate proficiently in conversational contexts may lack the language skills to read and write in disciplinary classrooms.[11]

Unique Challenges in Each Content Area. In addition to the common challenge across content areas posed by academic language, each subject area/discipline uses certain vocabulary, phrases, and ways of writing sentences that present additional, unique challenges to readers. These ways of using language are not arbitrary. For members of a discipline, these elements best support the communication of disciplinary content and ideas.[12] These agreed-on methods of communicating are dynamic and open to change as disciplinary knowledge and practice shifts.[13] However, grasping how familiar language is repurposed for disciplinary communication is a challenge for many novice readers. For example, everyday words can be used in discipline-specific ways (e.g., variable, source, or method), and general academic language can have particular ascribed meanings in the texts of each discipline. The word *significant*, when used in the social sciences, generally means *statistically significant*; however, in history, *significant* is synonymous with *important*.

However, students are not only navigating the language of disciplinary and academic communities. Secondary (middle and high) schools shape how subject matter language gets translated to students as they are apprenticed into disciplinary thinking. Schools exist as particular social contexts that demand particular language forms. But within schools, each subject area also makes use of a specific constellation of language features that mirror those used in the larger context of that discipline, but which have been "repurposed" for teaching.[14] These features are shaped by both the school context and what is considered developmentally appropriate for students. For example, when being introduced to genetics concepts, middle-school biology students may complete Punnett square charts to introduce them to the concept of how phenotypic traits are determined genetically. However, school texts and educators may use simplified language that suggests that traits are determined by single genes, rather than multiple alleles (of which genes are composed). These necessary adaptations shift in important ways how young people are introduced to disciplinary language and, as a result, come to understand disciplinary content.

Disciplinary Content: Common and Unique Challenges

Common Challenges Across Content Areas. The challenge of learning in the disciplinary classroom results simultaneously from the nature of the language and the content. In the average elementary school classroom, learners read narrative texts whose content often mirrors their own lived experiences. However, across content-area classrooms, the vast majority of texts read by adolescents are expository.[15] In contrast to the narrative texts, the content of expository texts is often abstract (as when reading in math), unobservable (as when reading in physics), or pertaining to the distant past (as when reading in history).[16] However, expressing this complex content often requires complex language, which is why we conceptualize teaching content and language as reciprocal instructional practices.[17]

All disciplinary texts begin with the common goal of *generating new knowledge* in that discipline and of establishing that this knowledge is credible, and so readers must uniformly approach these texts with a healthy degree of skepticism.[18] Evaluating whether the knowledge presented is trustworthy often involves engagement with multiple texts that present a range of perspectives, sometimes supported by contrary evidence.[19] Adolescent readers, who habitually view texts as *facts*, often become frustrated when presented with contradictory accounts and struggle with the task of evaluating an author's veracity.[20] Thus, it appears that a precondition for being able to weigh the credibility of text is whether students understand that knowledge, regardless of the discipline, is not static.[21] For example, evidence suggests that students who see science knowledge as subject to change and falsifiable are more likely to integrate new knowledge than their peers who view it as static.[22] This idea of knowledge as a moving target is also what underlies knowledge generation in all disciplines. Simply stated, if knowledge were static, there would be no need for new historians, scientists, mathematicians, or literary scholars.

Unique Challenge: Methods of Inquiry. Despite the universal goal of producing texts that can be trusted, the ways in which knowledge is constructed, vetted and re-imagined is an artifact of each discipline.[23] Students, often situated as consumers and not producers of disciplinary knowledge, may be unaware of what it means to generate new information as a scientist, mathematician, historian, or literary scholar, which impacts their ability to evaluate the quality of disciplinary content presented in texts.[24]

Students may not know what evidence, phenomena, or texts working scientists, historians, literary scholars, or mathematicians study. They may also be unclear about the methods and tools (both material and theoretical) that these experts count as evidence.[25] As Bransford, Brown, and Cocking explain: "The evidence needed to support a set of historical claims is different from the evidence needed to prove a mathematical conjecture, and both of these differ from the evidence needed to test a scientific theory."[26] For example, in math, readers might expect to see a numeric proof; readers of history are accustomed to seeing a number of corroborating primary source documents cited to support an assertion. If students understand both the sources and limits of knowledge in a discipline, they are better equipped to make informed decisions about what makes *good science, reliable history,* or *logical math.*[27] Given that students today have Internet access to sources that have not been subjected to peer review (as with articles published in most disciplinary journals), fact-checked (as with most newspaper articles), or edited (as with textbooks), developing this critical stance has become a primary challenge facing disciplinary educators.[28]

Unique Challenge: Ways of Organizing Knowledge. While experts have elaborate mental maps (information schema) of how knowledge in their domain is organized, students, as novices, lack this overarching understanding.[29] This is not to suggest that students do not possess knowledge—rather, they lack experience with the systems of knowledge like those found in the disciplines.[30] Joseph Schwab suggests the use of two key questions to deduce the information schema of a domain: What are the central concepts (or building blocks) of a discipline and how are these connected?[31]

In the sciences, new ideas are often subsumed under preexisting ones.[32] For example, Einstein's theory of relativity is the larger framework in which all theories of motion and gravity are nested. Similarly, mathematical concepts such as *addition* and *infinity* are central ideas that appear in all domains of mathematic inquiry.[33] On the other hand, in history and the social sciences, while information is organized chronologically, the theories used to explain events need not be hierarchically organized as in science.[34] For example, structuralism and modernism are not hierarchically related—each provides a useful lens and a set of language to make sense of historical events. These ways of organizing knowledge in a domain impact how writers present information in disciplinary texts and how expert readers interpret these relationships. We suggest that disciplinary literacy is not simply about acquiring the specialized language used to construct and share disciplinary information, but also about studying how knowledge itself is generated and organized (often through language) and learning how to mentally map this knowledge.[35] And while novices may not have access to the mental schemas of experts, we suggest that through reading the texts that experts write and attending to how authors organize knowledge through language, adolescents are offered a partial view of these elaborate mental maps.

Teaching Disciplinary Texts: Unique Opportunities

In spite of the challenges that complex disciplinary texts present, our experiences as teachers (in middle school and high school social studies, history, biological science, physical science, and ELA classrooms) and as collaborators with schools across the country has been that a focus on disciplinary thinking can make content-area classes more exciting and may help to improve student learning in content areas. In part, we believe that student engagement has the potential to increase in these contexts because, by demystifying the language of each content area, educators are inviting adolescents into the disciplines and providing them with the resources to express their opinions, ideas, and understandings. By supporting students as they assume disciplinary identities—to speak, think, and write like scientists, historians, mathematicians, and literary scholars—educators are not only teaching content in an authentic way, but they are also sharing with students the curiosity and engagement with which members of a discipline approach their subject.[36] Jerome Bruner describes the *sense of excitement* that students feel when the structure of a discipline is revealed to them and argues that knowledge of how information is organized in a discipline is necessary for recalling this knowledge at a later date: "The teaching and learning of structure, rather than simply the mastery of facts and techniques, is at the center of the classic problem of transfer."[37]

However, we also encourage teachers to view disciplinary literacy instruction as an opportunity to invite all students to bring their out-of-school language and knowledge resources into disciplinary communities.[38] Essentially, teaching students to navigate multiple discourse communities and learning spaces is one way that educators can promote access and equity in the classroom.[39]

Disciplinary Literacy Pedagogy: Our Proposal

Why are discipline-general literacy strategies and instructional practices not enough? Despite the common challenges identified across disciplinary texts, the unique challenges that these texts pose demand the use of a nuanced set of literacy skills. Fundamentally, providing only limited background about the ways in which knowledge is constructed in each discipline and focusing heavily on general reading strategies (vocabulary, fluency, phonics), cognitive strategies (predicting, inferring, visualization), and comprehension routines (summarizing, note-taking) fails to recognize the specialized nature of the demands of reading in math, science, English, and social studies.[40] By making these demands clear to students, educators will make the reading task easier for them.[41] It is critical that instruction intended to engage students in disciplinary thinking, practices, and communication (including reading and writing) be situated in the very disciplinary practices teachers hope to build. Although we focus on using disciplinary texts in this chapter, disciplinary literacy instruction does not begin with a given text, but with a meaningful question. Just as members of the disciplines do not randomly read texts about *topics,* but instead ask questions about phenomena or concepts, teachers of disciplinary literacy should begin with questions that engage students in the big ideas of the discipline and motivate relevant text reading and writing. It is these meaningful questions that should drive text selection.

Take, for example, a high school student required to take a course on physics. As is often the case, the instructor begins with a text selected to illustrate how thinking in the discipline of physics has shifted over time, in this case Aristotle's *Physics.* The instructor begins to fly through the assigned text without framing a reason for reading it. As a naive reader of a disciplinary text, the student might rightly wonder if the point was to understand intellectual history or the arguments themselves or question in what sense he should understand these propositions about the world as being true. And this instructor could recommend that the student use general reading strategies, such as rereading or summarizing, to tackle this complex text.

In contrast, a disciplinary literacy approach would frame a purpose for reading with an intellectual question, unpack the purpose of reading in a way that contextualizes the discipline-specific mission of the text (or her reading of it), and then integrate useful strategies for making sense of the text. For example, this instructor might pose text-dependent questions to guide students' reading, such as:

- *Paraphrase:* What is Aristotle's definition of "nature"? Using the text, locate evidence to support your answer.
- *Interpret:* How is this the same or different from how we define "nature" today?[42]

Drawing from Moje and Speyer, this instructor might support the building of *necessary knowledge* through discussion, close reading of texts, questioning, and the reading of other materials.[43] The teacher might engage her students in reading an accessible version of this text, provide purposefully designed graphic organizers, or engage her students in a discussion to help them make their way through the dense scholarly prose. She might also support her students by asking them to summarize the ideas or synthesize those ideas with other texts, all in relation to the questions that framed their reading in the first place. Furthermore, the instructor could model her thinking as she reads the text to demonstrate how an experienced reader of science literature approaches the text and evaluates Aristotle's propositions.

Several studies have provided evidence that such an approach can be effective. In a pattern that is generalizable to other disciplines, students' uptake of the strategies used by historians appears to result from strategy instruction in historical methodology.[44]

This kind of teaching takes time. The teacher described in the first example might argue that she did not have time for detailed framing and scaffolding because she needed to get to the theory of efficient and initiating causes or to Aristotle's teleological arguments by a certain date so that she could move through the curriculum. Many colleagues (and the authors of this chapter) would be sympathetic to this argument—

there are many constraints beyond the control of most teachers, including timing, assessment, and scheduling. However, as advocates for disciplinary literacy pedagogy, we would argue that without the framing of meaningful intellectual questions or purposes, not only are students not engaged in the kind of work that members of the disciplines (and professions) do, but they are also not learning the concepts and practices of the disciplines in robust, deep, and meaningful ways.

Some readers of this chapter may be thinking that the content taught in their discipline is not as abstract, nor the texts as challenging, as Aristotle's *Physics*. Many contemporary content-area teachers have colorful textbooks with user-friendly glossaries and online support with links to videos and podcasts. These books are carefully written to achieve an average reading difficulty at grade level and are often focused on general reading strategies.[45] However, such strategies are blunt tools for the task of making sense of disciplinary texts.[46] Many fail to acknowledge the ways in which scientific thinking differs from historical thinking or the ramifications of this for how students must read.[47] For example, we believe that even code-breaking skills (e.g., decoding, sight word recognition) may be applied differently when reading a math versus a science text. Although these early-acquired basic literacy skills are easily transferred from one domain to another and share commonalities with decoding and basic sight word recognition in nondisciplinary contexts, we believe that they may be applied in nuanced ways in the content areas.

Intermediate literacy skills (e.g., summarization, compare-and-contrast, comprehension monitoring) are also shaped by the demands of disciplinary texts. For example, summarization, as a general comprehension strategy, manifests differently for a math versus a science passage because the text structures and ways of highlighting salient pieces of information are uniquely disciplinary. Finally, there are a range of discipline-specific literacy skills that are highly specialized and thus not as easily transferred and/or adapted from one discipline to another. These literacy skills may not be applicable to the texts of another discipline. For example, knowledge of how to read a table in a science textbook may not be pertinent when reading a novel in English language arts. Given this conceptualization, we argue that literacy skills—at all levels—require that educators grapple with the ways that the texts of each discipline differ. In sum, educators must view and teach texts as artifacts of how members of a discipline think about the world and interact with the social context of their discipline.

The Importance of Disciplinary Expert Texts for Novice Readers

To this end, we encourage the use of disciplinary texts as the basis of content-area instruction. Notably, texts exist along a continuum from more- to less-disciplinary (figure 2.1).[48]

FIGURE 2.1

The continuum from less- to more- disciplinary texts

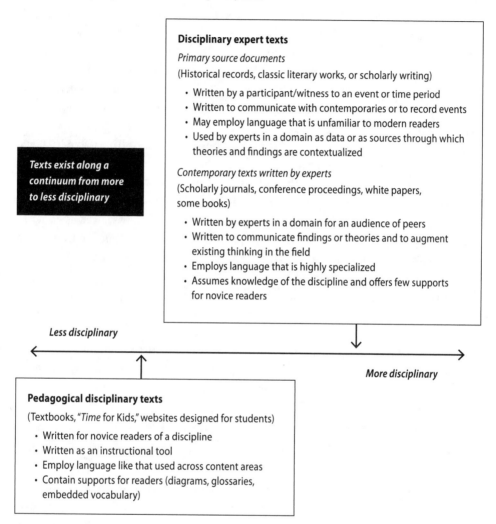

Pedagogical Disciplinary Texts Versus Disciplinary Expert Texts

At one end of the continuum are texts written for novice readers of a discipline (*peda-gogical disciplinary texts*) that employ more general academic language like that used across content areas (see Disciplinary Language: Common Challenges above). At the other end of the continuum are texts written for experts in a discipline or authenti-cally used by members of a discipline (*disciplinary expert texts*).

As shown in figure 2.1, the disciplinary expert texts fall into two categories. The first comprises primary source documents, which are used by disciplinary experts as data (in history or English) or as sources through which writers seek to contextualize their own theories and findings, such as when philosophers invoke Marx's writings or mathematicians reference Benoferoni's inequality proof. The second consists of contemporary texts written by experts in a discipline for an audience of peers (e.g., scholarly journals, conference proceedings, white papers, and some books). These texts have a high incidence of the language and sentence types that are employed in that discipline.

Strictly speaking, most textbooks are not considered disciplinary expert texts, rather these are pedagogical disciplinary texts intended to be used by novices. Similarly, news articles on science, math, and history topics do not qualify as disciplinary texts because they are not used authentically in the disciplines and are generally written for lay readers. While pedagogical disciplinary texts are widely viewed as easier to read, research has demonstrated that in simplifying sentences, textbook authors often exclude language that serves to link ideas and create dense sentences, making textbooks challenging to comprehend.[49]

This is not to suggest that textbooks and texts written for young people on disciplinary topics should not be used in classrooms. Though not easily accessed by all readers, they are useful references in any discipline and can provide essential background knowledge. Nevertheless, to acquire knowledge of how scientists, mathematicians, and historians engage with their area of study and communicate, we must also use disciplinary expert texts, scaffolded and sometimes adapted to support students' reading.

The Role of Disciplinary Expert Texts in Disciplinary Literacy Pedagogy

Below, we present examples that qualify as disciplinary expert texts. We suggest that while they cannot replace pedagogical disciplinary texts, they are an important component of any content-area curriculum because they provide students with authentic opportunities to read and think like experts and, equally important, provide teachers with opportunities to teach disciplinary reading and writing practices. Using disciplinary texts is akin to the notion of a *mentor text*, which provides guidance for novices in how experts write and think about their topic of study.

For example, many novice writers are taught to write literary analyses in English language arts classrooms. While essays written by peers provide a useful model, reading essays published by literary scholars offers students an authentic window into how experts marshal textual evidence to support a thesis and make use of language in specialized ways. Also, using disciplinary expert texts with students can provide opportunities to appraise texts as experts do with their peers' writing—a strategy that is vital in supporting novices to appraise their own writing in a discipline. For example, when reading scholarly publications, experts assess the strength of the research by asking whether the claims are supported by existing evidence and if the evidence presented is reliable.[50] These ways of appraising text can be modeled by educators for students when reading disciplinary expert texts.

Disciplinary expert texts also offer a counterpoint to textbooks, which have a tendency to portray disciplinary knowledge as static truths and the work of experts as following rigid patterns. For example, in the sciences, the differences between the scientific method portrayed in students' textbooks and the actual ways in which scientists think about data, discuss evidence, and revise their thinking are stark.[51] In fact, scientists report engaging in research in a much more iterative, collaborative, and creative way than is portrayed in textbooks, which emphasize a lock-step scientific method.[52] Textbooks also strip the voice of the scholar who produced the knowledge, rendering disciplinary arguments or claims as fact.[53]

However, using disciplinary expert texts is no pedagogical panacea. Simply using such texts, which can, at times, represent the *tidied-up* version of the research process, is simply not sufficient to help our students enter into the habits of mind used by experts in a discipline.[54] This is the role of structured and well-scaffolded inquiry activities that engage students in the study of primary source data in a discipline—reading primary source documents in history, engaging in a close reading of a poem in ELA, deriving a proof in math, or engaging in an experiment in science.[55] However, it is interaction with disciplinary expert texts that provides students with a notion of the final destination of disciplinary inquiry.

Our readers may also question whether there is utility in using very challenging disciplinary expert texts with students, many of whom struggle to comprehend less complex sources. This is a valid concern; learning to make use of disciplinary expert texts is no simple task for adolescent learners (or their teachers). In fact, evidence suggests that learning from research articles is quite challenging for novices and that students have difficulty identifying claims, appraising evidence, and attending to information about the source or author.[56] However, novices will only develop these skills if given the opportunity and the tools—this is the goal of the type of disciplinary literacy instruction described in this chapter. Chapter 10 of this book offers suggestions for how to use a diversity of texts in the context of the classroom.

How Do Disciplinary Expert Texts from Each Discipline Differ?
Demonstrating How Disciplinary Habits of Mind Are Realized in the Language of Disciplinary Texts

Now we turn to an examination of disciplinary texts written by experts for their peers to demonstrate how disciplinary habits of mind are linked with language practices. Other articles and chapters have examined the language of the disciplines as it manifests in pedagogical disciplinary texts (e.g., textbooks) or in the expert texts of a single discipline (e.g., science abstracts).[57]

Certainly, there is much diversity even within the disciplines in the language and text structures used by expert writers. Each text is a reflection of the writer's voice, the specifics of the audience, the purpose for which the text was written, and the nature of the content—all of which may vary within the writings of a single discipline.[58] However, we feel that the selected texts exemplify how the habits of mind of each discipline are realized through language. This section is designed to help educators to recognize these features as a prerequisite to planning instruction that uses disciplinary expert texts with adolescent readers. We also suggest that these disciplinary texts may provide additional knowledge not found in textbooks. For example, the history text selected could be used as a counterpoint to instruction on the Trail of Tears using textbooks, which often paint an incomplete picture of the larger sociohistorical context. While we do not suggest that educators use these *exact* texts, most likely, the disciplinary texts that educators might choose for the purpose of teaching disciplinary ways of thinking will share commonalities with these texts.

The Disciplinary Expert Texts of History and Science

First, let us compare the excerpts from disciplinary texts in history and science. We begin with an example from a history text.

Text 1: History Text

<u>*In the latter part of the eighteenth century,*</u> white **colonists** began to recognize that, especially *in areas of the South* where Africans and Indians outnumbered whites four to one, a great need existed "to make Indians & Negro's a checque upon each other least by their Vastly Superior Numbers, we should be crushed by one or the other."[33] In 1775 <u>John Stuart, a senior British official, complained</u> that "nothing can be more alarming to the Carolinians then the idea of an attack from Indians and Negroes"; he further believed that "any intercourse between Indians and Negroes in my opinion ought to be prevented as much as possible." [34] <u>Historian William Willis</u> states that one of the main reasons that the colonists curtailed Indian slavery was white **fears** of an alliance between Native Americans and African immigrants.[35] <u>Various mechanisms began to be developed throughout the</u> **colonies** <u>that served to differentiate between Africans and Native Americans.</u> A) Slave codes began to distinguish between them. B) Miscegenation laws were passed to restrict the intermarriage between the two. C) African slaves **were used against** "Indian **uprisings**"; Native Americans were used to quell slave revolts. D) The colonists offered bounties to Native Americans for capturing and returning runaway slaves. The policy of fostering **hatred** between the races became an enduring element in the relationships among the varied peoples of the South. E) The *Virginia Supreme Court codified this policy in 1814* when it made provisions related

to the natural rights of white persons and Native Americans, "but entirely disapprov-ing, thereof, so far as the same relates to native Africans and their descendants."[36]

Source: Excerpted from P. Minges, Beneath the Underdog: Race, Religion, and the Trail of Tears, American Indian Quarterly 25, no. 3 (Summer 2001): 453–479.

As evidenced in Text 1, historians rely on the following processes to share informa-tion, which we will discuss in turn: enumeration, corroboration, grammatical shifts, etc. Lemke suggests that in contrast to math and science texts, social studies texts are more "closely aligned with the ordinary personal world of human uncertainties, judg-ments, values, and interests."[59] He surmises that this is, in part, because such texts employ a chronological structure and a narrative voice. However, despite these simi-larities to narrative texts, reading social studies texts can be challenging, too, because students are unaware of the implicit mind-sets that have informed the construction of a scholarly text in this discipline.[60] In short, the work of a historian is to construct a coherent account of the past by making use of multiple documents, which may pres-ent disparate versions of historical happenings. Like the work of literary scholars, the work of historians is interpretive. Historians, in making these interpretive leaps, seek multiple source texts that serve as evidence. Thus, historians place value on *corrobo-ration*.[61] We are not surprised that the author of this scholarly work explicitly states the *identities of numerous sources* (see underlined portions of Text 1 for examples), from a contemporary historian to a British soldier who lived and wrote in the 1700s.

Another hallmark of history writing is the *enumeration of pieces of evidence* to support a central assertion.[62] In the text, readers can observe how the author's disci-plinary orientation toward idea development is manifest in his use of evidence (see items A–E) to support the assertion that "Various mechanisms began to be developed throughout the colonies that served to differentiate between Africans and Native Americans." However, although this is the author's subjective appraisal of historical events, he uses no personal pronouns (e.g., *I*, *me*, *my*) or markers of epistemic belief (words like *think* or *believe*). This is the great paradox of history writing. Although historians are assuming an evaluative stance toward the content they are studying, disciplinary conventions demand that historians articulate their subjective take on events in objective terms.

Unlike members of the math or science community, historians place value in avoiding *presentism* (applying a modern set of values to events occurring in the past) and seek to situate documents within the context of their creation (political, cul-tural, geographic) in a phenomenon called *contextualization*.[63] While the beliefs of the white Carolinians referenced in the passage are certainly unsettling to modern readers, the author of this passage avoids the use of language that would explicitly convey this view. Furthermore, the goal of establishing a narrative that is situated in a particular time and place is further supported by the frequent references to dates, years, and places (see italicized and underlined portions of Text 1).[64] Because history texts often refer to people in a collective sense, these texts also make use of the noun form of verbs and adjectives, in what Halliday and Matthiessen have dubbed *thingifying* (also called *nominalizing* in the discourse analysis literature).[65] In Text 1, references to uprisings (from "to rise up") is an instance of this type of *grammatical shift* (see bolded text in the example). Prominently, the author shifted the modality of the text by constructing a number of absent subjects and passive verb forms. For example, the author states "African slaves *were used against* Indian uprisings," (our italics) instead of "The colonists incited African slaves to put down Indian uprisings." Similar grammatical shifts also serve to support history writers in referring to abstract phenomena, such as emotions or social movements. For instance, in Text 1, a grammatical shift allows for the nouns *fear* and *hatred* to be used as adjectives to describe the emotional state of the white colonists. Finally, history texts, like other texts that we will examine below, attempt to avoid repetition. In particular, this tendency in history texts to refer to a single entity, person, or group through a series of different nouns can pose particular challenges to novice readers who lack the vocabulary breadth of expert readers (e.g., in this example, *colonists, Carolinians,* and *white persons* all refer to the same group).[66]

For contrast, let us turn to a science text.

Text 2: Science Text

Segment 1: The capability of animals to run over large obstacles and over a variety of terrains is aided by their *ability to modulate the stiffness of their compliant legs in reaction to changes in their environment* [12]. **Apparently** these animals can operate at or near optimal conditions for passive, dynamic <u>self-stabilization</u> because the **viscoelastic** properties of their passive mechanisms, termed **preflexes** [13], help stabilize their locomotion against **perturbations** [14], **apparently** with response times faster than could be attributed to reflex action [15]. We are interested in designing robotic limbs that can mimic or exceed *this performance* by understanding the animal legs' functional properties and by relating their passive properties to the controller design and ultimately a correspondingly designed machine's dynamic performance.

Segment 2: The robot **appears** to run faster and more efficiently with leg stiffnesses less than or equal to a 6L leg. This **suggests** that to uncover the value of tunable stiffness legs for this robotic platform the stiffness range must operate in this realm or lower. This exposes the <u>limitation</u> of the C-leg design and brings us to the second point: a <u>modification</u> to the C-leg design is necessary to overcome this <u>limitation</u>.

Excerpted from K. C. Galloway, J. Clark, and D. Koditscheck, "Variable Stiffness Legs for Robust, Efficient and Stable Dynamic Running," *Journal of Mechanisms and Robotics* 5, no. 1 (2013).

Like history texts, science texts show a series of characteristics that reflect the habits of mind shared by members of the discipline. For example, scientists use language to convey an attitude of *informed skepticism*, make use of *technical terms*, and try to *avoid repetitions*. One aim of science writing is to produce texts that embody scientists' beliefs: that all scientific knowledge is tentative, dynamic (versus static), empirically based, and theory-driven.[67] Text 2, which is excerpted from a journal article written by robotics engineers for an audience of peers, exemplifies this mind-set. This orientation of *informed skepticism* is evident in the double use of *apparently* in segment 1 to qualify the writers' claims about how animals move (see bolded and underlined words). Notably, this language of doubt is not explicitly present in the history text examined above, although some history texts bear this hallmark of academic language. In segment 2, use of words like *appears*, *suggests*, and *limitation* to describe the authors' findings further illustrate this tendency to regard results as tentative. We can see in this text how a theory of animal movement serves as justification for pursuing this robotic application, which is in keeping with the theory-driven way of thinking (epistemology) of this discipline.

Schleppegrell suggests that the succinct and precise representation of science findings is supported by *language that is abstract and technical* as well as by sentences that contain many clauses (set off by commas) and a high number of nouns, verbs, adjectives, and adverbs relative to spoken language.[68] In contrast to Text 1, Text 2 is packed with this technical language (*viscoelastic*, *preflexes*, *perturbations*) (see bolded terms). For members of the science community, these words communicate science concepts accurately and succinctly. For example, although the authors could have written at length about the material and mechanical properties that characterize animal muscles, *viscoelastic* serves as shorthand to specify these properties for their readers.

It is not simply these content words that make reading in the sciences challenging. In fact, words that refer to concepts are frequently highlighted in textbooks and explicitly taught by science educators. Rather, it is the use of familiar verbs and adjectives as nouns (thingifying/nominalizing, as described above) that poses difficulty to many novice readers of science texts (see underlined examples in Text 2).[69] For example, in segment 1, the authors use the verb *stabilize* and the noun form of this verb (*self-stabilization*). Functionally, this recasting allows information to be packed into a single clause (for example, the clause "help stabilize their locomotion against perturbations" can be drastically shortened with the term *self-stabilization*). The use of the prefix *self-* to modify *stabilization* represents another method used in science writing to pack large amounts of information into relatively compact sentences.

Members of the science community, like historians, also *value a lack of repetition in writing*. Typically, scientists will introduce a concept and then elaborate on it in subsequent sentences.[70] This is a problem for inexperienced readers of science texts because the central concept being discussed is rarely restated, so readers must hold the concept in mind as they read on. In Text 2, segment 1, we see this effort to avoid repetition in the use of the phrase "this performance" in the final sentence to refer to an animal's "ability to modulate the stiffness of their compliant legs in reaction to changes in their environment" (phrases italicized in Text 2) described in the first sentence.

The Disciplinary Expert Texts of Literary Criticism and Math

Now, let us turn our attention to the disciplinary texts of literary criticism and math. Like other disciplinary text types, literary scholars and mathematicians also construct texts in ways that reflect the epistemologies, or ways of constructing and valuing knowledge, of their disciplines. Again, we use two texts to illustrate these habits of mind, starting with an example of literary criticism.

We selected Text 3 because it comments on Shakespeare's "Sonnet 73," which is used as a Common Core standards exemplar text. Here, we again see how members of a discipline use language in specialized ways: this literary critic *assumes a less detached stance* than was observed in Text 1 or Text 2, *systematically structures an argument by making use of textual evidence*, and engages in *close examination of textual language*.

Text 3: Literary Criticism

> In me thou seest the glowing of such fire
> That on the ashes of his youth doth lie,
> As the deathbed whereon it must expire,
> Consumed with that which it was nourished by.

The last line of this quatrain yields alternative, incompatible interpretations, its crux being the preposition *with*. If *with* is construed as *by*, then the sense of the line is roughly conveyed in the paraphrase that the *New Variorum* attributes to Beeching (1904): "Choked by the ashes which once nourished its flame." Beeching's interpretation was based on that of Dowden (i88i) and was, in turn, supported by Tucker (1924), who cited what he believed to be the source of Shakespeare's line in this passage from *Lyly's Euphues and His England*: "the Torch turned downewarde, is extinguished with the selfe same waxe which was the cause of his lyght." Here *with* obviously means *by*, and the two passages would seem to express the same ironic idea: that the flame is consumed by its very source of nourishment.[1] In opposition to this interpretation, the *New Variorum* cites only Leon Kellner (1933), who read *with* as "simultaneously with" rather than *by* and paraphrased the quatrain thus (in Rollins' translation): "As the fire goes out when the wood which has been feeding it is consumed, so is life extinguished when the strength of youth is past."[2] Subsequent editorial opinion has overwhelmingly supported the *New Variorum*'s majority—Dowden, Beeching, and Tucker—as against the solitary dissent—that of Kellner—registered therein.[3] Criticism, in turn, reflects the editorial consensus; thus Hallett Smith, for instance, observes that "the ashes tend to choke the fire, though they represent former fire, former fuel."[4] **I think it can safely be said** that the orthodox interpretation of the line in question is the one that construes with as *by*; **my** present purpose is to offer support for the heterodox interpretation.

Excerpt from A. T. Bradford, "A Note on Sonnet 73, Line 12," *Shakespeare Quarterly* 26, no. 1 (Winter, 1975): 48–49.

Literary scholarship or criticism differs from other disciplines in that its boundaries are particularly porous (literary critics may use historical documents or draw on knowledge of language from linguistics) and ways of conducting literary criticism are not codified.[71] However, there is a shared assumption in this discipline that: (1) close engagement with texts can reveal qualities that are not immediately evident, and (2) all texts are constructed and thus are able to be interpreted in a multitude of ways.[72] Unlike science or math, where scholars aim to converge on a single solution, literary scholarship is an interpretive exercise "organized around the production of consensual and qualitative knowledge arrived at through contentions rather than the empirical testing of theories."[73] In Text 3, in which the writer comments on the use of particular language (*with* and *by*), this tolerance for varied interpretations is highlighted in the evenhanded discussion of other scholars' interpretations of this same language. As a result of the value placed on interpretations by members of this disciplinary community, some literary scholarship may have *a less detached stance* than the texts of other disciplines (see bolded examples in Text 3). For example, the author's use of a personal pronoun—*my*—in the last sentence as well as the phrase "I think it can safely be said" are indicative of this notion of findings as personal, which contrasts sharply with the detached stance observed in the text of other disciplines. While educators often teach that the third person is the preferred tense in academic writing, engagement with expert texts often illustrates that scholars adopt the first person as a way to assert ownership over thinking. Yet it is also this notion of interpretation that leads to the need for arguments to be clearly delineated and systematically supported.[74] Much like authors of the science and history texts above, this author makes his case by systematically presenting previous scholars' assessments of the true meaning of Shakespeare's language and then presenting evidence to support his own interpretation in subsequent paragraphs (not included here). This acknowledgment of scholars who have written before is a central way that disciplinary experts join what constitutes an ongoing dialogue in their domain.

Evidence suggests that critical theorists share a broad knowledge of and apply critical theories as lenses through which text is interpreted.[75] Given that texts are their object of study, literary scholars, like scientists, have a common method through which they build knowledge. Text 3 demonstrates the preference in literary scholarship for careful reading of the text—a hallmark of how literary scholars *do* the work of this discipline. While the notion of *close reading* has experienced resurgence in the parlance of educators as a result of the CCSS, there remains a debate in literary studies (and education) about what is attended to in the process of close reading and the role of readers in this interpretation.[76] Certainly, it seems that literary scholars agree that close reading involves attending to language as a feature of text that can have multiple meanings.[77] While this chapter takes no stance on the close reading debate, we suggest that use of textual evidence to support interpretations, can be accomplished only when students have minimally comprehended and thoughtfully engaged with the language of the text. In Text 3, the author's focus on single words demonstrates how this habit of mind is manifest in expert writing.

Finally, we turn our attention to a text produced by statisticians for a readership of peers.

Text 4: Math Text

After determining the optimal bandwidth, we estimate γ_{pass} and γ_{fail} by fitting linear probability models using *observations* within h^* on the appropriate side of the *discontinuity*. We can implement this process in one step, as follows,

$$p(GRAD_i = 1) = \beta_0 + \beta_1 MATH_i + \beta_2 PASS\_MATH_i + \beta_3(PASS\_MATH_i \times MATH_i) + \varepsilon_i \quad (1)$$

for the *i*th individual within six points on either side of the cut score. In this model, $\beta_2 = \gamma_{pass} - \gamma_{fail}$ represents the *causal* effect of passing the 10th grade MCAS mathematics examination on the population probability of high school graduation for students at the margin of passing. If its estimated value is statistically *significant* and *positive*, then we know that classifying a student at the cut score as passing the high-stakes test, as opposed to failing it, causes the student's probability of graduating from high school to increase *discontinuously*.

Excerpt from J. P. Papay, R. J. Murnane, and J. B. Willett, "The Consequences of High School Exit Examinations for Low-Performing Urban Students: Evidence from Massachusetts," *Educational Evaluation & Policy Analysis* 32, no. 1 (2010): 5–23.

In this disciplinary math text, we note a number of distinctive features: the *presence of symbols*, the *extreme lack of redundancy*, and the *use of everyday language in disciplinary ways*. Unique to math writing and other disciplines that make use of mathematical knowledge is the use of mathematical notation in the form of meaningful symbol systems and Greek alphabet letters to represent math concepts (see bolded examples in Text 4). In part, this language allows for mathematicians to succinctly communicate formulas. However, a secondary function is to support the dual communication of mathematical thinking through both the written and symbolic modes. This dual system of communication is a necessary facet of written discourse in mathematics-based fields because mathematicians value transparency in how proofs have been derived and problems solved, which can be challenging to accomplish through writing alone because the content can be so abstract (e.g., infinity, inverse operations, negative numbers). In Text 4, the Greek letter γ (which readers familiar with this type statistical analysis will recognize as representing the dependent variable) is paired with text explaining the mathematical process: "After determining the optimal bandwidth, we estimate γ_{pass} and γ_{fail} by fitting linear probability models using observations within h^* on the appropriate side of the discontinuity." While it thoroughly and precisely explicates the writer's process to peers engaged in similar work, this construction can be particularly problematic for novice readers.[78] Formulas are one of the most succinct forms of disciplinary communication, but can be a challenge for readers of math texts, because they are not able to benefit from the author's elaboration on the ideas as when reading in other disciplines. In addition, math texts also make use of vocabulary in unique ways.[79] Mathematics demands a special vocabulary to communicate; however, many everyday words often have particular meanings within the mathematics literature; in Text 4, such words include *observations*, *discontinuity*, *causal*, *significant*, and *positive* (see italicized examples).

Quantifying the Challenges of Reading and Writing Disciplinary Texts: A Question of Learning Opportunities

The four diverse texts just discussed, which capture only a portion of the ways that language is used in disciplinary writing, certainly present challenges to adolescent readers. Nevertheless, when taught in purposeful and supportive ways, they also provide novices with access to how insiders to a discipline construct knowledge and communicate ideas. Our recent research, discussed below, suggests that these opportunities are rare for most adolescent learners; however, this does not have to be the case.

Our research of students and teachers in schools in two urban communities in the Northeast provides data about students' exposure to subject-area texts in five middle schools. We asked sixth-grade (n = 140) and seventh-grade (n = 151) students how much time they spent reading in class and for homework in each content area. Students were asked to report how often they engaged in reading activities during one month at school according to a 7-point Likert scale (figure 2.2). Not surprisingly, students reported spending more time reading in English class than they did in the other content areas. However, they reported spending a great deal of time reading in each of the content areas, and the total amount of time that they spent reading in science, social studies, and math classes combined was far more than what they reported reading in English class alone. Thus, reading in the disciplines remains an entrenched part of schooling for adolescents and a component of the curriculum that should be attended to by all educators.[80] A version of this survey is freely available at http://cals. serpmedia.org.[81]

We also collected data on the types of texts that students read in each content area. Notably, adolescents in our study reported reading a range of genres across content areas (figure 2.3). However, they described spending much more time reading pedagogical disciplinary texts (magazines, textbooks, notes, newspapers) than reading texts that might qualify as disciplinary expert texts (maps, tables). Students reported reading no primary source documents or trade books. These data suggest that students in this sample likely faced many of the challenges outlined above: (1) they frequently read expository texts (a less familiar genre for most adolescents); (2) they read pedagogical disciplinary texts that likely contained some of the challenging language features highlighted in this chapter; and (3) they had little exposure to disciplinary expert texts that might have supported them in understanding the ways of structuring knowledge through specialized language used in each content area. However, these data are also heartening because they suggest that students are reading each day across content areas, which implies that there are ample opportunities for integrating the type of text-rich disciplinary literacy instruction we describe above.

Responding to the Challenges and Opportunities of Disciplinary Reading: What Is a Teacher to Do?

If the challenges presented by disciplinary texts demonstrated above are considered in light of these findings, then the task of teaching youth to read, comprehend, and write disciplinary text is enormously challenging.

I. Collectively Recognizing the Challenges of Disciplinary Reading for Middle Graders

One of the greatest challenges educators face is recognizing that even middle grade students are novices to expository reading. Math, science, and social studies educators must confront the fact that while students may have been reading for six to ten years, they have, on average, been reading nonfiction texts similar to those used in these disciplinary classrooms for only one to four years.[82] Not surprisingly, they are not very sophisticated readers of expository text.[83] The task is equally great, however, for educators in the field of ELA. Students often come to the ELA classroom with

FIGURE 2.2

Student self-reported time engaged in reading at home and in school on a Likert scale from 0 (never) to 7 (every day for more than one hour each day)

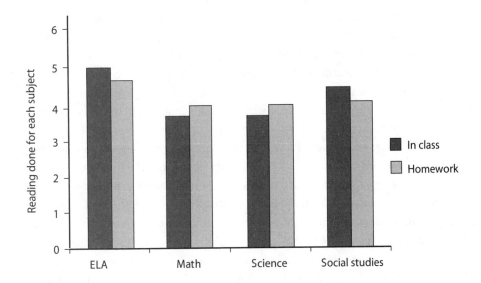

FIGURE 2.3

Student self-report on time engaged in reading various text types in each discipline on a Likert scale from 0 (never) to 7 (every day for more than one hour each day)

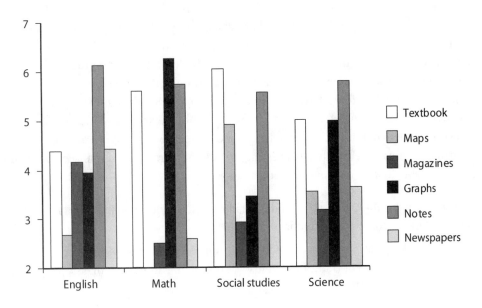

a great deal of experience reacting emotionally to fiction text, but little experience engaging in close reading or analyzing language.

It seems, then, that all educators are equally responsible for promoting literacy, although each discipline has its own brand of literate thinking. In addition to the cross-disciplinary challenge of reading expository texts that contain general academic language and more abstract content, we have suggested that the texts of each discipline present unique challenges—the language, which students are expected to comprehend, differs according to the purpose, audience, and epistemologies of each discipline.[84] For adolescent readers, who have little understanding of the ways of generating or sharing knowledge in the disciplines, this language requires unpacking by skilled educators.

Given the diversity of reading levels of most middle-grade classrooms, we suggest that instruction using disciplinary expert texts might involve read-alouds of these texts by the teacher, rich text-based discussions, and repeated exposure to such texts across multiple lessons. As Wells suggests opportunities to use the language of disciplinary texts in oral communication bolsters disciplinary understanding: "(Language) has an essential role to play in mediating pupil's apprenticeship into the discipline, both as a medium to respond to and prepare for work on written texts . . . and, more generally, as an opportunity for 'talking their way in' (Halliday, 1975) to ways of making sense of new information."[85] However, integrating these supportive practices into the instructional fiber of all middle school classrooms represents a significant challenge given that dialogic approaches are under utilized in many classrooms.[86]

Finally, educators themselves may face challenges from peers who see print-based pedagogies as less relevant for today's learners. Some have argued that disciplinary literacy is irrelevant in a digital age, where disciplinary information is always a keystroke away. That view, however, is shortsighted for two reasons. First, unless students learn to engage in disciplinary practices—including reading practices—who will become the new members of the disciplines? More centrally, educators need to be concerned that all students have the opportunity to build both digital and disciplinary literacy skills so that youth from a broad range of backgrounds and experiences can contribute to building new disciplinary knowledge. Second, even readily available information must be evaluated, suggesting that disciplinary literacy skills will be even more valuable in a digital environment.

II. Making Explicit the Differences (and Similarities!) Between Disciplinary Texts and the Purpose for These Differences

As we have demonstrated above, the language employed by disciplinary expert texts is not simply a matter of tradition, but also of function. Although it may be tempting to turn to ELA colleagues to support this work, for the most part these teachers, as members of the language and literary disciplines themselves, do not understand what it means to read complex natural science, social science, or math texts in the same ways or at the same levels of understanding as a content-area teacher may. They lack the expertise and therefore the habits of mind and norms of practice that content-area teachers may be trying to develop in students.[87] In fact, we encourage teachers of English to develop students as readers and writers within their own discipline, which has unique ways of applying lenses (e.g., feminist, Marxist) to understand character motivations and themes. So, while reading specialists may be able to support students who have difficulties in basic literacy skill development and cross-discipline initiatives may be able to boost students' general academic knowledge or general strategy use, the content-area teacher is best positioned to provide the discipline-specific understanding of a text in a nuanced way that aligns with the fundamental instructional goals of a course. To be clear, we are asking every teacher to be a teacher of reading, but in this case teaching "reading" means focusing on the content-specific approaches to reading that align with each discipline.[88] We suggest that by making explicit the differences between disciplines, teachers help to manage the lack of coherence that adolescent learners may feel when navigating middle and high school, where different ways of knowing, speaking, thinking, and writing govern the norms of each classroom.

III. Providing Opportunities for Students (and Teachers) to Read Disciplinary Texts Written for Experts and Novices

This chapter has only served as an introduction to the unique and common challenges of teaching disciplinary texts. We recognize that the approach we outline demands that educators radically reimagine texts not only as tools for teaching disciplinary content, but as models for exposing students to disciplinary thinking and language. For educators, beginning to select and teach disciplinary expert texts from the universe of available resources requires an investment of time. However, this is not work that disciplinary educators should engage with in isolation. For principals and instructional leaders, we suggest that creating communities of *disciplinary* practice, where teachers of each discipline might explore these ideas together, is a promising initiative (see chapter 3 of this volume).

Certainly, for students, becoming a scientist, mathematician, historian, or literary scholar also takes time. Educators should not expect that students would begin to accurately produce the language found in disciplinary expert texts after a single exposure (or even after numerous exposures!). However, in this chapter, we suggest that students are best supported in grasping the nuances of disciplinary thinking and language through instruction that highlights how texts are both alike and different. We envision a classroom context where these authentic texts of the disciplines are interspersed with textbooks, magazines, and visual media sources. In the chapters that follow, we suggest strategies for creating multiple opportunities to think, read, and write like members of a discipline.

3

Disciplinary Literacy in Practice

The Disciplinary Literacy Network as a Vehicle for Strengthening Instruction Across Content Areas

LISA MESSINA

In my various roles as English teacher, department chair, Title I coordinator, and literacy coach at the elementary, middle and high school levels, I have had fifteen years of experience observing instruction in a variety of contexts, as well as the ways in which students navigate—with varying degrees of success—the varied curricular demands they encounter across disciplines, curricula, and instructional approaches. Teaching and coaching at an urban high school from 1996 to 2006, I observed many students who struggled with reading and writing in various disciplines. I also worked with many teachers who struggled to address this issue, ultimately abandoning the reading and writing in their curriculum. For the past five years, I have worked as a district-level literacy coach, providing professional development and coaching for literacy coaches and teachers in K–8 schools. My experiences have shown me that a solid foundation of literacy instruction throughout elementary, middle, and high school is essential if we expect all students to master the varied reading and writing demands across the disciplines.

Disciplinary literacy instruction is particularly critical at the secondary level. Middle and high school students must master discipline-specific ways of knowing and learning, mentored by teachers who have a strong grasp of effective literacy instruction and their own personal literacy skills and dispositions. Yet, many secondary teachers embark on their careers with nothing more than a mandatory course on reading instruction and receive little professional development in this area. The Common Core State Standards may help us focus on the integral role literacy plays in learning in all disciplines, but this shift requires a great deal of professional support for teachers across content areas. Disciplinary literacy instruction is not just about remediation for those who struggle. Disciplinary literacy at its core is about mastering skills that are essential for advanced study and careers in the various disciplines. No reform, no matter how thoughtful and well executed, will lead to high achievement for all students without addressing their literacy development across disciplines. We can no longer work in departmental silos, hoping ELA teachers address our students' literacy needs. Districts need a collaborative, systematic approach to the implementation of disciplinary literacy instruction. The Common Core standards require this, and students deserve it.

Disciplinary literacy requires broad ownership of the work. Therefore, successful districts build networks of educators across the disciplines who can envision, implement, and sustain the instructional transformations necessary to move beyond the sporadic infusion of literacy strategies by a select group of teachers to the powerful implementation of effective literacy instruction across disciplines and classrooms.

Building the Network

As my district embarked on restructuring our middle schools to raise student achievement and close achievement gaps, I believed that an intense focus on literacy instruction in all disciplines was essential to achieving these goals. To facilitate this work, I created the Disciplinary Literacy Network (DLN), a professional development and leadership group designed to strengthen disciplinary literacy teaching and learning, as well as provide leadership for effective, discipline-based literacy education in our new schools. This initiative is a multiyear commitment requiring widespread participation and implementation, but it had to begin with a broad group of committed leaders—administrators, coordinators, instructional coaches, and teacher leaders— who were willing to learn together and lead together. We needed to articulate what it meant to learn in each discipline, unearthing shared responsibilities for students' literacy development as well as areas that must be owned by experts in each discipline. To gather participants who had the vision and content expertise necessary for this work, I asked each department (science, math, social studies, ELA, and bilingual education) to create a team that included the coordinator, instructional coaches, and two to four teacher leaders. Together, these teams formed a powerful network of people who could craft a cohesive vision of instruction and shape essential elements of our plan for student achievement—coaching, professional development, curriculum design, and cross-departmental collaboration.

Gathering together a cross-section of district and school-level leaders who have the necessary content expertise to articulate a vision of disciplinary literacy instruction and make that vision a reality is the first step. In the remainder of this chapter, I describe the DLN in detail, including the essential conditions for creating a DLN that can raise student achievement through a collaborative focus on disciplinary literacy instruction.

A Structure for Deep, Sustainable Collaborative Learning

We cannot expect educators to do this work without carving out time for collaborative learning. Participants need time to come together for sustained periods of professional development, followed by time to try things out in classrooms and reflect on learning. Amid the chaos of designing new schools, we carved out four professional days for the entire Network to convene, as well as three two-hour professional development sessions when departmental teams could meet to examine literacy in each discipline (appendix A outlines the content of these sessions). The Network sessions focused on building a shared understanding of disciplinary literacy and collaborative relationships across departments. Departmental meetings engaged teams in exploring literacy in their particular disciplines by analyzing texts their students were expected to read, designing and videotaping lessons to develop students' disciplinary literacy skills, and embedding the literacy practices discussed in the Network into curricula. Alternating between cross-discipline sessions and smaller, discipline-specific meetings allowed participants to develop a broad understanding of disciplinary literacy while working with content-area peers to examine practical applications in their own disciplines and classrooms. Several weeks in between sessions allowed teachers to experiment with new ideas, work with coaches, and complete readings or other activities assigned for the Network. This structure was based on the belief that, ideally, participants should meet regularly enough to gain momentum and build relationships while also having time to process and reflect on the complexities of disciplinary literacy instruction.

A Vision of What Disciplinary Literacy Is, Why It Matters, and What It Takes to Make It a Reality

Clearly, creating a shared understanding of what disciplinary literacy is and why it matters for student learning is essential at the outset. Reading a text together can provide an important foundation for building this shared understanding and anchor conversations about practice. It is important to choose a text that presents the complexities of disciplinary literacy yet is accessible to a wide audience and includes practical applications to the classroom. I chose Doug Buehl's *Developing Readers in the Academic Disciplines* as the core text for the DLN.[1] Grounded in principles I value deeply—an apprenticeship model, the concept of communities of practice and the gradual release of responsibility—this text does an excellent job of defining disciplinary literacy while providing many practical instructional strategies, presented through the lens of each discipline.

The apprenticeship approach to literacy instruction is an important foundation for secondary literacy reform. The door to working with content-area teachers opens when we ground the work in the demands of their discipline and their own experiences as learners in the discipline. Powerful literacy instruction requires teachers to apprentice students in their disciplines through modeling, metacognitive conversation, and the gradual release of responsibility. It is essential, then, that teachers are cognizant of their own skills and behaviors as master learners—readers, writers, speakers, and listeners—in their disciplines. I began the Network, as I do all of my work with secondary teachers, asking participants to reflect on the following question: *How has literacy played a role in your own learning in the discipline you teach?* Sharing these insights with each other helps build relationships and provides everyone with a meaningful entry point into the work ahead.

Using their own experience as a foundation, content-area teachers must articulate what it means to master the ways of reading, writing, and learning in their discipline. What do scientists, historians, and mathematicians read and write? What are the skills required to tackle these texts effectively? To begin this conversation, I engaged the group in an activity from *Reading for Understanding: A Guide to Improving Reading in Middle and High School Classrooms* to help them uncover their disciplinary reading lens.[2] As each participant read, online, a challenging, discipline-specific text that I selected, they noted their reading processes in four areas: what they tend to focus on, the types of questions they ask themselves, the images they form and the predictions they make while reading. Participants then shared their processes with members of their own discipline and created a poster that included shared characteristics in each box. Examining these posters side by side revealed vast differences in both reader behaviors and text characteristics in each discipline. English teachers, for example, noted their attention to metaphorical language, rich images, and the ability to "accept confusion" as they believed things would become clearer as the plot unfolded. The mathematicians, however, focused heavily on precision of language and meaning, interpreting mathematical symbols, and understanding how visuals such as charts and graphs related to the written text. Several participants commented that English teachers, who approach texts with a literary lens, are not in the best position to teach the specialized reading of other disciplines.

For this work to be successful, teachers must not only be able to articulate these specialized ways of reading, writing, and thinking but also see themselves as the experts in the field who apprentice students in the ways of literacy in their discipline. Classrooms must be seen as communities of practice in which this apprenticeship unfolds. As students move from subject to subject, they must be mentored as they become "insiders" who can participate successfully in each discourse community. I find this to be a new idea for many secondary educators, who see the English class as the place to develop these skills. I created a visual to help the group envision this concept and convey that each community of practice bears responsibility for helping students develop as critical readers, writers, thinkers, and speakers in *each* discipline who can access, apply, critique, and integrate information *across* many disciplines, texts, and contexts.[3]

Since this work is still uncharted territory in many districts, the Network needs a clear vision for how departments will collaborate in order to make this vision of instruction a reality. Appendix B outlines a vision for the long-term collaborative learning across departments that I believe is critical to building a cohesive vision of instruction and realizing full implementation of that vision across classrooms. Teachers need to feel both responsible for developing students' literacy skills within their own disciplines and part of a larger team of teachers, coaches, and district personnel who are collectively responsible for supporting students across the disciplines. A network such as the DLN builds both the individual and the collective knowledge and sense of responsibility necessary for successful, widespread implementation.

A Clear, Realistic View of the Role of Content-Area Teachers in Literacy Instruction

We've come a long way from the old adage "Every teacher is a teacher of reading" to a powerful conception of disciplinary literacy instruction. The model of disciplinary literacy presented by Shanahan and Shanahan helps conceptualize the content-area teacher's role in developing students' literacy skills as well as the limitations of this work in secondary classrooms.[4] While we are asking secondary teachers to rethink the way they teach their disciplines, it is not realistic—given the content demands of their discipline, large numbers of students, limited class time, and lack of training—to expect them to teach basic literacy skills. Students who need basic literacy development beyond elementary school require the support of trained interventionists, positions sorely lacking in many secondary schools, including ours.

We should expect content-area teachers, however, to understand the reading and writing processes as a foundation for their instruction. As a way to begin examining the reading process, I asked a literacy coach to model a think-aloud using a very challenging text. Several participants cited this as the most powerful activity of the day for the very reason I intended: it exploded the notion of reading, allowing us to hear the complexities of what happens in the mind of a reader as she processes information and setting the stage for the complex work ahead of us. I then asked each participant to practice a think-aloud with a partner.[5] Modeling the process and providing time to practice helps teachers unpack their own complex reading processes and increases the likelihood that they will use it in the classroom to model their processes for students and allow them to articulate and hone their own processes as readers.

Strong Collaboration Between Literacy and Content Experts

The Network must include leaders who can provide the literacy expertise necessary to guide and support this work. If your district has not already built this capacity, I strongly recommend investing in training as well as partnering with local universities or organizations that can help guide the work as you build the capacity for long-term sustainability. Literacy coaches highly trained in the instructional underpinnings of powerful literacy work—such as the gradual release of responsibility, the reading and writing processes, and the needs of struggling readers—are instrumental in the DLN; but they cannot lead this work alone. The *Standards for Middle and High School Literacy Coaches* outlines what coaches must know about literacy in all content areas to support teachers effectively, and is an important document to examine in a DLN. Yet, given these standards, we must ask: how many certified reading specialists do we know who are intimately knowledgeable about every discipline, including the content, curricular expectations, and philosophical underpinnings that create each disciplinary lens? My district is fortunate to have well-trained literacy coaches *and* content coaches in each core content area but, prior to the DLN, they had rarely worked together. My central goals in designing protocols and activities were to: (1) increase our literacy coaches' understanding of content areas aside from ELA; (2) increase content-area coaches' understanding of literacy; and (3) perhaps most importantly, to build the relationships necessary for these educators to work together productively on an ongoing basis. For example, as departmental teams engaged in analyses of texts, lessons, and units of study in each discipline, literacy coaches and teacher leaders from the ELA department participated in the conversation to build their own understanding of the disciplines as well as uncover how the literacy work they have been trained to do through an ELA lens might support other disciplines. Uniting the domains of literacy and content development in this way is a critical shift not only for our district but also for districts nationwide.

Examination of Both the Role and Demands of Texts in Each Discipline

Many secondary teachers have told me that they avoid the use of complex texts because they do not have the instructional expertise or the time to help students access them. The implications of this decision are great. First, it creates a vicious cycle: students can't access the texts so teachers do not expect them to learn from texts, and their dexterity with texts becomes more and more impoverished each year. Second, it perpetuates the notion that texts do not play an integral role in the ways knowledge is accessed and constructed in a discipline. For work on disciplinary literacy to be meaningful, this cycle must be broken. Educators must articulate the role text plays in their discipline and what the expectations are for student interaction with these texts as budding historians, mathematicians, scientists, and literary critics. In our first small group session, I asked each department to articulate what texts they feel students *must* be able to read and write to engage in their discipline effectively. These lists articulate a unique set of textual expectations in each discipline, and setting them side by side at the following Network meeting served as a powerful reminder that the textual expectations placed on students across disciplines require them to be adept at navigating a wide range of complex texts.[6] It was also very clear that English language arts teachers, intent on their students' developing a literary life, are probably not spending much time helping students read their science texts aside from occasionally discussing some general nonfiction reading strategies.

To help students tackle the demands of these texts, teachers must know how to uncover text challenges and plan instruction to support them. To that end, I created a protocol to help departments analyze texts used in their discipline (appendix C). Each department chose a challenging text from their curriculum and completed the protocol with members from the department and literacy specialists. Obviously, teachers cannot go through an in-depth process such as this with every text they use. Rather, the goal is that teachers internalize the analytical process and become more conscious of the text demands students must navigate. One science teacher commented at the end of the year that she has internalized this process and is now much more aware of the challenges and strategies she can use to help students navigate them.

A Shift from Selecting Generic "Strategies" to Disciplinary Literacy Instruction

The wave of "reading strategy" work that I grew up with as a new teacher in the 1990s was very powerful in many ways. We teachers were finally articulating for students what "good readers do" and attempting to teach them how to do it. Aside from the fact that many of us (including me) began teaching strategies almost distinct from content or student thought, the result was that many of us adopted important strategies for guided practice—KWL (what students already *k*now, *w*ant to know, and ultimately *l*earn), anticipation guides, writing-to-learn strategies, and so on. Teachers who did not live through the growing pains of the strategy wave are now being asked to leap forward a few decades—straight to the concept of disciplinary literacy instruction. And much of what teachers will still find in terms of resources are generic strategies designed to be used in any discipline, as if there were no significant differences between them, or, even worse, strategies that were designed for the ELA classroom. The development of discipline-specific strategies is only in its infancy; for now, teachers need to, in Buehl's words, adopt a "translator orientation" in order to "translate generic literacy practices into more discipline-specific variations that approximate what insiders do as readers and writers in their discipline."[7] For the final DLN session of the year, I asked participants to select a generic literacy strategy from a set (anticipation guides, graphic organizers, vocabulary activities, etc.) and work with colleagues from their discipline to transform the strategy into a discipline-specific variation using the literacy lens they had developed in the Network. They then shared that strategy and, more importantly, the rationale for designing it the way they did. As I walked around the room, I was delighted by the rich conversations the activity generated about teaching and learning in the disciplines—and the practical ideas teachers proposed for their colleagues.

We must move, however, from simply selecting a strategy we can insert into our existing lessons to a model of teaching and learning driven by this question: what is it that students will be able to do as *readers* or *writers* as a result of this lesson or unit that they will be able to utilize when they encounter the next reading or writing task in my discipline? The Common Core standards move us closer to articulating the answer. However, standards are just standards. They outline what all students should know and be able to do at the end of a grade. Content-area teachers must still unpack the standards by articulating the underlying skills and behaviors necessary for mastery of the standards—a critical step in disciplinary literacy instruction.

In collaboration with literacy and content experts in each discipline, we used a protocol I designed to unpack one literacy standard in each discipline for one lesson that would be videotaped and shared with the Network (appendix D). We then used a similar protocol to examine the larger demand of a unit of study in each discipline (appendix E). Designing lessons and units as a collaborative team proved to be some of the most important activities in the DLN, uncovering several important aspects of this work. First, it illuminated the fact that these standards are very complex, with many different skills underlying their mastery. Figure 3.1 shows *some* of the skills unpacked for one Common Core standard in ELA.

Second, it provided a structure for participants to explore concrete strategies together, building relationships as they shared their varying content and literacy expertise. Finally, unpacking the units of study highlighted the hidden complexities of what we are asking students to do in our curricula and the numerous literacy skills required to complete these units at advanced levels. Pinnell and Fountas's *The Continuum of Literacy Learning, Grades K–8: A Guide to Teaching* can be a helpful resource for teachers in this process.[8]

At the end of the day, however, these skills must be taught in a meaningful framework of instruction that includes modeling/explicit instruction, guided practice, and a focus on student independence through a gradual release of responsibility. Moving from explaining or assigning to modeling and guiding toward independence is a huge challenge, one that requires a great deal of professional development for content-area teachers beyond year 1 of this kind of initiative.

FIGURE 3.1

Underlying skills for one Common Core standard in ELA

ELA CCSS	Examples of underlying literacy skills necessary for mastery
W.3: Write narratives to develop real or imagined experiences or events using effective technique, well-chosen details, and well-structured event sequences.	Writers develop an outline to use while they draft.
	Writers think carefully about how to start their stories.
	Writers create believable, complex characters as the foundation of their stories.
	Writers think about the genre, setting, and audience for their stories.
	Writers decide on a focused conflict and brainstorm possible resolutions.
	Writers choose a point of view for their stories.
	Writers use dialogue to reveal their characters to the reader.
	Writers use sensory details to help readers visualize the setting of the stories.
	Writers problem solve while drafting.
	Writers think carefully about how to end their stories.
	Writers reread their work and cut or add in order to keep the stories focused.
	Writers make choices about verb tense when writing sentences.
	Writers reread their work to ensure consistency of tense.
	Writers reflect on how they have grown as writers.

Job-Embedded Professional Development in Real Classrooms

Teacher leaders are crucial to the success of an initiative such as the DLN that asks teachers to make great shifts in their practice. Not only is it their instruction that ultimately matters, but their classrooms also provide the necessary context to develop effective, discipline-specific instructional practices through job-embedded professional development. These teacher leaders also play a critical leadership role as they share their work with colleagues. Additionally, it is critical to ground the work in real classrooms in your district, avoiding the temptation to say, "This is great but it wouldn't work with *our* students." Teachers participating in the DLN agreed to collaboratively design, teach, and videotape a lesson to be shared with the larger group. In order to build a trusting community, I designed a protocol that required participants to view the lessons as learners, not experts charged with critiquing the work of the teacher (appendix F). This proved to be one of the most important learning tools in the Network, and teachers have agreed to allow their classrooms to be laboratories where literacy coaches, content coaches, and teachers can engage in classroom observations to analyze student learning more closely in the future. Laboratory classrooms such as these are essential if we hope to move from occasional workshops to the development of effective disciplinary literacy instruction in our schools.

Addressing the Most Important Question (Again and Again)

Inevitably, no matter how much people are committed to this work, the conversation returns to the limited time content-area teachers have to cover everything they need to cover. This eternal tug-of-war is only a symptom of a larger tension, a central question that must be answered: Is literacy instruction something "extra" or is it an integral part of what it means to learn in a discipline? Year 1 of the DLN found us returning to this question periodically, ending the year examining a quote from Elizabeth Moje, who I think sums it up best: "Without careful attention to what it means to *learn* in the subject areas and what counts as knowledge in the disciplines that undergird those subjects, educators will continue to struggle to integrate literacy instruction and those areas."[9]

Year 2 of the DLN will focus on building a solid understanding of what it means to learn in each discipline and articulating the learning theories each department is operating under as they design their day-to-day instruction. It is my hope that as we articulate these contexts and dig in to terms that we all use (such as *inquiry*) we will discover what I already suspect—that disciplinary literacy instruction is just good teaching across disciplines.

Results of Year 1

Although it is unrealistic to expect radical shifts across classrooms in one year, the results thus far have been promising. The group is in the right state of disequilibrium—we have raised some huge, somewhat daunting questions about the role of literacy in each department and have some momentum to do the difficult work of finding answers. We have begun to build a foundation of understanding and buy-in with a core group of individuals and develop the leadership necessary to implement disciplinary literacy instruction in all content areas, the first step in building the capacity we need to address the Common Core standards and improve student achievement.

Coaches and teachers across disciplines are having meaningful discussions about literacy, beginning to incorporate literacy practices into curricula, and working together in ways they never have before. Of course, all this work is for naught if we do not see concrete evidence of enhanced student performance in the disciplines. I am proud to say that we now have a window into how this work can impact student achievement through small, yet powerful, shifts in instruction as a result of the collaboration between literacy and content experts. For the final DLN session, a group of teachers and coaches across disciplines presented their work together and explained the impact it had on student achievement, even in its infancy.

The collaboration between the literacy coach, science coach, and science teacher was particularly thrilling, as they had seen results in only a few collaborative sessions. The teacher had identified a problem of practice—students were struggling with the assigned scientific writing. They then analyzed student writing for evidence of these concerns. Borrowing a common practice from our ELA classrooms, the team decided that students needed mentor texts—models of the kind of writing they were expected to do. Recognizing the dearth of useful exemplars for students, the team drafted their own—using one student's actual data—as the literacy coach guided the process through an interactive writing technique and the science coach provided content expertise. They then designed two lessons around this exemplar. In the first lesson, the teacher shared the exemplar with students, allowing them to uncover characteristics of science writing through an inquiry approach (e.g., "What do you notice?"). Students then discussed those characteristics and had time in class to experiment with using those techniques in their own writing. A follow-up lesson addressed a specific characteristic that required further instruction: how to incorporate data into their writing. Both the science and literacy coaches observed the lesson (videotaped and shown during this presentation) then met with the teacher to analyze student work for evidence of growth. I might not have believed the results had they not brought student work to show the fruits of this collaboration. Drafts of student writing before and after the two lessons showed impressive growth in the skill and sophistication of their writing. The writing techniques students "borrowed" from the mentor texts—complex sentence structures, proper citations, and high-level terminology used in scientific writing—added to both the precision and sophistication of their writing. I have to admit I shed a few tears of joy, reassured that we were engaging in work that would ultimately raise student achievement, albeit with a *long* road ahead. In year 2, the DLN will work hard to build this culture of collaboration and evidence-based reflection across our new schools.

Perhaps even more promising is this: when literacy coaches were only funded half-time for the new middle schools, a team of teachers from ELA, math, science, and social studies spoke at school committee about the critical role of literacy in their instruction and the need for full-time literacy coaches who can to support them in their literacy work with students. Now that is something I had waited a long time to see—and it was worth it!

Additional Resources

Coleman, David, James Patterson, Susan Pimentel, and Susan Wheltle. *Massachusetts Curriculum Frameworks for English Language Arts and Literacy.* Malden, MA: Massachusetts Department for Elementary and Secondary Education, 2011.

Fisher, Douglas, Nancy Frey, and Diane Lapp. *In a Reading State of Mind: Brain Research, Teacher Modeling and Comprehension Instruction.* Newark, DE: International Reading Association, 2008.

International Reading Association. *Standards for Middle and High School Literacy Coaches.* Newark, DE: International Reading Association, 2006.

Lee, Carol D., and Anika Spratley. *Reading in the Disciplines: The Challenges of Adolescent Literacy.* New York, NY: Carnegie Corporation of New York, 2010.

APPENDIX A
DLN Dates and Session Overviews

When	What	Reading/Preparation for Meeting
November 15	Network Session 1 (8:30–2:30) • Overview/Expectations • Disciplinary Literacy: What, why and how? • Apprenticeship and the Metacogntive Classroom • Reading Through a Disciplinary Lens	*Developing Readers in the Academic Disciplines* (Buehl, 2011): • Chapter 1 (pp. 1–30) • Part of chapter 2 (pp. 30–53)

Between November 15 and January 13	Discipline-Specific Team Meeting (2 hrs)
	• Analysis of text(s) in my discipline
	• Instructional implications
	• Preparing for video lessons and units of study
		Developing Readers in the Academic Disciplines:
		• Choose one section from the remainder of chapter 2:
		   Science (pp. 54–57)
		   Social Studies (pp. 57–61)
		   Mathematics (pp. 61–66)
		   ELA (pp. 66–71)
		"Reading in the Disciplines: The Challenge of Adolescent Literacy" (Lee and Spratley, 2010)

February 1	Network Session 2 (8:30–2:30)
	• Discuss reading.
	• Share text analyses for each discipline: So what?
	• Video—A classroom example: Examining these practices in ELA
	• The Common Core and an example unit of study (ELA)
	• Mini-lesson Statements: Generative Learning across the Disciplines
		Developing Readers in the Academic Disciplines:
		• Chapter 3 (pp. 71–93)
		  Choose one section from the remainder of chapter 3:
		   Social Sciences (pp. 92–97)
		   Science (pp. 97–101)
		   Mathematics (pp. 101–105)
		   ELA (pp. 106–110)
		• Chapter 4 (pp. 120–162)

Between February 6 and March 16	Discipline-Specific Team Meeting (2 hrs)
	• Planning for video lesson in collaboration with content coaches and ELA/literacy team.
		• Brainstorm 10 statements (5 for reading and 5 for writing) that articulate disciplinary literacy skills in science, math, or social studies.
		• Read sections of *Standards for Middle School and High School Literacy Coaches* (IRA) for your discipline or the discipline you are supporting:
		   "What Adolescents Need" (pp. 1–3)
		   Literacy Standards: ELA (pp. 19–22)
		• CHOOSE ONE:
		   Literacy Standards: Math (pp. 23–25)
		   Literacy Standards: Science (pp. 27–30)
		   Literacy Standards: Social Studies (pp. 30–34)

When	What	Reading/Preparation for Meeting
Between March 16 and April 10	Videotape Lesson for April 10 Network Session	• Teachers videotape lessons and then meet with the content and literacy coaches to prepare for presentation.

Tuesday, April 10	Network Session 3 (8:30–2:30)
	
	Watch CPS classroom lessons that develop disciplinary literacy and content knowledge using protocol for feedback.
		DUE: Video of Lesson
		
		Developing Readers in the Academic Disciplines:
		• Chapter 5 (pp. 163–187)
		• CHOOSE ONE:
		    History (pp. 188–192)
		    Literary Fiction (pp. 192–198)
		    Science (pp. 198–203)
		    Math (pp. 203–208)
		• Chapter 6 (pp. 216–263)

Between April 23 and May 18	Discipline-Specific Team Meeting (2 hrs) • Designing units of study in collaboration with content coaches and ELA/literacy team.	Pages 9–54: *In a Reading State of Mind* (Fisher, Frey, and Lapp)
Thursday, May 31	Network Session 4 (8:30–2:30) • Examination of units of study using tuning protocol. • Planning for Year 2: Crafting a vision for literacy in the upper schools.	DUE: Units of Study *Developing Readers in the Academic Disciplines:* • Chapter 7 (pp. 263–279)

APPENDIX B
A Vision for Disciplinary Literacy Work in the Upper Schools

- A well-articulated, shared vision of curriculum and instruction that supports students' development of disciplinary literacy (reading, writing, thinking, speaking) across all content areas.
- Effective literacy practices are field-tested by in-house experts in the content areas with support from coaches and colleagues.
- These practices/scaffolds are included in the curriculum, addressing the Common Core in meaningful ways.
- All teachers understand the role of readers, texts, and literacy teaching in their disciplines.
- In every classroom, teachers are apprenticing students in their disciplines, modeling their thinking and strategies for learning, and engaging students in metacognitive conversations as they become skillful readers and writers in that discipline.
- All teachers utilize effective instructional practices/strategies to help students develop disciplinary reading, writing and thinking skills:
  - Explicit instruction
  - Modeling
  - Supported/guided practice
  - Independent practice
  - Small group instruction
  - Discussion
  - Sharing and student reflection
  - Read aloud/shared reading
  - Use of multiple, diverse, multileveled texts
- Students gain fluency with texts across all disciplines through wide reading of texts at their *independent level.*
- Students tackle *instructional-level* texts strategically with support from teachers and peers.
- Students develop strategies to use when encountering *difficult texts* across disciplines.
- Students are supported by instruction as they develop as writers within and across disciplines.
- Students write extensively across disciplines, both as a means to process content knowledge and to demonstrate content knowledge.
- Literacy coaches and content-area coaches collaborate and share their expertise in order to support all teachers effectively.
- All teachers receive job-embedded professional development that includes individual and group coaching as they reflect on practices that support students' literacy development.

- Educators across all disciplines, special education experts, and ESL/ELL experts share a common vision and collaborate to ensure all students reach high levels of achievement.
- Teacher leaders deepen their understanding of the role literacy plays in their disciplines and serve as classroom laboratories where teachers and coaches can develop discipline-specific literacy practices in meaningful, content-specific contexts.
- Teacher leaders provide leadership through the facilitation of team meetings, and participation on leadership teams.
- Content-area teacher teams meet regularly to:
    - Examine how to support students' literacy development within their discipline.
    - Use protocols to explore how teacher work can best support students.
    - Use protocols to analyze and assess student work to inform instruction.
- Cross-content area teacher teams meet regularly to:
    - Articulate literacy demands and expectations across the day.
    - Collaborate on how to support all students across disciplines.
    - Use protocols to explore how teacher work can best support students.
    - Use protocols to analyze and assess student work to inform instruction.
- Structures are available that support leadership and communication:
    - Ongoing collaboration and leadership from the *Disciplinary Literacy Network*.
    - A *school-based literacy leadership team* that includes all content areas and provides direction and support for literacy development through data and program analysis.
    - A *district-based literacy leadership team* that includes representation from each school in order to collaborate on a common vision and support schools.

APPENDIX C
Inquiry with Content-Area Text

Adapted from the Strategic Literacy Initiative Protocol, West Ed.

Goals:

- To surface the challenges that a particular content-area text may present for students
- To inform our thinking about resources students might use to help them navigate a complex text
- To explore different instructional supports students might need to help them make meaning of challenging content area texts generally

I. *Choose a facilitator (2 minutes):* The group chooses a facilitator to guide them in the inquiry process. The facilitator's role is to help the group focus their questions and thinking on the demands of the text.

II. *Present the text (5 minutes):* The teacher who is sharing presents the text and how it fits into the curriculum. Group members listen and take notes. Some things to address with group:

    – What is this text? Why was it chosen?
    – Why is it important that students read it?
    – How does it relate to the major themes or topics in the curriculum?
    – *What should students know and be able to do as a result of working with this text?*

At the end of the teacher's presentation, group members may ask clarifying questions about the context or goals for reading the text.

III. *Surface text challenges (10–15 minutes):* The presenting teacher distributes copies of the text. The group reads a passage of the text and takes notes using the following questions as a guide:

    – What do students need to know to make sense of this text?
    – What challenges might this text pose for students?
    – Which of these challenges are discipline specific, if any?

The group (including the presenting teacher) discusses their observations, continuing to focus their discussion on the text itself rather than their experience with students.

IV. *Discuss possible instructional supports (15 minutes):* The group discusses instructional supports that would help students engage with and make meaning of the text. As with every other part of the inquiry, the discussion here should focus on the text and related reading task, with all members of the group (including the teacher who brought the text) participating equally. This is *not* a time for the group to interrogate the presenting teacher about what he/she did or plans to do with the text. Use the following questions to help guide your discussion:

- What instructional scaffolding would help students succeed with this reading task?
- What can you explicitly teach students about reading in your discipline that might help them deal with not only the challenges of this specific text but also the challenges of text in your discipline generally (e.g., readers of literature should be comfortable with ambiguity)?

V. *Reflect (5–10 minutes):* Group members write individually using the following prompt as a guide:

- What did you learn from this discussion that can inform your instructional planning?
- What will you do to follow up on what you have thought and heard?

Group members share their responses.

APPENDIX D
Protocol for Tuning Content-Area Lessons

This protocol was inspired by the SRI Tuning a Plan protocol.

Essential Question:

How can this lesson best teach content through/alongside disciplinary literacy skills?

I. Presentation of the Lesson Plan (5–10 minutes)

The presenting teacher shares the lesson plan, considering the following questions:

- What are the content objectives for the lesson? What will students know (or be able to do) as a result of this lesson?
- What reading and/or writing are students expected to do (*or could they do*)?
- What prior knowledge might students need?
- What vocabulary is essential to understanding the concept(s)?
- Are there any literacy/instructional strategies you are already thinking about using? If not, do you have any particular questions about how to use disciplinary literacy strategies to increase content learning?
- How will you provide feedback to students? How will you assess student learning?

II. Clarifying Questions (3–5 minutes)

Participants ask "clarifying" questions if information has been omitted in the presentation that they feel would help them understand the plan. *Clarifying questions are matters of "fact." Save substantive issues for later!*

III. Uncovering Potential Literacy Challenges (15 minutes)

The group examines the draft lesson plan and brainstorms: What potential challenges might this present for a reader/writer in this discipline?

- Participants brainstorm potential challenges.
- Presenter is silent.

IV. Aligning Lessons with the Common Core (10 minutes)

The group selects potential Common Core standards that may be addressed in this lesson (if the teacher has not already selected a standard).

- Members individually review the Common Core State Standards for Reading and/or Writing in the appropriate discipline.
- Each participant shares one standard and offers a rationale and/or example of how that standard may be addressed in the lesson.

V. Teacher Reflection and Selection (3–5 minutes)
The presenter reflects on what s/he has heard and selects a standard to be addressed in the lesson.

VI. Unpacking the Common Core and Articulating Generative Learning (10 minutes)
The group (including the presenting teacher) breaks down the Common Core standard:
- What are the underlying literacy skills and behaviors that must be taught/learned in order for students to master this standard?

VII. Discussion of the Lesson (15–20 minutes)
- Participants discuss the lesson and explore suggestions for tuning. Some questions to consider:
  - What suggestions do you have for "tuning" this lesson to *better support disciplinary literacy skills*?
  - What specific literacy strategies would you recommend utilizing in order to support readers/writers and increase content learning?
- Participants will write for 3–5 minutes before sharing ideas with the group.
- Presenter is silent.

VIII. Presenter Reflection (5–10 minutes)
The teacher has an opportunity to reflect on what s/he has heard.
- What ideas did you hear that you would like to explore further?
- What strategies are you thinking of embedding? Why?
- What questions do you have or advice would you like as you try to tune this lesson?

APPENDIX E
Protocol for Tuning Content-Area Units of Study

This protocol was inspired by the SRI ATLAS protocol.

Goals:

- To learn about units of study in each discipline.
- To explore ways to embed/articulate literacy teaching in units of study.
- To provide an opportunity for literacy and content experts to collaborate around curriculum and surface implications for future collaboration.

Essential Question(s)

- How do/can our units of study support the development of students' disciplinary literacy skills?
- How is/can literacy work be articulated in our units of study to support teaching and learning?

I. Presentation of the Unit (5 minutes)

The presenter shares the unit, considering the following questions:

- What are the content objectives for the unit? What will students know (or be able to do) as a result of this unit?
- What reading and/or writing are students expected to do (*or could they do*)?
- What vocabulary is essential to understanding the concept(s)?
- Are there any literacy/instructional strategies already infused in the unit? If, not, do you have any particular questions about how to use disciplinary literacy strategies to increase content learning *in this unit*?
- How will you provide feedback to students? How will you assess student learning?

II. Clarifying Questions (3–5 minutes)

Participants ask clarifying questions if information has been omitted in the presentation that they feel would help them understand the plan. *Clarifying questions are matters of fact. Save substantive issues for later!*

III. Aligning Instruction with the Common Core (10 minutes)

The group examines the Common Core State Standards for Literacy addressed in the unit or brainstorms potential standards that could be addressed in the unit.

- Members individually review the Common Core State Standards for Reading and/or Writing included in the unit.
- If Common Core standards are not included, each participant shares one standard and offers a rationale and/or example of how that standard may be addressed in the unit.

III. Unpacking the Common Core and Articulating Implications for Teaching (10–15 minutes)

The group breaks down the Common Core standards in ways that make them teachable:

What are the literacy skills and behaviors that must be taught/learned in order for students to master this standard?

IV. Discussion of Instructional Implications (15 minutes)

The group examines the unit and brainstorms:

What might be taught and/or included to support disciplinary literacy skills (reading, writing, and speaking) in this unit?

- Consider:
  - Specific lessons (reading and/or writing)
  - Instructional practices
  - Instructional strategies
  - Models that may be included (e.g., a model of writing)
- Participants will write for 3–5 minutes before sharing ideas with the group.

V. Reflections (10 minutes)

Each member (including the presenter) has an opportunity to reflect on what s/he has heard.

- What ideas did you hear that you would like to explore further about units of study in your particular role (teacher, coordinator, coach)?
- What questions do you have or advice would you like about units of study in this discipline?
- What implications does this have for our work together moving forward?

APPENDIX F
Introduction to Video Observations

We are each engaging in these video protocols as learners—not critics or experts, or even critical friends. The purpose of each video observation is to enhance our *own* understanding of literacy instruction in a particular discipline and explore how that impacts *our work* (as teachers, coaches and coordinators). Presenting teachers also have an opportunity to share with us some of their learning and thinking as they reflect on their lessons as well as the takeaways of participants. We are very fortunate to have the work of teachers and students, in CPS classrooms, as a lens through which we may learn together.

As a community, we are trying to gain insight into the following questions:

- What does it mean to teach "generative" literacy skills, behaviors, and dispositions in my discipline?
- How can I ensure that students learn skills and behaviors as readers and writers that they will be able to utilize as they encounter new reading and writing tasks in my discipline?
- How does this impact my role as a teacher, coach, or coordinator?

Protocol Guidelines
- Stick to the protocol!
- Keep the focus on unpacking your *own* learning.
- When noting evidence from the video that relates to your own learning, remember that we are only seeing a snapshot of a classroom:
    - Keep your language tentative. Language such as "*I am wondering . . .*" "*Perhaps . . .*" "*It seems like . . .*" reflects the spirit of this work.
    - Avoid sweeping conclusions about what you see or don't see (e.g. "Students obviously did not understand *X*, which makes me think . . .")
- Don't be afraid to ask each other questions about your learning. Part of the value of these conversations is exploring our learning together.
- Try to push yourself, and take risks with your own learning.

Protocol for Observing Content-Area Lessons
This protocol was inspired by those used by the SRI as well as the Cambridgeport School Lab Classroom Protocol, Cambridge, Massachusetts.

I. *Overview of the Lesson (5 min):*
The teacher provides an overview of the lesson so participants understand what they are watching.

II. *Examination of Lesson Documents (3–5 min):*
Participants read texts or documents used in the lesson, if available.

III. *Viewing the Lesson (8–20 min):*
Participants observe the lesson and note evidence of what they see/hear and any wonderings or thoughts about their own learning.

IV. *Examination of Student Work (if applicable) (5 min):*
Participants analyze student work to deepen understanding of the work that students are doing in this lesson and discipline in general.

V. *Writing and Reflecting (5 min):*
Participants take time to reflect on their own learning. Think about:

 – What evidence did I see that helps me think about my own learning?
 – What can I learn about myself (as a teacher, coach, coordinator) through this observation?
 – What new questions or wonderings do I have about generative learning in my discipline as a result of this observation?

VI. *Observers Share Reflections (15 min):*
Participants share highlights from their reflections, remembering to focus on their own learning rather than providing suggestions for the teacher or critiquing the lesson. *Presenters are silent.*

VII. *Presenting Teacher Shares Reflections (5 min):*
The presenting teacher shares highlights from his/her own reflections and new learning from the lesson experience. *Participants are silent.*

VIII. *Protocol Debrief:*
The larger group will debrief the process after all videos have been completed.

Lesson Observation Note-Taker

Focus questions:
• What does it mean to teach literacy skills, behaviors, and dispositions in my discipline? • How can I ensure that students learn skills and behaviors as readers and writers that they will be able to utilize as they encounter new reading and writing tasks in my discipline? • How does this impact my role as a teacher, coach, or coordinator?

Observations: "I noticed/saw/heard…"	Reflections: What does it make me think/wonder about my own practice?

4

Research in Vocabulary

Word Power for Content-Area Learning

JOSHUA FAHEY LAWRENCE, BRIDGET MAHER, AND CATHERINE E. SNOW

As content-area teachers, we recognize that teaching our students to comprehend the difficult content-specific texts that we use in our classes requires careful attention to supporting students' vocabulary knowledge. Often technical words—like *photosynthesis, executive branch*, and *distributional property*—grab our attention, since they are tightly connected to our content area. Teachers also know that there are important general academic words that are used across content areas, but that sometimes have specific connotative meanings in each and can certainly affect students' understanding of content-area readings; examples include words like *nonetheless, alternatively, subsequently, iteration*, and *categorize*. In this chapter, we argue that teaching academic words is one of our essential responsibilities as content-area teachers, since doing the work of historians, mathematicians, literary critics, and scientists in the real world requires the ability to comprehend challenging disciplinary texts. This does not mean teachers should halt the curriculum in their classes to teach word definitions; rather, they utilize research-based supports and content-specific uses of words when they occur naturally in their texts.

Purposes for Teaching Vocabulary

Many people think of vocabulary instruction in connection with standardized test preparation. This is indeed a common purpose for vocabulary instruction and one that drives an approach to teaching low-frequency words that are likely to be assessed on certain standardized tests but not often encountered in reading. A completely different reason for vocabulary instruction is to improve knowledge of more general words that are likely to be encountered in the generic texts used in reading comprehension assessments. For most content-area teachers, the most important reason to teach vocabulary is to help their students read and write disciplinary texts in nuanced ways. We believe that the specialized training and experience of the content-area teachers allows them to explain the meanings and connotations of discipline-specific and general academic words and how these words are employed in math, science, social studies, and literary texts.

One of the biggest challenges facing teachers is determining which words to spend time teaching and how much time to spend on each one. There are several studies of vocabulary instruction that help educators understand the possibilities for vocabulary instruction and how to choose words to teach. The most well-known heuristics suggest that words fall into three tiers: (1) words that are well known by all native speakers (such as *banana, ice, car*); (2) academic words that might be seen in text from any discipline but are less frequently used in speech and often hard to define (like *however, anticipate, incorporate*); (3) words that are found only in texts written for certain disciplines (like *hypotenuse, photosynthesis*, and *appellate court*).[1] In this chapter, we will discuss the importance of teaching tier 2 and tier 3 target words, examine if these distinctions exist in the writing of middle school students, and review some of the research on how vocabulary can be taught across content-area teams.

Vocabulary for Content-Area Reading

Content-Specific Vocabulary

Most teachers in each content area already understand the need to teach content-specific vocabulary and spend time doing so. Content-specific words often fall into the "need to know" category of learning. These are often words evoked in content standards and essential questions. Indeed, it is hard to imagine what it would mean to teach the water system in a secondary science classroom without teaching the technical meanings of *evaporation, condensation*, or *precipitation*. Content teachers often open their lessons with either a discussion or hands-on activity to provide students with an understanding of the key terms. When they do, students may encounter the word in text only after having had a pretty clear introduction to the meaning of the word from their teacher. Sometimes we introduce students to new technical vocabulary by connecting technical terms to ideas students already know. However, we also know that while a hands-on introduction to the concept of weight using a scale may suffice as a warm-up activity, understanding the scientific meaning of *weight* and the technical difference between *weight* and *mass* requires a more precise definition of the two. It is this precise understanding that we work hard to help our students to grasp. This is a common instructional challenge in teaching content-specific vocabulary and different from the challenge faced in teaching content-general vocabulary in important ways.

An additional challenge faced by content-area teachers is that most of our students don't discuss the water cycle, the distributive property, or hexamic pentameter with their friends and family. When young children learn the word *banana*, they don't forget it. It's a conceptually simple term, and they hear it again and again. When a high school or college student finishes a class, however, it is a different matter; knowledge of concepts and names atrophies in the months and years after instruction.[2] We need to be sure to help students activate knowledge of technical words when we begin our units, just as we help students activate background knowledge. We can also help students maintain rich vocabulary by maintaining a language-rich classroom, as Christina Dobbs describes in chapter 5.

Content-specific vocabulary can be especially challenging for ELLs. Providing these students with first-language (L1) definitions has been found to improve essential target word knowledge and comprehension and to help prevent learners from making incorrect inferences about word meanings.[3] L1 definitions can also be used to highlight, for example, Spanish language cognates of English vocabulary words; knowledge of Spanish-English cognates has been shown to be related to the reading comprehension of upper elementary Spanish-speaking ELL students.[4] Another strategy for teaching content-specific target words is to provide visuals in combination with definitions to help comprehension of the vocabulary terms. Research suggests that while visual aids may not improve vocabulary learning over and above definitions alone, the combination of visual supports and written definitions results in improved reading comprehension of topically related texts.[5]

Content-area teachers typically do spend time helping students master the key words in their instructional domain, but our observations suggest that they sometimes over-rely on textbook glossaries and definition-focused instructional practices. Although we want students to be able to understand and use precise definitions for content-specific terms, research suggests this is a good strategy for coalescing understanding of a new word, but not as effective for establishing an initial understanding of it. The discussion of the differences between *weight* and *mass*, followed by several readings and then an examination of the technical definition, is likely to result in better outcomes than the same sequence in reverse order.

General Academic Vocabulary

General academic words present a different challenge for teachers and students. These words are not typically focused on in content standards, and they often go by unnoticed as teachers in each discipline focus on those words that they see as essential for content learning. (Example words include *abandon, abstract, academy, access, accommodate, accompany, accumulate, accurate, achieve, acknowledge, acquire, adapt, adequate, adjacent, adjust.* The complete word list can be found at http://www. victoria.ac.nz/lals/resources/academicwordlist.) Even when we do teach these words, we find that it can be difficult to provide precise definitions, and if that has been the focus of our vocabulary instruction, we might struggle. Just as an example, try coming up with a cogent definition of *nonetheless* or *notwithstanding*! Fortunately, knowing a clear definition of these words is not requisite to being able to understand texts that use them, or even use them well ourselves. Not surprisingly, although students are required to define content-specific words on assessments, they are rarely if ever assessed on their formal knowledge of general academic words.

Multiple exposures to the target word in different contexts is one of the best-researched predictors of word learning.[6] A student has a 6 percent chance of learning the meaning of a new word from a single exposure when reading for fun and a 10 percent chance when reading to understand a topic.[7] In other words, some students will learn key features of some words just from one exposure without a formal definition at all. When they encounter a word for a second, third or fourth time they get additional opportunities to infer word meaning. When students have a chance to participate in a discussion that uses a target word, their chances of learning the new word further increase.[8]

Although they should not be used as the primary instructional tool, *student-friendly* definitions are part of good vocabulary instruction. Student-friendly definitions are not complete, but provide at least one common meaning of a target word in a definition that does not use words that are harder than the target word. Many students find it hard to learn from dictionary definitions; they learn much better from student-friendly versions.[9] There are some great online dictionaries that provide definitions using only high-frequency words, such as the *Longman English Dictionary* (http://www.ldoceonline.com/). Student-friendly definitions help monolingual students establish decontextualized understandings of words, understandings that distill the core meanings that they begin to infer from initial encounters.[10] Language-minority students also benefit from a combination of definitions and exposures to words in context.[11] Accessible definitions also provide a way to review words easily (although they are not a great tool for teaching words by themselves).[12]

Even when students have received multiple exposures to a word and are then introduced to a user-friendly definition, they may not maintain a complete and thorough understanding of the word. Indeed, one of the clearest insights from vocabulary research is that word knowledge is not a bimodal outcome—words are not simply "known" or "unknown." When we first encounter a word, we can usually be sure that the word is an English word, and we can often determine the part of speech of the word, but we may know almost nothing else about it if we have not encountered it before and there are few context cues in the sentence or passage it is used in. After a second encounter, we may come to understand that it is related to a particular topic (e.g., the judicial system) or is one of a class (e.g., a type of lizard). Only after multiple exposures and opportunities to discuss the word may we come to a semantically precise understanding of a word. Just as students' knowledge of a word accumulates gradually, it seems to atrophy slowly over time as well. This can be particularly noticeable during the summer, when differences in summer activities and resources across students seem to relate to their maintenance of vocabulary knowledge.[13] Second-language learners may have steep trajectories of vocabulary learning in their second language, but they may also be particularly susceptible to summer setback.[14] As teachers, we need to be patient with students when a word is on the "tip of their tongue" and as they build up solid and precise knowledge of new vocabulary. We should not jump to conclusions about their knowledge of target words too quickly and must understand that providing a definition is not the only, or even a good, measure of if a student knows a content-general word.

Related Research

In this section, we share results from some of our ongoing research projects into vocabulary use and instruction. First, we describe a project intended to help us understand the overlap and complications between the tiers of vocabulary terms as they are actually used in middle school classrooms. Next, we present results from a quasi-experimental evaluation of the Word Generation vocabulary instructional program, a cross-disciplinary academic language instructional program designed to help students learn general academic words.

Cross-Content and Content-Specific Word Use in Middle School

We were intrigued by the fact that although there are theoretical arguments behind the distinction between *content-specific* and *general academic* words, there had not been much of an empirical basis for this distinction from sources collected in secondary classrooms. Was it possible that this distinction is not as salient in middle school as it might be in college texts?

To understand the range of words and academic language that middle school students were actively using, we examined the words that appeared in their content-area notebooks. The students attending the school we sampled from used notebooks in each of the content areas on a daily basis.[15] We sampled 16,984 words, contained in twelve content-area notebooks (including English language arts, social studies, math, and science) belonging to three middle school students. Netty and Sandra were seventh-grade students.[16] Netty had received a designation of "needs improvement" on the state assessments of reading and math. According to state tests, Sandra was a relatively strong math student ("proficient") but had scored "needs improvement" on her English language arts standardized assessment. Her teachers characterized her as social and hardworking. Her notebooks featured writing produced with colored pens and florid doodles. Millie was a competent and serious Latina eighth-grader who had scored "proficient" on both reading and math standardized tests. Teachers identified Millie as an academic standout who was making strong progress during the year in which we conducted this study. While they demonstrated a range of math and reading skills, the three students shared a reputation for regularly attending school and being active participants in classroom instruction and, as a consequence, wrote in their notebooks on a daily basis. On average, between fourteen hundred and fifteen hundred words were sampled from each student's notebook and entered into a database. The first step in our analysis was to identify terms with the same root (e.g., *definition* and *define*). Then we established the frequency of root words and inflected forms as they were used in notebooks within each content area, and also across content areas.

Table 4.1 presents some basic descriptions taken from the student notebook analysis. In each column, we present the common words per subject and the number of instances we found. We analyzed the trends within and across content areas. Like

TABLE 4.1

Frequency of the most common words sampled from content-area notebooks collected from seventh- and eighth-grade students

Math		Science		ELA		Social Studies	
Word	*Count*	*Word*	*Count*	*Word*	*Count*	*Word*	*Count*
equation	171	equation	19	response	19	resources	17
variable	37	elements	19	analyze	11	affected	12
factors	25	periodic	19	definition	9	assessment	12
negative	10	reaction	9	symbolize	9	analyze	10
coordinates	9	variables	8	techniques	8	areas	10
dimensions	9	phases	8	visualize	8	located	8
maximum	9	formulas	5	themes	7	cultural	8
expanded	6	variable	4	conclusion	5	location	7
location	6	chemicals	4	prediction	4	features	7
corresponding	5	evidence	4	authors	4	constitutions	7
equations	5	transportation	4	consequences	4	diversity	7
evaluate	5	procedure	3	symbolism	4	economic	7

previous researchers, we found words that occurred in only one content area and also those that occurred in math, science, social studies, and English notebooks. Interestingly, we also noticed that there were many content-general words that, while maintaining the same basic core definition in each content area, also had distinct connotative meanings in each. Words in another group have technical meanings in different content areas with a very broad core definition. We review examples of each of these kinds of words taken from our notebook corpus below.

Content-Specific Academic Words. The sampling from middle school notebooks revealed that although there were words used in only one content area, there were also many words that were used in both math and science notebooks. For example, the term *theme* was used exclusively in English language arts middle school notebooks; it represents an example of what researchers commonly think of when they talk about content-specific words. However, the terms *equation* and *volume* occurred in both math and science notebooks and expressed the same concepts (table 4.2). These findings suggest that disciplinary texts may not be as specialized in secondary classrooms as they are in the college texts, and collaboration between dyads of math and science teachers may be useful in teaching words that are important in both disciplines.

Cross-Content Academic Words. We found some words occurring across all content areas and that these words were basically the same words found in the academic word list developed from college texts. The terms really become part of the glue of an academic text—maybe not used to explain a critical content-specific concept, but rather utilized to organize the text. One example of this type of term includes *summary*, which in all content areas means "a brief explanation of a concept." Additional examples of terms within this category include: *analyze/analyzing/analysis, create, data, definition/define, environment, evidence, identify/identified, image, infer, investigate, locate, objective, positive, predict, process, response, similar, symbol, topic, variable/varied, vocabulary.*

TABLE 4.2
Words used in both math and science notebooks

Equation
Coordinate
Volume
Intercept
Exponent
Graph
Perimeter

Content-General Words with Strong Disciplinary Connotations. We also found words that students used across all content areas, but that had different connotations depending on usage and discipline. For the most part, although the connotative meanings of the terms varied in each discipline, the base understanding of the term informed all the uses. For instance, the word *distribute* has a general meaning that might be found in any content-area text. It also has a precise meaning that typically occurs in math classes (as in the distributive property) and a general meaning with rather strong connotations in social sciences or political contexts (wealth distribution). We also found examples of the word *fraction* (from the Latin root for *broken*) used in a math notebook in problem solving, but found *fraction of the population* in social studies and the word *fracture* used in science notebooks (see table 4.3 for more examples).

Content-General Terms with Distinct Meanings in Each Subject. Another closely related category of word we found contains content areas that will utilize the same term in very different ways (see table 4.4). Students need to be skilled in navigating terms within content areas and able to comprehend multiple meanings of the same term according to context and content area. One key example of such a term is *cell*, which, depending on discipline, could mean "a small biological structure," "a prison room," "a phone," or "a part of a whole." Teachers can increase comprehension by teaching

TABLE 4.3

Content-general words with disciplinary connotations

Climate	Conclusion	Distribute	Energy	Fraction	Prime	Physic	Substitute
Climate change; social climate	Conclusion (final outcome); conclusion of a paper	Distributive property; distribution of wealth	Energetic; alternative energy	Fraction of the population; fraction (numbers); fracture	Primary; prime number; prime example	Physical; physics; physique	Substitution property; substitutes (replacing)

TABLE 4.4

Content-general terms with distinct meanings in each discipline

Author	Cell	Culture	Feature	Probable
Authoritative; authority; author	Biological structure; prison room; small component of a whole; small phone	Cultural phenomenon; culture of bacteria; culture of a society	Geographic feature; feature presentation; feature (prominent or special)	Probability; probably

the term within the discipline, but also reinforce the definitions possible in other content areas. Students can also utilize context clues in readings to reason through potential definitions/meanings for the discipline that may be different from their previous knowledge or understanding of a word.

Word Generation Project

There is no doubt that students are exposed to a variety of specialized vocabulary and academic vocabulary constantly in school. The sampling from middle school notebooks reveals that students are encountering terms that have varied and complex meanings within and across content areas. In order to create cohesion across content areas and assist students in vocabulary learning, teaching teams can utilize word lists and vocabulary integration activities that engage students, while still moving the relevant curriculum forward.

One such integrated vocabulary program is the Word Generation Project, which encourages cross-content-area vocabulary instruction through brief, engaging activities for students. The Word Generation curriculum was developed through a collaboration between the Strategic Education Research Partnership (www.serpinstitute. org) and Boston Public Schools, and originally implemented in five Boston middle schools. The program introduces students to selected academic vocabulary words in the context of a high-interest passage about a controversial topic such as "Where are the women in math and science?" "Do professional athletes deserve multimillion dollar salaries?" or "Should the government impose a mandatory year of service after high school?" Each week, as students explore the topics in fifteen-minute sessions in each content area, they are also introduced to five content-general words (figure 4.1).

The program was designed so that each week students would encounter the five words in different content areas so that if a word has a different meaning or connotation in math than it does in social studies, they would have a structured encounter with the word and opportunities to discuss its meaning in each class. We hoped that teams of teachers working together to teach general academic words could improve student learning, even though the program was implemented for only fifteen minutes per day.

To test if students learned words from participating in the program, our research team began a quasi-experimental study in which academic word learning by students in five schools implementing the Word Generation program was compared with academic word learning by students in three schools in the same system that did not choose to implement the program. The results presented here have been described in greater depth elsewhere.[17] All students in the treatment schools received the intervention; both pre- and post-test data were available on 697 sixth-, seventh-, and eighth-grade students in the five treatment schools, and 319 students across the

FIGURE 4.1

Word Generation curriculum

The Word Generation materials define a list of key elements that are used to organize instruction. Those elements include the following (from wordgeneration.org; see website for more program details)

- Day 1—*Launch* (English teacher)
  - Introduction of passage, target words, and a controversial topic that can support discussion and debate
  - Comprehension questions to guide the class in checking understanding of the passage and to invite students to tap into their personal beliefs about the week's topic
- Day 2—*Debate* (Social studies teacher)
  - Use of academically productive talk to argue positions
  - Identification of reasons and evidence
  - Development of positions on issues
- Day 3—*Micro Experiment* (Science teacher)
  - Science-related background information gives students more practice using different forms of the words.
  - Fictional experiments reinforce scientific thinking.
  - Students interpret data and draw conclusions.
- Day 4—*Word Problem* (Math teacher)
  - Mathematics problems similar to standardized test items
  - Use of some of the target words in math context
  - Problem is related to weekly topic
- Day 5—*Essay Writing* (English teacher)
  - Writing activity: "Taking a Stand"
  - Prompt provided to inspire persuasive essay
  - Opportunity to use target words in writing
  - Evidence and reasoning included in essays in order to support position

---

three comparison schools. Of these, 438 students were classified as language minority (i.e., students whose parents reported preferring to receive materials in a language other than English). The vast majority of students in both treatment and comparison schools were low income.

Multiple regression analyses demonstrate that participants in the program learned more words than nonparticipants ($\beta = 0.166$, $p < .001$). The average effect size of program participation on the researcher-developed vocabulary assessment was 0.49 (controlling for the improvement attained in the comparison schools). We also wanted to determine how well students maintained their word knowledge after the end of the program, and so we followed up with them at the start and end of the following school year. We were able to use data from 1,665 students in the study in five schools implementing the Word Generation program and four comparison schools.

We saw the anticipated improvement during the instructional year in knowledge of target words, and that this improvement was evident even a year after the end of instruction. We take these results to mean that whole school approaches to general academic vocabulary instruction can have sustained impact on student word knowledge of these key vocabulary words.[18]

Implementing a School-Level Vocabulary Program

The Word Generation program can be downloaded and used for free. Schools are encouraged to try it out in one teaching team or grade level, even if only for one unit. Alternatively, teams of teachers could collaborate to implement a cross-content vocabulary program on their own. General academic words can be chosen at the school level and should be integrated into content-area classes for multiple grade levels. If the lists cannot be compiled at a school level, cross-content teaching teams can select general academic words for instruction. In order to select words, teaching teams should:

- Assemble, select words for the list, and plan the implementation
- Print out the lists of general academic words provided in the resources section (see http://www.victoria.ac.nz/lals/resources/academicwordlist)
- Determine as a group which words to teach and when, with input from all members of the team
- Discuss the different meanings and uses of vocabulary words across content areas

The integration of general academic words into multiple content areas will increase the likelihood of comprehension and deeper understanding by students.

Conclusion

We are gratified to see the increased focus on vocabulary in the Common Core State Standards and the national trend toward thinking about how to improve vocabulary instruction and support student vocabulary learning. We think three of the biggest insights from research are: (1) word learning is granular—there is a range of ways that students can know a word; (2) students cannot necessarily make the vocabulary knowledge they have explicit; and (3) word learning is supported by active use of words in high-interest contexts. We have also learned that supporting vocabulary learning is challenging for many content-area teachers, even when they are to committed to it. In chapter 5, Christina Dobbs presents some of her practice-tested suggestions for creating a language-rich classroom, which we enthusiastically recommend to you.

Vocabulary in Practice

Creating Word-Curious Classrooms

CHRISTINA L. DOBBS

In my work as a professional development coach, I visit many content-area classrooms and see many teachers working hard to teach students a variety of skills and concepts. In most of those classrooms, there is an understanding that vocabulary is important, that knowing the words and language of a subject are keys to unlocking that subject for students. But when it comes to implementation, the how-to questions of vocabulary (along with the how-much and how-often questions) are the ones most frequently asked. And they are excellent questions. What does strong vocabulary instruction look like in a secondary content-area classroom?

It is no wonder that teachers wrestle with these important issues. I have wrestled with these very questions in my own experience as a high school language arts teacher, a reading specialist, and now as a literacy coach. Now, as I move through schools and classrooms as a coach, I find that many packaged curricula provide defined words in text but often lack strategies for teaching those words or providing a broader approach to word learning in the context of a particular discipline. Struggling readers typically lack background knowledge and need to learn many words, leaving teachers with many words to teach and many difficult questions about which words are most important and which they should teach. This chapter tackles these questions in the hope that classroom teachers find a clear and streamlined approach to fostering word learning. This way, they can use their limited time to maximize students' vocabularies.

A traditional approach to vocabulary instruction is to have students define words that might be unknown in a particular chapter or unit. Students often define words bolded in text, and sometimes they must use them in sentences. Next there is some sort of quiz at the end of the unit to try and determine whether words have been learned. And this is not a bad place to start. However, if we want students to learn words independently and retain them beyond units or sections of text, we need a different approach.

The Promise and Pitfalls of Explicit Vocabulary Teaching

Content-area teachers are rightly concerned about how much material they have to cover, how many skills there are to teach, and how many varying student needs they must address each day. As we try to figure out how vocabulary fits into a picture that is often crowded and complicated, eventually someone asks, "How am I supposed to have enough time for this, along with all the other stuff I've got to do?"

The answer, while not simple itself, is to focus on building up vocabulary in a variety of simple ways beyond teaching words explicitly. Though teaching words explicitly is a valuable component of a vocabulary-rich classroom, it is not the only way to make a classroom into a place where words are learned. Explicit teaching is necessary, but not sufficient for developing strong vocabularies in students.

A New Vocabulary Approach in Three Parts

We need an approach that is well rounded and goes beyond the traditional ways of teaching words. This chapter proposes a classroom approach to teaching vocabulary in three parts. To foster real vocabulary growth in students, a teacher and classroom community must think of vocabulary instruction as something to be addressed on three different fronts. Picture a stool with three legs (see figure 5.1)—without all three, it is not possible to sit down. Those three legs provide the foundation that all of the weight rests on. So much of what happens in a content-area classroom relies on this strong base of language, because skill and content knowledge must be built on a base of being able to think and talk using the language associated with a particular discipline.

This chapter will spend time on each of the three legs:

- Create a language-rich, word-curious classroom.
- Teach word-learning strategies.
- Strategically choose which words to teach.

We will begin with the two legs that might seem less familiar to many teachers but that set the stage for explicit word teaching that really makes a difference. Each section will introduce some strategies that are low-preparation and engaging routines to support each of the three legs.

Vocabulary instruction should not require teachers to plan elaborate or complicated lessons with many materials; instead, strong instruction relies on simple ways of talking, thinking, and writing that call attention to words and how to learn them. Clear approaches to word learning will encourage curiosity and independent motivation for words with students. In order to be as engaging and powerful as possible, the

FIGURE 5.1
Robust vocabulary instruction

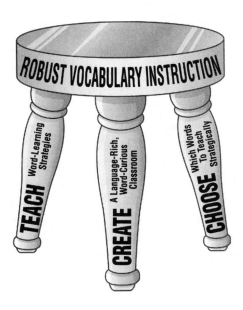

techniques selected will include collaborative strategies for word learning and strategies that can be embedded into the texts being used in any classroom.

Leg #1: Create a Language-Rich, Word-Curious Classroom

The first step in building a strong vocabulary-learning classroom is to create a classroom space that is both language-rich and word-curious. An environment where there is lots of language learning, curiosity about words, and discussion and talk is one where students can feel comfortable learning new words with each other and on their own. It is not a place where students learn words only when a new chapter begins or only on one day of the week, but a classroom that provides opportunities for students to use the language they know and the language they are learning in repeated and meaningful ways. So what does this mean? What does it look like on the ground?

Build Word Consciousness in Your Classroom

The first thing teachers can do to achieve first goal is to build word consciousness daily in the classroom. Anderson and Nagy define word consciousness as having three pieces to develop. These include:

- Both a cognitive and an affective stance toward words
- A motivation to learn words
- An awareness of how language is used in particular situations[1]

This motivation and affective stance means that students cannot look on the work of vocabulary as "boring" or otherwise "uncool." Instead, our classrooms have to be places where being curious and interested in words is an ordinary part of our day-to-day way of being.

Much has been written about how to foster word consciousness with younger children, and suggested strategies include building word walls, promoting word play, and print-rich classroom environments.[2] It is not hard to envision how this looks with younger students, who often meet in classrooms where they have one teacher for many content areas. But less has been written about adolescent learners, who often attend classrooms that are compartmentalized by subject and taught by teachers who typically specialize in the discipline being taught. Even so, we can imagine how we might extend these word-consciousness principles to adolescent content-area classrooms. Here are some extensions for those word-conscious strategies in the adolescent classroom:

- *Make a print-rich environment:* Find as many ways as possible to make your classroom a print-rich space by including lots of text from your content area. Make sure to display a variety of print on the walls; this environmental print might encourage even older students to read and learn the terms of a content area. If your discipline requires that you typically display formulas or algorithms, you could label the pieces with terms like *variable*, to reinforce those terms for students. But a print-rich classroom also includes the availability of text and having texts on display throughout your room. Students should have a choice of a wide variety of content- and language-rich texts in a truly print-rich environment.
- *Set routines and rewards for word finding:* Establish routines that reward students for finding and learning new words or attempting to use those words in their speech and writing. You might keep track of students who try to use new words in their assignments, or you might institute a reward system for students who find new words or additional meanings for known words. And, even when students use new words in ways that are not entirely correct, you should reward and encourage those adventurous attempts that mark a student trying to integrate new words into his/her vocabulary.
- *Model sophisticated talk:* Perhaps the most important step you can take in your classroom is to use sophisticated words in your talk with your students and talk explicitly about your language choices. The complexity of the words and sentences used by teachers is ultimately related to students' vocabulary learning, so it never

hurts to use a high level of vocabulary in a supportive way, defining words as needed.[3] Students need to know the discourse differences between how you speak in a particular discipline in school versus how you speak outside school or in another discipline. By explicitly discussing these patterns, you will help students understand what language is most appropriate and expose students to a variety of terms.

- *Build a content-driven word wall:* And finally, a simple and oft-suggested but infrequently adopted tactic in the upper grades is to build a word wall specifically for your content area. Often the difficulty for students in content-area classrooms lies in learning academic, highly specialized, and/or technical vocabulary, and often these terms build on one another and must be retained to move forward. A word wall to help reinforce these terms provides continual exposure to them. You could color code words by part of speech or create webs to show conceptual relationships (e.g., words related to *energy* or *motion*, literary terms, etc.).

If you implement even a few simple word-consciousness strategies, you should plan not to spend lots of time on them; instead, you should think about putting a few word-consciousness routines and tools in place early in the year that you reflect on occasionally. In the end, you can expect to see a classroom in which you find a friendly and encouraging atmosphere for word learning, setting a tone that will draw students in and push them to expand their vocabularies. Then you will have set the stage to move to the second leg of vocabulary instruction, encouraging vocabulary-rich talk in your room.

Create a Talk-Friendly Classroom

When I began teaching high school language arts, I had large classes and lots to cover. So all too often, in an effort to be efficient and get everything covered, I demanded that students work silently at their desks, not only as they were reading but also as they assessed their reading, wrote about it, and did research. I realize now that this was not likely the best approach to encourage my students to try out new words and language.

Today I think differently about encouraging word learning in classrooms. Language is a collaborative process, designed to communicate messages from one person to another, and I now place importance on providing more opportunities for such collaboration in my classroom. You will read in other chapters of this book about the importance of discussion and the variety of skills that can be built by encouraging students to talk; however, here are a few thoughts about how you might use discussion specifically in service of word learning:

- *Construct definitions and sentences collaboratively:* We know many students lack the background knowledge they need to appropriately discern the meanings of words.[4] Why not allow groups of students to compile their tidbits of knowledge to compile definitions and work with words in a way that is more generative? Often in my own classroom, this looks like pieces of chart paper with target words in the center, going through a process that is similar to a Frayer Model. Then students fill in categories around the target, such as writing a definition in their own words, illustrating the word, thinking of related words, coming up with synonyms/ antonyms, and/or using the word in a sentence or series of sentences.

- *Explicitly encourage groups to talk about the text at hand using the words:* You can encourage students, as they do group work for other purposes like practicing skills or analyzing text, to use learned words in their discussions. In debates or other classroom discussions, you can set up rewards for students who incorporate words into their comments. If you give students opportunities to plan what they might say ahead of time, you give them opportunities to use words that are not automatic to them yet. In a social studies formal debate lesson, I have seen students, in the interest of winning the debate, carefully plan what they might say in a discussion to make sure they use the words properly and to maximize the clarity of their comments.

These strategies for building word consciousness and encouraging talk might seem too simple or low-stakes to really push vocabulary learning in your room. But in fact, it is simple, ongoing, clear strategies that have the most power for students, and we cannot underestimate the power of setting up a classroom where language-richness and word-curiosity are normal, everyday ways of being.

Leg #2: Teach Word-Learning Strategies

The second important leg of the stool in content-area classrooms where students effectively learn vocabulary is the teaching of *word-learning strategies*—routines and procedures that students can use independently to learn words they do not know. Many people have speculated and studied vocabulary, and though their estimates vary, generally it is thought that students need to have learned around fifty thousand words by the end of high school.[5] If this is indeed the case, we could teach words all the time, around the clock, to the exclusion of all else, and we still might not reach this number. And of course, we cannot simply put aside all the other material we need to teach in content-area classrooms in the interest of learning words.

This means that students need the skills and strategies of independent word learning in their toolboxes, so that when they do need to know a word not being explicitly taught, they can figure out what it means. In classrooms with incredible diversity along almost every dimension, teachers would find it a difficult, if not impossible, task to teach all of the words that are unknown by at least one student in a classroom. Instead we need to add word-learning strategies to classrooms that are already language-rich and word-curious.

Often, when a student is unsure of a word, the typical response is to tell the student to ask someone or look it up in the dictionary. Asking someone is not a bad strategy, though there is always a chance that a student could ask someone who is also unsure of the word. But the dictionary strategy is often a fallible, if not impossible, one for students, especially strugglers. Dictionaries require that students know base forms of words and word spellings in order to even begin looking up a word, and even then, the language used in dictionary definitions is often opaque to students. Students need strong word-learning skills before they can begin looking up words in the dictionary. There are several ways we can help students develop stronger word-learning strategies, including being considerate of multiple meanings, teaching about word parts and morphemes, teaching students to be aware of when they know a word and when they do not, and giving students routines for finding word meanings when they are unsure. These word-learning strategies and instructional habits are described in more detail below.

Be Conscious of Multiple Meanings

Often, when I am discussing the comprehension of a text with a student, I realize that a struggle around a particular point stems from confusion about words that mean more than one thing. We have to train ourselves as teachers to be on the lookout for these words so that we can help students learn to be aware in a similar way. There are many content-specific words that have more general meanings in other contexts, so sometimes we can explicitly teach students about these multiple meanings. A math classroom I worked in had words listed on the wall, and underneath each word was the common meaning of the word and then the mathematical meaning (e.g., *cut*—common: "divide into pieces with a sharp implement"; math: "reduce").

However, we can also build awareness of multiple meanings by pointing them out as we talk about other content and skills with students. Much of this informal mentioning of multiple meanings hinges on the teacher reading the text ahead of time with an eye toward words that have multiple meanings. For instance, *solution* in chemistry class means something quite different than when discussing conflict in literature; this is easy to point out quickly as it comes up in introducing solutions to students if you are in the habit of thinking this way. Then, you can use ways of tracking learned vocabulary (e.g., adding to your word wall, keeping lists of learned words in journals) to add additional meanings to words you have defined.

Teach Students About Morphemes

Often the words that students struggle with as they move up in grades are less common and contain multiple syllables. You can teach students to approach these words by teaching about morphemes. Morphemes are the smallest units of words that carry meaning, so not all syllables are morphemes. But morphemes can convey a great deal of information: an -s at the end of a word makes that word plural; -ment can make a word into a noun. Morphemes also include those base words that carry basic meaning. Take for example, the word *contradict*. It consists of two morphemes—*contra-* (meaning "against") and -*dict* (meaning "to speak"), building a word meaning "speak against." Breaking down those complex words into parts that carry meaning can help students to figure out and take educated guesses at words they do not know. Teaching even a few common morphemes can lead to large word-learning growth for students.[6] Then you can teach students a simple procedure to decipher words once they know a few morphemes:

- Recognize that you need a deeper understanding of a word.
- Analyze the word for any morphemes you recognize (sometimes morphemes can change the sound or spelling of a word, so this can be tricky).
- Hypothesize the word's meaning if you add up the parts.
- Check your hypothesis to see if it makes sense in the passage context.[7]

Once students know this procedure, they will have another tool to use when they run into unfamiliar multisyllabic words.

Help Students Be Aware of What It Means to Know a Word

Another way to help students sharpen their word learning skills is to help them be more attuned to what it means to know a word. Knowing a word is much more complicated than a simple "yes I know it," or "no I don't." Knowing a word can range from some general familiarity of what the word has to do with, to a deep word knowledge. Deep word knowledge can include the word's connotation in various contexts, words related to the word, and transformations of that word to all sorts of other forms.

It is easy to begin this process of building awareness by showing students a basic heuristic to know when a word is known or unknown. As you introduce new words, ask students to rate the word on a scale by a show of hands or on the list of words you are working with:

1—I've never heard the word before.
2—I've heard that word, but I don't know what it means.
3—I think I know it, and it has to do with . . .

4—I know what it means and can use it in this context.

5—I know lots about this word, including other meanings.[8]

This sort of awareness can help students become more metacognitive about the words they know and do not know.

Give Students a Routine for Finding Meanings for Unknown Words

Establish a list of steps and possible strategies for finding the meanings to unknown words. Too often, the typical strategy students use when they do not know a word is to skip it. This does not lead to word learning, and students need a series of steps they can take that do foster independent word learning. This list can include all sorts of steps, such as considering whether the word meaning is essential for understanding the text, using text clues or text-provided definitions or glossary, using the morpheme strategy to dissect the word, asking others for help with the word meaning, looking for other instances of the word in the text or on the word wall, or even looking at the dictionary if the root word is transparent. Each content area might have a slightly different approach to the order of the steps on this list, but the important piece is for students to know what the plan is when they realize they need to know a word's meaning to understand text.

If these simple strategies are in place early on in a classroom, then students can begin building strong skills for determining when they need to learn words and how to go about learning words independently, freeing up teachers to focus on particularly important terms and concepts explicitly with students.

Leg #3: Strategically Choose Which Words to Teach

The first two legs are simple routines and ways of thinking that can go quite a distance toward building a strong vocabulary-learning classroom. But using them does not mean that teachers should abandon explicitly teaching words to students. In ways that the other legs do not, explicit teaching can help students comprehend the text they are reading if the words taught are chosen with purpose, taught well, and used multiple times.[9] Being strategic about which words to teach explicitly is the final leg to the three-legged stool of building a classroom where many words are learned.

All too often, vocabulary instruction simply becomes asking students to define lists of words appearing in a text or even lists of unrelated words. This practice, although a start, does not maximize the little time we have to teach students words explicitly; if we know we will not be able to teach all of the words students need, we need to concentrate our attention on the most important and useful words to make best use of our time.

Here are a few essentials to remember when choosing words to teach:

- What is your lesson focus? Choose words that serve your lesson purpose.
- What words are necessary to comprehend the text? Choose words that are essentials for passage comprehension.
- Which words are academic words or words useful in many contexts? Choose words that students will encounter again and again as they move from class to class.
- Which words are interesting but not essential to understanding the passage? Choose to leave these words for another day of teaching.

For example, in a lesson about iambic pentameter using a poem, the words *iambic* and *pentameter* (which are unlikely to even appear in the poem) are essential to achieving the lesson's learning goals. But, if students are learning about the variety of ways that Shakespeare wrote about the theme of love, it is possible that the words *iambic* and *pentameter* are not necessary for the lesson purpose. If we choose a smart list of words, then we will get more mileage out of our explicit vocabulary instruction.

Simply being strategic in choosing the words is not enough, however, to maximize explicit instruction. We must also determine how much time we will spend teaching each word and when we will teach each word. Flanigan and Greenwood suggest a great framework for determining which words to teach and how long to spend on each.[10] They ask teachers to look over a text and make a list of words they think students might not know. Then they sort those words into four bins, driven by the learning goal:

- *Bin #1—Critical "before" words:* These are the one to three words most important for understanding a particular text or concept. They should be introduced prior to reading with high levels of support; teachers may even spend ten to twenty minutes making sure students have plenty of knowledge about these words.
- *Bin #2—"Foot in the door" words:* These words are important for comprehending the text, but students need less depth of understanding of these prior to reading. A teacher would introduce them briefly for a few minutes prior to reading and move on. Words that students already have some background knowledge about or new labels for known concepts are good ones for this bin.
- *Bin #3—Critical "after" words:* These words are useful, but not essential for students to understand a particular passage. They can be taught as students read or following the reading with varying amounts of time. High-utility academic words that occur across content areas and words defined explicitly in the text are good candidates for this bin, since students will be able to initially comprehend the text without support.

- *Bin #4—Words not to teach:* These words are not essential to teach at any point during the work with a particular text. It can be difficult to choose which words to leave out completely, but words that do not serve the instructional goal for the day or words that students already know are ones that can be left out of explicit teaching.

The power in teaching words explicitly lies in choosing words well and then using those words repeatedly. By being strategic in choosing which words to teach, we are able to maximize how much students can comprehend as they read, thus exposing them to more words and helping them to have a broad base of words in each discipline.

Conclusion

There are no silver bullets when it comes to vocabulary teaching, and strong vocabulary teaching is not about letting vocabulary take over. Powerful vocabulary teaching does not just teach words explicitly. It also relies heavily on teaching word-learning strategies and building a language-rich, word-curious environment. The strategies that students learn must be simple, so that students can do them independently and often, and, because not all strategies are likely to work for all students, an important part of good vocabulary teaching is building a repertoire of strategies from which students can choose the ones that work best.

If all these pieces are in place in a classroom, you will have an environment where learning words happens regularly and in deep and lasting ways. You will have built a base that is strong enough to build (or sit) on as you focus on all the other pieces of your particular discipline.

6

Research in Discussion

Effective Support for Literacy, Content, and Academic Achievement

CATHERINE J. MICHENER AND EVELYN FORD-CONNORS

Classroom discourse incorporates a range of goals and features, but its core consists of the teacher's instructional talk, which scaffolds students' learning experiences and frames students' interactions with instructional tasks, texts, and each other. The examples shown in figure 6.1 of actual instructional talk in two classrooms both focus on reading comprehension around content-area texts. What is plain, however, are the different ways that these teachers structure their instructional discourse; among them, who talks, when, and for how long; the kinds of questions the teachers ask; the teachers' responses to student ideas; the opportunities for students to respond to each other; and how both teachers and students treat the text. Even the lengths of these excerpts of instructional talk differ.

On the left is a pattern of instruction that you will undoubtedly recognize. The turn taking is a straightforward "teacher-student-teacher-student" pattern. The teacher's questions check for comprehension by eliciting a limited range of answers drawn directly from the text. Students' responses are short and stick to the text material, and the teacher's responses to student answers consist of either approval or a follow-up question that seems to limit the range of possible answers ("Migrating, good. What does that mean?").

Compare this with the pattern of talk on the right. Here, the pattern is still generally "teacher-student-teacher-student," but with some important differences. The teacher's questions are posed less to check on students' comprehension of the text and more to extend their thinking on responsibility and Internet use, topics addressed in the text. The questions pick up on the preceding student's responses, the student responses are lengthier, and the teacher acknowledges contributions with little evaluation ("Mm-hmm"), which seems to encourage more student talk and offers time for one student to clarify his or her thinking. This is a pattern of discourse that we all recognize as well, but don't see in as many classrooms. It happens frequently in our daily

FIGURE 6.1

Instructional talk: Two examples

Classroom 1—Science: Instructional talk around a text on animal adaptation	Classroom 2—ELA: Instructional talk around a text on online safety and social networks
Teacher: Just hold on. [*Student stops reading aloud*]. What does it—what does it mean by winter survival now? Xavier?	**Teacher:** Okay, so does MySpace the company have any responsibility?
Xavier: Survive—trying to—ways to survive in winter.	**Gregory:** Yes, Tom. Tom. Tom.
	Teacher: Who's Tom?
Teacher: Ways to—can somebody give me an example of what an animal has to try—their survival skill, sometimes they to try to do to survive? Leila?	**Gregory:** He's the creator, he made MySpace.
	Teacher: Tom should be responsible?
	Students: Yeah. [*unintelligible*]
Leila: The sheep—I mean elk. The elk travel in [*inaudible*] they travel with their family because they're getting food.	**Teacher:** What's Tom supposed to—let's get back. Gregory? Shhhh. None of the separate conversations. Hold on. How should Tom monitor millions and millions and millions of people?
Teacher: Okay, Xavier?	**Gregory:** Have millions and millions and millions of computers?
Xavier: Migrating.	**Naeem:** He should call the cop—he should tell the cops to monitor and the schools.
Teacher: Migrating, good. What does that mean?	**Teacher:** Mm-hmm.
Xavier: Moving to a different place.	**Naeem:** To monitor the cops, I mean, cops monitor computers.
Teacher: Good. Heather, what else do animals do?	**Teacher:** So basically we agree, it's a problem, right? Somebody's gotta monitor it?
Heather: They going to migrate in lower altitudes.	**Ariella:** I think he should pay—I think he should pay the police to monitor it, or for him to have MySpace, 'cause then if stuff happened or those molesters and stuff they get on and start talking to girls and stuff, or boys, they should stop it.
Teacher: What does it mean by lower altitudes?	**Teacher:** Can I ask a question?
	Students: [Yes.]
Heather: To the lower, like grass.	**Teacher:** How many in this class are monitored when they're on their computers?
Teacher: Lower area, right. Good.	**Wilson:** My mom got hawk eyes. She watch me all the time.
	Teacher: And how many are unmonitored?
	Students: [*crosstalk*]
	Teacher: Alan, what did you say unmonitored was again?
	Alan: Um, under adults—
	Naeem: No adult super—
	Alan: Yeah.
	Teacher: No supervision.
	Alan: Yeah, nobody's watching
	Teacher: So you say you're going on the computer unmonitored?

lives: when discussing politics over a drink after work, when exploring curriculum ideas in faculty meetings, or when talking to family members about a pressing issue. Our daily adult conversations have a dialogic and reciprocal nature as ideas are freely exchanged among active participants.

Do these differences matter for students' content learning and academic literacy development? Most research over the last twenty-five years suggests that, yes, discussions like the one on the right are more engaging and strengthen student learning. Across grade levels, classroom environments rich in oral language correlate with higher levels of student academic achievement.[1] Researchers who have evaluated specific discussion-based programs or observed teachers facilitating discussions in the course of their instruction have found that students' regular participation in productive discussions leads to gains in content acquisition and literacy learning.[2] Yet despite these positive findings, such productive, engaged discussions occur infrequently in our classrooms. Although middle and high school teachers report that "discussion" is their primary instructional format, in a study of 112 eighth- and ninth-grade language arts classes, researchers found that students engaged in less than one minute of true discussion per hour of class.[3] Clearly, implementing effective discussions is a challenging aspect of our craft as teachers.

Before we turn to the evidence for the instructional use of academic discussions, a brief note about our terminology is in order. We all use the words *discuss* and *discussion* every day to mean just about any kind of talk, from conversations and lectures ("I'd like to *discuss* your tardiness, young man") to debates and academic papers ("In the conclusion, we will *discuss* the implications for teaching"). Curricular guides often suggest that we "hold a *discussion*" of key ideas either before or after reading, but what this means is often unclear.

At its best, classroom discussion can be thought of as a free exchange of information between students and (likely) their teacher.[4] In these discussions, the content is less tightly regulated by teachers, which allows room for students' ideas to emerge.[5] Others have characterized discussion similarly: Dillon defined discussion as "a particular form of group interaction where members join together in addressing a question of common concern, exchanging and examining different views to form the answer, enhancing their knowledge or understanding."[6] Discussion has also be described as what it is not, namely recitation, a pattern of classroom talk characterized as *initiation-response-evaluation* (IRE) where the teacher *initiates* talk with a question, receives a *response* from a student, and then *evaluates* whether the answer is acceptable or not.[7]

These definitions all share a key characteristic: high-quality academic discussions that contribute to student learning are reciprocal, meaning that the talk consists of a dynamic give-and-take of ideas. These discussions are typically collaborative, sometimes exploratory, and usually open-ended. In the classroom, such discussions encourage students to share their various perspectives so that comprehension of a text or content becomes a process of reconciling potentially competing perspectives to illuminate each other, helping to generate deeper student understanding.[8]

In this chapter, we share the research on academic discussion and examine some important characteristics of these dynamic, reciprocal interactions. We look closely at the ways that teachers use their instructional talk to strengthen student learning, and we share findings from our own research on patterns of classroom talk. Our chapter is guided by three questions: (1) Why is discussion thought to be a powerful academic support for student literacy achievement? (2) What are the characteristics that distinguish high-quality discussions (the pattern of talk in the right-hand example) from the more run-of-the-mill instructional discourse patterns like IRE (the pattern in the left-hand example)? and (3) How do teachers create the conditions for these productive interactions around content to take place?

Oral Language: A Bridge Linking Reading to Learning

Reading and writing competence is fundamental to academic work. To succeed in school, students must read with enough skill to comprehend their classroom texts, reflect on the ideas presented in these texts, and produce coherent written responses. Such academic proficiency is based in students' oral language knowledge and skills, which underlie and foster these critical academic skills.

When young children enter school, oral language skill is a prerequisite for successful classroom interactions and contributes to young children's reading development.[9] As students advance into the upper grades, texts become more consistent sources of academic language development and vocabulary knowledge. The language and ideas found in texts and content are much more decontextualized and abstract than in the early grades, with greater complexity, richer and more varied vocabulary, and denser sentence structures.[10] These types of content and language are not always available in our students' daily lives, placing adolescent readers in a unique position compared with their younger peers: as readers, adolescents not only have to rely more on their language knowledge, but they must know more language that is not readily available in everyday contexts. Compounding this challenge is the fact that by middle school, most students receive little, if any, explicit reading instruction to help them grapple with disciplinary texts.[11] When students are unable to comprehend the texts they read, they cannot command the academic content they are expected to master. Students' use of oral language can be a strong bridge between the abstract and decontextualized language of school and texts and acquiring secondary content knowledge.

Two broad perspectives have been used to explain the relationship between oral discourse and literacy skills. One emphasizes oral language skill as fundamental to students' participation in the classroom interactions that enable the development of literacy skills and reading comprehension.[12] The other draws from the idea that oral interaction with others, using scaffolds (such as texts or a more knowledgeable person), will eventually be internalized and used in literacy activities.[13] Whatever the perspective, researchers agree that to develop the language competence necessary to access texts and understand the content of the higher grades, students must regularly engage in dialogic interactions that promote increasingly complex language skills.[14] Engaging students in productive academic discussions offers a support for such skills.

By managing the discourse of the classroom, teachers set the tone for how knowledge and learning are treated.[15] In this way, they create classroom environments that can substantially raise the intellectual rigor of the classroom while increasing students' engagement in learning. In the following sections, we consider the traits that distinguish high-quality discussions. These characteristics have been studied by observing secondary classrooms and through interventions using specific programs that incorporate or centralize text-based discussions. Both types of studies have shown strong relationships between discussion and students' literacy achievement, engagement, and quantities of productive talk.

Some Nuts and Bolts of Productive, Academic Discussions

High-quality, productive classroom discussions do not occur by happenstance or luck. Rather, they are the result of careful planning and a teacher's skilled facilitation. While various instructional models illustrate a range of possible approaches for constructing fruitful discussions, they all share the guidance of a skilled teacher and a high-quality text with sufficient complexity to make engaging discussions possible.

Quality Matters: Models of Productive Talk

Teachers and researchers have developed a number of instructional models that have encouraged the strategic use of classroom discussion as a teaching and learning tool to support students' active engagement in reading (for a brief description of some well-known models, see appendix A). These models share a common emphasis on the teacher as collaborator and sometime discussion facilitator, with the goal of furthering students' engagement with the text and with each other. The form of discussion in these models also disrupts the traditional IRE pattern of instruction.[16] While discussion-based programs vary in the amount of teacher control over discussions and in their stance toward texts (critical and questioning, informative, or aesthetic), there is consensus that such discussion-based reading instruction is more helpful than traditional recitative or reading-strategy instruction.

In an analysis that compared the effectiveness of nine established discussion-based models (e.g., Collaborative Reasoning, Paideia Seminars, literature circles), researchers found that overall, these approaches led to greater gains in student learning than conventional teaching approaches.[17] Many of the interventions promoted students' reading comprehension, and some supported students' critical thinking and reasoning about text, although fewer were effective for *both* increasing student literal comprehension and critical thinking. Interestingly, these text-based discussion programs had stronger effects on students with below-average academic ability than other students, possibly due to a greater need among these students to develop stronger reading skills. Additionally, more research is needed to understand how productive discussions function in classrooms of students with special needs and English learners (see appendix B for a brief review of current research). Finally, this analysis showed that although the nine programs all increased student talk, this did not necessarily result in reading achievement gains, suggesting that the quality, not just the quantity, of student talk matters.

A second study of the same discussion-based programs found that the most productive discussions were framed by the teacher in ways that encouraged students to talk about texts and content and to sustain that productive focus for relatively lengthy periods of time.[18] When critical-analytic perspectives toward texts were emphasized, students exhibited higher levels of reasoning and critical thinking. Students talked more when asked authentic questions and when discussions had high levels of teacher uptake (questions or responses that incorporate a previous response, like: "Say more about *that*"). From these two analyses of popular discussion-based programs, it would seem that students need sufficient time to talk about texts and content, spurred by questions that help students maintain topical focus and encourage analytic and critical thinking. Thus, both the quantity and quality of talk are important characteristics of discussions that impact positively on students' learning outcomes.

Leveraging Questions to Improve Learning

Teachers' questioning patterns are important supports for student learning across the content areas. Questions can strengthen the academic rigor of a lesson and the degree of student engagement in high-level thinking. Questions can encourage students to wrestle with complex texts and look for text-based evidence, an important component of the Common Core State Standards. *Authentic* and *open-ended teacher questions, uptake questions,* and *student questions* have been linked to instructional episodes characterized by higher levels of student engagement and intellectual rigor, increases in critical thinking, self-reflection, skillful scientific argumentation, and literacy achievement.

Many researchers have found that *open-ended* and *authentic* questions, questions that allow for a range of possible answers, correlate with higher levels of student engagement and literacy outcomes across content.[19] Authentic questions have also been linked to students' writing achievement and productive discussions.[20] Consider the difference in two questions posed by a teacher during her language arts lesson on the meaning of a poem (figure 6.2)

In the exchange on the left, the teacher simply asks her student to find the answer in the text, and Lucas answers accordingly, using the words directly from the text. During the same lesson, the teacher asks for Adia's thoughts, and receives her inference and interpretation. Questions with higher levels of academic rigor elicit higher levels of thinking and greater displays of knowledge from students, including critical thinking and scientific argumentation.[21] In contrast, when teachers pose questions requiring simple answers or only factual information about texts and content, they elicit narrowly focused answers or simple recitations of facts.[22] These narrow questions are indeed necessary at certain points in a lesson, and it matters how teachers and students use them, but if we are to provide students with more opportunities for deeply considering content and displaying their knowledge, questions that elicit a range of possible answers should be emphasized during instruction, despite the increased demands on instructional time and the challenge for teachers to interpret and synthesize students' comments to keep lessons cohesive.

Uptake questions that incorporate some element of a student's idea or previous answer have also been shown to correlate with student literacy and content learning outcomes.[23] Uptake questions in science and language arts have been shown to promote extended student talk, more reflective and critical thinking, and student engagement. Consider the examples shown in figure 6.3.

Uptake questions shift responsibility for thinking back to students, to position students' ideas centrally during instruction and show students that they are being taken seriously through this reciprocity in instructional talk.[24] Uptake of students' answers can encourage student elaborations, and challenging students' answers can increase critical thinking and student engagement.[25] This back-and-forth questioning and reasoning between students and teachers seems to be a key characteristic of classrooms where productive discussions are happening.

Discussions that include *student questions* can also result in increased student learning. In a study of discussion in middle-school science classes, students' abilities to engage in scientific thinking, including making arguments and claims, were linked with the quality of the questions they asked.[26] Figure 6.4 shows an example that

FIGURE 6.2

Narrow versus open-ended questions

Narrow		Open-ended	
Teacher:	In these two lines we're talking about the skin. **What color is this person's skin?**	*Teacher:*	**What are you thinking, Adia? Tell me what you're thinking when you read these first two lines.**
Lucas:	Brownish, pinkish, yellowish, and white.	*Adia:*	I'm thinking that she's one way, and she don't like 'em, so she change her hair, her eyes, even her skin to suit her.

FIGURE 6.3

Teacher uptake

ELA: writing test-prep lesson		Math: lesson on central tendency	
Ellie:	I think it's supposed to be kind of like sum all the evidence and details and then be, like, an end to something.	*Teacher:*	What information is important here?
		Rafael:	They give the grades before and after the rule is in place.
Teacher:	OK. So part of it, yes, it's summing it up. **What's another way to say that?**	*Teacher:*	**OK, so students' grade information before and after is the information we've been given. What should we do with this information?**
Ellie:	The closing sentence kind of has to restate what your—the topic sentence is.	*Luis:*	Well we gotta know if there was an effect, like, did it make any difference to the kids who wanted to play on the team—so did they study more after the rule was put in place, and work harder, and did they get better grades?
Teacher:	Right. And as you get more into writing pieces like this, you'll get better at restating your actual topic sentence using almost the same exact words, but in a different way.	*Teacher:*	**Right, so Luis says that we need to see if the rule had an effect on their grades, right? So, Luis, how will we calculate that?**
		Luis:	Either use the mean or median.
		Teacher:	**OK, Luis tells us to find either the mean or the median. So let's think about the purpose of each one** and then we can decide which is more appropriate in this case . . .
		Adrienne:	Well, the mean will give the average, so, yeah, that will work here.
		Teacher:	**And why is that so?**
		Xavier:	Well, because we just need to find the average and then we can compare before and after the . . . rule.

reveals both the importance of a student's question for spurring cognitively engaging talk, and for creating an opportunity to construct an argument (however imprecise!).

This example of a short scientific discussion that began with David's intriguing question is demonstrative of the possibilities for more careful thinking and the aca-

FIGURE 6.4

Building on student questions in discussion

Science: Student question during a text talk about air pressure
David: If you jumped on a trampoline from more than 1,000 feet, would the trampoline break? Would the bouncy part break?
Teacher: Depending on how strong those springs and the metal that holds the bouncy part to the actual frame. It probably depends on how much you weigh, too. That's a physics question. [*crosstalk, inaudible*], and weight and speed. Manuel?
Manuel: One thing about that is I saw this thing once on the Internet. What it said was that all objects get accelerated by gravity at a rate of 9.8 meters per second squared.
Teacher: So it doesn't have anything to do with your weight, your mass?
Manuel: Well, yeah, because there's an eventual—actually, it does slightly . . . It's the relationship of surface area to weight, and eventually the pushing of air on you against the speed will just stop you from going any faster. Well, it's pretty much like— you'd have to drop from 20,000 feet to actually reach that certain dead point.
Teacher: The point where you don't continue to speed up. I see what you're saying . . .

demic talk that students can create themselves if we follow up their questions with attentive and authentic questions, restatements, and encouragement. The following section looks at these follow-up talk moves in more detail.

Say More: The Importance of Follow-up Moves

Follow-up moves are teachers' responses to students' answers and contributions. These moves can be evaluations in the classic IRE sense ("Yes, 2, 3, and 5 are examples of prime numbers. Good."), repetitions of student answers, as in the left-hand column in figure 6.5 ("Slaves. So she might be treating . . . slaves . . . "), or brief corrections ("Well, sick people . . .) that do not deviate from the teacher's line of questioning. Alternatively, follow-up talk moves may be used to integrate or extend students' contributions. On the right-hand side of figure 6.5, the teacher follows up a student's question or contribution three times by posing clarifying questions, and then offers her interpretation using Ariana's own term ("different countries").

Some researchers have argued that what happens in this third turn (evaluation, the "E" position in the IRE pattern) is one of the most important elements in conducting productive discussions, particularly when these moves encourage students to extend or qualify their contributions.[27] It is here that teachers can steer the course of the discussion and model the level of intellectual rigor they expect from their students. It is also in this third turn that teachers can open up the discussion and invite more students to participate: "So who has something to say about what Amaya just said? Who can build on that? She said it's a privilege to play sports, so . . . " If teachers avoid

FIGURE 6.5

Examples of teacher follow-up moves

Social studies class		ELA sheltered English immersion class	
Teacher:	Yes. So who was she treating in Richmond, Virginia? Who was she probably treating? Sick people who may have also been what, Sanjit?	*Sofia:*	What does this mean, "to shake hands with yellow men, and red men"?
Sanjit:	Hurt people?	*Teacher:*	**What page are you on?**
Teacher:	**Well, sick people probably would be hurt, yes . . . They're sick, they're injured, they're hurt. What else? What kind of people might she be treating?**	*Sofia:*	65.
		Teacher:	**. . . "he met many people along the way, he shook hands with yellow man and red man, black man and white man." What'd you think that's showing?**
Lucia:	Soldiers?	*Ariana:*	It's like different.
Teacher:	**She might be treating soldiers, but more importantly,** who would have just been newly free?	*Teacher:*	**Different what?**
		Ariana:	Different countries.
Student:	Slaves.	*Teacher:*	**Yeah, people from different countries. We all have different-colored skin. I think that they're just trying to show you how different all the people are [here].**
Sara:	**Slaves. So she might be treating who used to be slaves, but who were now free.** Remember, it said . . .		

evaluating students' contributions and instead seek clarifications, explanations, and justifications, students are more inclined to participate because the role of primary knower has shifted to them.[28]

There are a variety of follow-up moves teachers can use. Teacher *revoicing*, a talk move through which the teacher incorporates some aspect of a student's idea in her response, has been shown to clarify and elaborate ideas, change students' utterances into more academic language, and broadcast important ideas for the class to consider.[29] In the following example, the teacher revoices her students' ideas and then elaborates as they discuss the meaning of *maintain*:

Teacher: So what does it mean to maintain something?

Evie: Like to maintain being focused in class.

Teacher: Maintain being focused in class. And when I come around and talk to you about maintaining your focus at home, what does that mean? Johnson, if we say, "maintain your focus at home," what are we talking about? We want to make sure you get what done?

Johnson: Your work done.

Teacher: Your work done. So you keep it up. You concentrate on your work, and you keep going until it is all . . .

Students: Done.

Teacher: Done. Okay.

Recasting moves, where the teacher restates students' contributions in more academic language, can help scaffold content and academic discourse like historical terminology and inquiry:

Teacher: Fester . . . and what does it mean?

Michael: To get infected.

Teacher: Okay, infected, decay, rotten.[30]

However, too much scaffolding can be detrimental: in one study, when teachers regularly offered hints about an answer, narrowed questions to get to an answer, or did not examine students' responses, students tended to have lower scores in reading comprehension.[31] Above, the teacher narrows her questions to elicit fill-in-the-blank answers (*Teacher:* " . . . and you keep going until it is all . . . " *Students:* "Done."), precluding an opportunity for extended student talk.

Like some kinds of questions, teachers' follow-up moves have been positively related to reading comprehension scores and are seen as effective scaffolds for academic language acquisition. They can validate students' thinking, position students as active participants in their own learning, and focus students on important elements of the content. Follow-up moves that extend, challenge, or press students for more elaboration have been shown to scaffold and model disciplinary thinking and inquiry work. Despite their potential, more research is needed to identify productive follow-up moves and how they work to enhance student learning.

The Potential of Peer-Led Discussions

Until now, we have mainly talked about contexts where teachers direct and contribute to classroom discussions. Like authentic questions and some follow-up moves, peer-led discussions have been lauded as moving teaching away from the IRE pattern of instructional discourse to give students more opportunities to talk about texts. However, peer-led talk can be messy and chaotic, as figure 6.6 shows.

The students in this example needed monitoring and some instruction around facilitation and questioning to hold productive discussions. This challenge may deter our investment in peer-to-peer talk. There is conflicting evidence that peer discussions are increasingly used in secondary classrooms: some researchers have documented that discussions are very rare, but in a series of studies of secondary ELA teachers, more than half of the teachers reported using cooperative grouping patterns to increase interactions among students and reinforce important concepts.[32] Although

FIGURE 6.6

Example of peer-led discussion

ELA class, text-based discussion	
Mia:	What have you guys been thinking about this book?
Teacher:	Tina, are you listening to her?
Tina:	Yes. I think it's very good [*inaudible*].
Carter:	The movie is better than the book [*crosstalk, unintelligible*].
Mia:	What do you guys think of the book? [*off-task response*]
Mia:	What do you guys think? I think—
Robert:	I think I liked this book, but the things that happened—like why would somebody like her wanna run away from home? Why would you wanna run away if you have parents that support you?

student outcomes were not analyzed, many teachers believed that these grouping patterns strengthened students' learning and created opportunities for students to learn from each other.[33] These teachers may be right: in an analysis of student outcomes on the National Assessment of Educational Progress (NAEP), researchers found that students who had opportunities to respond to texts through discussions with peers at least once a week showed better comprehension than students who did not engage in these practices.[34] Secondary students themselves have reported that peer discussions were valuable for their own vocabulary learning.[35]

As we have previously noted, we cannot say that simply increasing student talk leads to better student outcomes: the *quality* of classroom talk may be more important for students' text comprehension.[36] In a recent review of the effects of inquiry-based science teaching, classes that included social activities like discussion and collective reasoning in groups had the highest effect on student outcomes. However, teacher-led inquiry programs showed better effects than student-led conditions, suggesting that teacher guidance is important for students to "generate, develop, and justify" scientific explanations in the process of learning content.[37] So while there is evidence that peer discussions may lead to more elaborated or complex student talk in math and reading, more research needs to examine the qualities of productive peer-led discussions in secondary classrooms and how students apply these discussions to their individual learning.[38]

Current Research

In our own research, we have studied the quality and quantity of teachers' instructional talk in math and language arts classrooms. Catherine's research takes a broad look at features of dialogic instruction, and Evelyn's work provides an in-depth look at how teachers can foster discussion. Our work reinforces some of the research presented above.

Catherine's Study: Some Indicators of Dialogic Instruction

Catherine looked at the instructional talk in thirty-one classrooms.[39] The findings presented here are from eight fifth-grade classrooms where the shift toward more decontextualized and abstract texts can become a pressing issue for teachers preparing their students for the transition to middle school. Like previous findings in secondary classrooms, these classrooms showed a lack of academic discussion and a predominance of teacher-managed question and answer (Q&A) instructional talk that followed an IRE pattern. Teachers talked a lot, speaking an average of seventy-six words per minute (with a standard deviation of 32), and posed almost one question per minute (standard deviation of .40). This Q&A genre of talk was characterized by a low rate of authentic questions, and more low-quality questions that asked students to recall or recite information directly from the text or from prior knowledge. Despite this, and the overall lack of discussion-oriented instruction, there was a relationship between high-quality questions and instances of extended student talk by individual students during this IRE pattern. High-quality questions were those that asked students to infer, generalize, synthesize, or evaluate textual information, which seemed to allow for increases in student talk amount within this Q&A pattern.

The few segments of talk that fit our definition of discussion as dynamic, give-and-take exchanges of ideas tended to begin with high-quality teacher questions or, as in the example provided in figure 6.7, when a student interrupted the whole-class read-aloud to ask a vocabulary question.

In this brief discussion, the reciprocal nature of the talk is clear as students respond to each other and the teacher. The teacher encourages this talk pattern by positioning herself as a participant ("I know I was thinking that . . . he survived") rather than an authority and by providing no evaluative follow-ups ("Yeah." "Mmm.") to let the discussion unfold. Unsurprisingly, this sort of discussion tended to happen with unabridged informational and narrative texts and rarely with test materials, form-focused worksheets, or review work.

These general findings from eight language arts classrooms suggest that instructional materials and the genre of instruction talk (read-alouds, Q&A, small-group text talks, etc.) tended to influence the talk moves that teachers employed. Texts with complex content seemed to allow for the possibility of discussions, and questions that got students to talk more about their thinking seemed to "loosen" the IRE pattern of talk to allow for more dynamic, reciprocal talk between teachers and their students.

FIGURE 6.7

Reciprocal teacher-student interaction

Dylan:	What does bilge water mean? On page 18.
Teacher:	The—okay, get a dictionary. I want you to look it up.
Angel:	Oh, I have a question too. What happened to the captain, 'cuz there's no humans?
Max:	Right.
Teacher:	I know I was thinking that when we read it, because I thought he survived.
Victoria:	That's not when they said the fifteen ponies. All it said was the fifteen ponies.
Teacher:	Yeah.
Victoria:	Because it said that—in the book, he got swept by the ocean at sea.
Teacher:	That he tried to grab onto the horse's tail, but I thought he made it. In the back of my mind I was like, "He made it," because they didn't say specifically he did. We'll have to read on. You could be right.
April:	I think he didn't. I thought that it took him—that the sea took him with it and it took him. It said the sea started coming down.
Teacher:	Mmm. The storm had left.
April:	Oh.
Teacher:	Can you get the dictionary please? . . .

Evelyn's Study: How Teachers Encourage Discourse to Develop Students' Vocabulary Knowledge

Evelyn studied classroom discourse during teachers' implementation of a vocabulary intervention known as Word Generation, developed by the Strategic Education Research Partnership (2008/2009).[40] Word Generation (WG) is a middle school instructional program whose primary objective is to develop students' knowledge of academic words and encourage word use during discussions of high-interest topics. WG implementation typically occurs on a schoolwide basis with each content-area teacher at a particular grade level taking responsibility for vocabulary instruction once a week. Data for this study were collected in the classrooms of several experienced math teachers in two urban middle schools as they implemented their weekly WG curriculum. Evelyn analyzed teachers' audio- or videorecorded instruction during their WG lessons and data from interviews with teachers.

Although teachers worked with curricula and instructional objectives that were the same or very similar, their approaches varied widely, both in instructional focus and in predominant discourse patterns. In particular, there was a noticeable contrast between discussions in the classrooms of Ms. Sol and Ms. Jenson (both names are pseudonyms). Ms. Sol organized her discussions primarily as *knowledge display*, that is, the classroom talk unfolded as a series of loosely related student answers to Ms. Sol's questions or prompts, with little teacher talk to link them together. Ms. Sol responded to students' contributions mostly with comments like "Okay," or "Good" rather than encouraging students to build on their classmates' ideas, to connect their ideas to the content, or to elaborate. As a result, each student's contribution seemed to reflect existing knowledge rather than something new about the content. Since she infrequently responded to students' utterances to modify, question, or strengthen their ideas, it is easy to imagine that students left the classroom with little *new* knowledge of target vocabulary, mathematical solutions, or topical ideas.

In contrast, discussions in Ms. Jenson's classroom had a *knowledge-building* character as students generated ideas around a central concept. As she negotiated students' various responses, Ms. Jenson explicitly connected their ideas to previous learning or to important concepts, periodically summarizing key ideas and information. In this way, ideas were cumulative and related to one another in a logical progression that moved participants into new academic territory. Ms. Jenson's elicitation of input from multiple students also positioned them as potential resources for each other in their explorations of content.

In addition, through her flexible use of a repertoire of talk moves, Ms. Jenson was successful at engaging students in sustained conversations about content during each segment of the lesson. Her discourse featured uptake through revoicing and repetition, strategic questioning, connecting, and frequent explanations and elaborations that furthered the discussion and promoted students' engagement with the content and with each other.

Ms. Jenson's knowledge-building approach also contributed to an ongoing process of formative assessment. Discussion allowed her access to students' current knowledge and made it possible for her to keep track of their developing understandings, based on their participation and ability to contribute ideas to the discussion. If she discovered that some students were confused, she could extend the discussion and provide additional explanation. Her knowledge-building approach also effectively engaged a wider cross-section of students, even the reluctant or less skilled, through the scaffolding she provided.

Implications for Practice: Academic Discussions Are Worth the Effort

Implementing, encouraging, and managing academic discussions is not an easy task. We know that transitioning instruction in all content areas from the traditional IRE pattern to more discussion-oriented patterns of talk is challenging; the tension between providing opportunities for students to collaboratively build understanding of content and text and maintaining control and authority to scaffold key information is not easily resolved.[41] Furthermore, having discussions, or even simply asking a question that pushes a student to explain his/her thinking, takes time. Teachers are already pressed for time to cover more content, increase test scores, and teach students with a wide range of backgrounds and abilities. Despite these challenges, there is a general consensus that discussions are worth the time and effort to provide some big payoffs for students and teachers alike. Both Catherine's and Evelyn's work affirm this.

This chapter has emphasized the central role that discussion can play for improving student learning and literacy outcomes in content-area classrooms. Certainly, teachers' ideas about knowledge building matter. Some authors have argued that student achievement may depend less on discrete teacher actions (question types, follow-up moves, etc.) than to a teacher's stance on knowledge building. In other words, if a teacher thinks of learning as receiving content from an authority or from texts, her teaching will tend toward IRE patterns of discourse with little room for student talk. However, if the teacher believes that students construct important knowledge through inquiry and collaborative talk with peers and adults, then his teaching may more readily use discussion. Of course, teaching is never quite so dichotomous, so fundamentally, it is important to consider how talk moves are used within the teacher's larger instructional framework.[42]

In closing, we note that the features of instructional talk reviewed here all share a common emphasis on increasing opportunities for student talk in academic work by shifting from teacher-dominated instruction toward a collaborative and inquiry-driven classroom discourse. Creating opportunities for students to voice their thinking is both a means to an end (i.e., as a teaching tool, discussion has been correlated with higher vocabulary, content understanding, engagement, and reading outcomes), and an end in itself, as we all want our students to be capable of expressing themselves in academically appropriate ways. The degree to which teachers understand and strategically control the discourse in their lessons can profoundly affect their abilities to teach effectively. As schools implement the Common Core standards, demand will grow for instruction that strengthens students' abilities to participate in the high levels of reading, writing, and speaking that the Common Core standards require across content areas. Academic discussion and the instructional talk that facilitates discussion hold great promise to help all students meet those demands.

APPENDIX A
Discussion-Based Instructional Models

Below are some well-known discussion-based literacy instruction programs.

- *Reciprocal Teaching (RT)*: RT moved the traditional teaching of reading strategies from teaching isolated skills to contextualizing them in small-group discussions about texts across subject areas. RT has been shown to be a successful tool for building knowledge and improving students' comprehension of text.[43]

- *Questioning the Author (QtA)*: QtA uses "queries" to explore important ideas in a text in conjunction with discussion moves. Research on QtA has shown increases in student talk and questions, better recall and text interpretation in upper elementary and middle school students, and significant effects on students' engagement and text comprehension.[44]

- *Instructional Conversations*: Developed by teachers and researchers to support English language learners (ELLs) as they transition into English-only classrooms, this model has been shown to improve story comprehension of ELLs and fluent English speakers, with stronger effects on narrative texts in the fourth and fifth grades.[45]

- *Collaborative Reasoning (CR)*: This model encourages a more critical-analytic stance toward texts: as students respond to key questions about narrative text, they develop positions, gather evidence, and consider the arguments of their peers. CR has been related to increases in student-directed talk about content and more sophisticated oral reasoning and written argumentation.[46]

- *Concept-Oriented Reading Instruction (CORI)*: Instruction is organized around an interdisciplinary theme. Studies have shown CORI students at intermediate and middle school levels increased their reading engagement and made significant gains in reading and content comprehension.[47]

- *Paideia Seminar*: Teachers act as facilitators of civil discussion about a previously read text by asking some open-ended questions. One study documented a teacher's struggle to reconcile appropriate scaffolding and leaving the students to co-construct under-standings of honors-level literary texts.[48]

- *Word Generation (WG)*: WG is a discussion-based academic vocabulary development program that introduces high-utility words each week across the four core-content classes. Researchers have found small but significant effects of WG on students' learning of target words, including language-minority students, who showed greater growth than English-only students.[49] In a study comparing WG with control classrooms, researchers found that classes with engaged discussion had more widespread student engagement and a structure that supported students' interactions with target words.[50]

APPENDIX B
Research on English Language Learners and Discussion

As our classrooms become increasingly diverse because of immigration trends, demo-graphic shifts, and inclusion policies, teaching content-area literacy skills is undoubtedly more of a challenge. It is surprising, therefore, that few studies have looked at discussion-based reading interventions for students with learning disabilities or for secondary English language learners. Two studies of Reciprocal Teaching showed inconsistent findings on learning-disabled students' reading scores.[51] Studies on the effects of discussion on English learners' literacy achievement have mainly involved elementary students (see Instructional Conversations in appendix A). A small study of upper-elementary ELLs has suggested that they may benefit more from questions tied closely to the text (and less authentic and open-ended) to support their language development.[52] It has been established that ELL's second-language (English) oral proficiency is related to reading comprehension and writing in English, but there are few studies that have looked at first-language oral proficiency and second-language reading comprehension and writing achievement, despite the obvious fact that English oral proficiency cannot be an assumed skill when teaching reading and writing to ELLs.[53] There is evidence that students' first language is related to their first-language reading comprehension, which is directly related to their second-language reading comprehension.[54] These findings are intriguing because practitioners could make the case that ELLs either need to improve their first-language literacy to indirectly improve their English reading, or that ELLs need to improve their English to better support their reading in English. Current practice in most schools in the United States suggests that teachers have chosen the latter route, but it is still unclear if this is a more effective program than bilingual instruction.

Discussion in Practice

Sharing Our Learning Curve

ABIGAIL ERDMANN AND MARGARET METZGER

Discussion is the queen of lesson plans: an essential, prominent, but often undertaught tool for the classroom teacher. Although discussion is the most difficult classroom format to plan and to manage, it is also the ultimate bridge between reading and writing. Nothing in the secondary classroom is harder to plan and lead effectively, except perhaps differentiated instruction. No one is born knowing how to lead discussion—it took us years in the classroom—but it can be learned. We hope this chapter helps others shorten their learning curve.

When we began teaching decades ago, there were no literacy programs, no Common Core State Standards, no state standardized tests. We were on our own. Yet we had the clarity, maybe just the common sense, to want our students to become better readers, writers, and thinkers. We knew that discussion would help students clarify their ideas and would motivate them to engage with the material and each other. We wanted democratic discussions where everyone engaged enthusiastically and all opinions were welcomed, where the conversations felt purposeful and intellectually challenging, where students would be increasingly willing to reveal their assumptions and question each other and the material. On some days, when students had failed to do the reading or they put their heads on their desks, these goals seemed like pie in the sky.

It took us decades of teaching high school to achieve authentic, lively, impassioned discussion in which even the quietest students participated and we genuinely wanted to know what students thought. Error by error, we learned how to plan and lead discussions. Sometimes we still feel inadequate. Sometimes discussions still flop. Yet, at each stage of our learning, we saw how we could improve. Then, just when we thought we had mastered discussion, we were humbled by switching grade levels, courses, populations. In retrospect, was it worth spending so many hours of our careers working on discussion? Did our effort pay off for our students? Yes, and yes. Frankly, we would invest those hours of planning all over again. For us, it has been a slow learning curve. We hope this chapter can help others be more effective discussion leaders, wherever you are in your development as a teacher, particularly as leading discussions becomes a major nationwide focus under the Common Core standards.[1]

Though we can share clever techniques and smart questions from our classrooms, these are not the key elements of genuine, strong discussion. The willingness to speak out in a group, to risk exploring what you think, to listen openheartedly to someone with whom you disagree—these qualities of effective discussion grow out of the most important part of a discussion: *relationship, relationship, relationship.* As many teachers would agree, the ideal discussion is democratic because it gives each of our students—quiet or verbal—a genuine investment in grappling with difficult issues, with each other, and with the material. For this to happen, students must feel intellectually safe with the teacher and each other. Respect must be modeled, taught, and practiced—over and over. Only then can teachers and students reap the intellectual, academic, and affective rewards of rich classroom discussions.

Why Discussion? What Are the Benefits?

When deciding whether and when to engage students in discussion, we always consider the possible benefits: helping students clarify their thinking, increasing motivation around particular concepts and genres, and introducing new ideas and ways of thinking about those ideas. Discussion can light the intellectual fire.

A major reason for any discussion is practicing articulating ideas. The very act of putting opinions into words forces all of us toward more clarity and depth. Thinking improves when we must explain ourselves, articulate vaguely held opinions, support our assertions, define our terms, and clarify our values and perceptions. We can encourage disciplinary habits of mind in our students by requesting that they continue thinking and articulating their ideas. Even simple questions help: "I don't understand what you're saying. Can you give an example?" "Can you generalize from that statement?" "How would you argue against yourself?" "Say more."

Students will disagree with each other. That's fine. But they need to be taught how to disagree: the phrase, "I see it so differently," invites difference and clarification; "That's stupid," shuts off conversation. We talk with students about how to handle disagreements on the first day or when needed. We teach students to base their contributions on what was said previously, to disagree without condescension, to never ridicule another's confusion. Sometimes we use prods like, "Can you restate that using a different tone?" or, "You can say, 'I have another way to solve this problem,' rather than saying, 'I have a better way to solve the problem.'" We explain that always being right doesn't further the flow of a discussion where the class, together, figures out a truth.

Beyond helping students clarify their thinking, discussions also serve as a motivating force in secondary classrooms as new ideas and content are introduced. When students find any topic interesting, their motivation increases. A dynamic discussion can introduce students to topics they might not care about yet—just as a movie or documentary or blog can initiate interest. A class can get swept up in the energy of the subject. A lively discussion feels infectious; students become interested in what their classmates say and thus care more about the topic, and are motivated to return to the material for evidence, justification, and new ideas. Before beginning *Lord of the Flies* or *A Separate Peace*, a teacher might ask students if they have ever witnessed bullying, been bullied, or bullied. Discussions about general topics allow everyone to participate and show that the topic central to the book matters. The same is true of ethical questions from science. Even simple questions like, "Do individuals recycling affect global warming, and how would you prove it?" motivates and energizes students.

Thoughtful, sustained conversation is so unusual in contemporary life that learning discussion techniques becomes even more urgent for developing the complex thinking needed in college and the workplace. Walk into any Starbucks and observe how few people are talking directly to each other. Watch the dynamics of a faculty meeting. Notice how dysfunctional our present government is. For each person's education and for a rational democracy, we all need to learn to talk and listen well. If students don't practice talking and listening in a classroom, which includes interacting with and respecting people who are really different from them, they may never learn it.

A Description of Our Learning Curve

In our first years of teaching, our own inadequate planning caused the most problems. Like many new teachers, we wrote lesson plans that said, "Discuss." We quickly learned that our vague plans to "discuss" resulted in chatter, chaos, silence, or hostility. So we worked to craft specific questions that would support our goals. At first, despite our good intentions, our questions remained oral quizzes. We knew the answers; we were just checking whether the kids knew the same material. Our questions had right and wrong answers, of which we were the gatekeepers. Students felt put on the spot—because they were. Sometimes kids refused to answer, even if they could. When the whole class knew the answer to an easy question, the student who answered, even to help out the hapless teacher, could be seen as a teacher's pet.

Over time, we learned that oral quizzes have a use, as long as we acknowledged the purpose: "I'm going to ask you some *teacher questions*, questions where I know the answer, and I'm just making sure you have the basic information/plot/facts. Then we will go on to *real questions*, where we will think about/interpret/debate those facts."

After this our students talked a lot and classrooms looked engaged, but talking was not enough. Teenagers talk all the time—think cellphones and hallways. We asked ourselves about the quality, not the quantity, of talking. What were they talking about? Did they listen to each other? Risk new thoughts? Build on the each other's ideas? Generate their own questions? Evaluate and reflect? Or repeat what they already knew?

When we taught different sections of the same courses, we worked together for hours creating "perfect questions" for both of our classes. It never occurred to us to plan for the class in front of us. Could we plan for the dynamics, chemistry, and interests of the different classes? Like professional curriculum writers, we assumed a perfect set of questions would elicit good discussion. We didn't yet understand that the students matter more than the questions. We needed to think about each class's knowledge base, competence, interest, and experience: Where do the students want to begin? How much time does this group need to calm down from the previous class, or lunch? Do they need to be energized? Are we sure they understand the basics? What will encourage more abstract thinking with this class of concrete thinkers? What questions will challenge their assumptions, draw out the non-speakers, and support the concepts and skills being taught? Finally, which questions interest us, the teachers?

Like many teachers learning how to lead discussions, we soon moved into a stage of *serial dialogues*. The teacher and one student talk while everyone else waits; then the teacher moves to another student who seems to know the right answer and starts another dialogue while the rest of the class sits. Students don't talk with each other. Most responses last for only one or two sentences. Our classes followed this pattern.

The research overwhelmingly shows that teacher talk dominates classrooms (see chapter 6). Students speak very little. We hoped our classes were different, but when we asked students to time our speaking versus the class speaking, we were horrified by how much we still monopolized conversations.

Besides talking far too much, we also still did most of the mental work. We figured out the questions in advance, thought on our feet, responded to comments, reworded, and lobbed the discussion ball in new directions. We did the mental work while the students watched, complied, regurgitated information, guessed, or acted out.

Often we held too tight a rein, too much control over which ideas were rewarded or dismissed. True, we needed a strong plan, with big questions, but we also needed the courage to deviate from our plan. When we came in with an inflexible lesson plan, the students' thoughtful questions never got asked. A brave student once asked Margaret, "Are you through with your questions? We're waiting to ask each other something else." With a rigid lesson plan, we focused on getting through the lesson, rather than on supporting student learning. Once, as a new teacher, while leading a discussion, Margaret urged the class to "think, think, think" while tapping her own temple. Her smart supervisor observed the irony: the answer lay in her head, and the students' job was to guess it. They were not thinking. She had stayed with the original plan, and was waiting for the right answer/her answer.

It took a long time for us to feel confident enough to let go of intellectual control and allow student thinking to dominate the class. Finally, although we still monitored the group dynamics, reinforced the content, and taught the concepts at hand, we no longer assumed we had all the answers. This helped us transition from serial dialogues to more open, authentic, student-led discussions. But first we had to be clear on the purposes and appropriateness of real discussion.

Deciding When Discussion Is Appropriate

As teachers across all content areas know, discussion is not always appropriate to meet the learning objectives of a particular lesson. Sometimes lectures are a more efficient way to convey basic information. It doesn't make sense to discuss photosynthesis when a lecture would more clearly and logically explain the process. We want students to know facts so they can use them for thinking. But facts themselves do not warrant a discussion. We admire social studies teachers who write the facts and dates at the top of an exam, indicating that knowing facts is not the final goal. The exam asks students to evaluate and interpret the facts. To check on planning, every day, for every lesson we asked ourselves: "Why do we want a discussion here? Why not some other format? What will they learn by talking with each other?"

Discussion seems most effective for critical thinking, inference, wondering, exploring, and hypothesizing. Perhaps most important, discussion demonstrates how other people think differently than we do. There are many ways to solve a math problem; many ways to critique a scientific finding; many ways to evaluate art or music. Through discussion, students learn to value mental flexibility in discovering different approaches. Solutions and new meaning are enhanced by multiple answers. We try to teach students to keep thinking, even when they have a possible answer. We often say, "Great. Now keep going. What other answers are possible?"

So, before planning a class discussion, a teacher's task is to decide whether discussion is appropriate and efficacious. Will students benefit from hearing different opinions? Does the topic lend itself to multiple interpretations? To preserve our own energy, we made a list of lesson formats—debate, demonstration, experiment, performance, etc.—and then chose the most effective format to reach the learning goals. Wiggins and McTighe convincingly argue that teachers should plan backward: figure out what students need to learn, and then construct a series of lessons that will achieve that end.[2]

Students, like adults, want to discuss the *big questions*—questions that require complex judgments and multiple answers. If the teacher can create an abstract, open-ended question from the topic at hand, discussion may be useful. Here are a few samples of big questions: Are there any limits to what scientists should research? Do animals have rights over human needs? Do individuals or ideas change history? When does a nation run out of choices? How does dictatorship affect children? What is the difference between trauma and tragedy? Define forgiveness. How do we assign responsibility? What forces drive a decision?

Once we understood when to use discussion and how to frame a real question, then we had to learn how our responses to student comments could deepen and broaden the discussion.

Learning How to Respond to Student Comments

During early discussions, we automatically responded to every comment with predictable teacher-statements like "That's right," "Good idea," "Nice work," "Great question," "Interesting," or "Anyone else?" Our well-intended phrases quickly became annoying to the students. We tested this pattern on ourselves. We tried talking for five minutes, with the listener interjecting a teacher-response at every pause. The comments were so infuriating that we could not sustain the conversation for even five minutes.

Instead of stock phrases, we learned to trust silence, that the next student can and will speak without an evaluative comment from the teacher as a transition. We self-consciously practiced a ten-second wait time, which involves the teacher silently counting to ten before moving on. Pausing during discussion is particularly helpful for students who have processing problems. Wait time gives everyone, not just the verbally adept students, a shot at involvement. If wait time is agreed on by the whole class, it both respects the quieter student and asks for thoughtful, rather than automatic, responses from all students. Midway through a discussion, we ask students to raise their hand if they haven't participated yet, giving the shyer, less confident students the floor to voice their thoughts. It also visually reminds us of who has not spoken.

We learned to respond honestly in discussions: "I never thought of that." "Alicia, can you build on what Jose said?" "I have no idea how you got there. Can you explain your thinking process?" "Does that idea contradict what we said before?" "You've lost me. Please explain more." "Let's create five more possible theories."

Some phrases help any teacher who facilitates discussion. Probably the most empowering phrase is "Say more." When a student makes a short comment and we want to understand it, we encourage them with that simple phrase. Verbal students don't need this, but quiet kids need help. Once the quiet student has dipped his toe into the discussion, "Say more" helps him wade out into deeper waters.

Some protection and encouragement happens behind the scenes, especially with the quietest kids: "You've been in the class for months, and you haven't spoken. What would make it easier for you? Do you want to come with a comment to contribute? Do you want me to pave the way by asking others to be silent to make room for you to speak? Do you need smaller groups?" Or, for the kid who dominates a class: "Do you realize that you are taking a lot of the conversational space? Can you track how much you talk? Can you write down your best comments before you speak? Can you take notes on what others are saying, rather than listening to yourself?" Such conversations outside the classroom are more effective than in-class confrontations or corrections, which may seem humiliating and prevent future participation.

Across all disciplines, repeated phrases help create disciplinary habits of mind: "If this, then what?" "What question is being ignored, and why?" "Whose voice is not heard?" "Give an example." "Give a counterexample." "What ethical issues arise from this situation or discovery?" And the killer question: "So what? Why does this matter?" We reinforce these habits of mind by using the same phrases for writing assignments and in feedback on students' writing. In any discipline, these open-ended questions signal that students can be real thinkers, not just repeaters of the teacher-given truth.

Refining Discussions: Small Groups, Shorter Times, and Written Responses

Depending on the goal of the class, we learned that discussion did not always need to be in a whole-class format. If the goal is to promote diversity in every small group, counting off by four and reconfiguring into four groups insures that students sit and talk with new people, not the ones they usually sit with. Other times, the goal may be to create safety and awareness. If students self-divide into groups of "talkers" and "non-talkers," the non-talkers often feel freer to express themselves. If you take down the big tree in the forest, the smaller ones sprout up. If all the talkers sit together, they find out how difficult it is to get a word in edgewise. In Abby's class, in preparation for writing a paper about gender, students broke into same-gender groups in order to free each group to be more honest. After a lifetime of mixed gender public education, the smaller groups felt tremendously liberating. The discussions were raucous as members gave voice to thoughts and experiences they would never have felt confident sharing with the other gender. One boy noted about group dynamics, "When you put all the boys together, we just yelled at each other. We need the girls." A girl said, "Now that I know other girls feel the same, I can be more honest in my paper." Another said, "I was so sure I was right. Now, I'm not so sure."

Margaret taught a unit about language reflecting and creating character. Included in the unit was an essay about losing one's first language through immigration. Margaret asked students to pair off: students who were immigrants with those who were not. She asked whether the essay resonated with their personal experiences. Suddenly those who had been self-conscious about their English talked animatedly about the accuracy of the essay. Simply pairing these groups reversed the usual talking/listening dynamic. Also, the immigrants noticed parts of the text that the other students ignored. For example, one immigrant focused on the description of initially losing humor when you lose your first language. Other students said, "I never thought of that. That would be terrible—not to be able to laugh with friends." After hearing what resonated with each other, they reread the original essay and thought about additional examples.

Similar to the notion that discussions needn't be whole-class, we also learned that effective class discussions did not need to last the entire class period. As new teachers, we practiced with ten- to twenty-minute discussions, which were about all we could manage. Longer discussions began to meander. An announced, shorter time frame focused the conversation and left the students wanting more, sometimes even continuing the conversation outside the classroom.

Another suggestion concerning timing, is the "parking lot" used in the powerful Empowering Multicultural Initiatives workshops. During a discussion, many topics are left hanging. Students need to know that their questions and thoughts matter. We can propose an intellectual parking lot, where unfinished ideas and unexplored questions are written, perhaps on the board or on chart paper. Those questions sometimes become the basis of the next day's work or can revitalize a flagging discussion later in the class.

After a time, we noticed that students' interesting ideas often evaporated if we did not include some written responses as part of the discussion. With nothing written down, discussions seemed less important than lectures. Years of teacher-dominated classrooms train students to value what the teacher says over what their peers say. The teacher speaks, and students listen and take notes. But in discussion, everyone speaks and usually no one takes notes. We affirmed and modeled that we valued student input by listening carefully and taking notes on students' comments during class.

We also learned to reaffirm the importance of the ideas in discussion by asking everyone to take a few minutes at the end of class to summarize the main points of the discussion, often in writing. Other times students focused their end-of-class responses with sentences like, "Before I came to class, I thought X. Now I think Y." This reinforces our expectation that discussion should expand our ideas. Also, this information helps us plan for the next class. One student said, "This was a shocking class for me. Americans can criticize the government; that was never possible in my country." Another student said, "Before, I thought all the colonists hated the British. Now I understand that some people didn't want to break from England. I'll bet they argued."

Another variation of the end-of-class question is: "Fill in this sentence. The most impressive/startling/controversial or confusing comment today was . . . " All of us in the room learned that different parts of a discussion make different impressions on other people. We do not think alike. Some of these end-of-class written reactions become the basis of longer, more formal papers.

Building Curriculum

When the curriculum jumps from topic to topic, or from book to book, students have difficulty constructing meaning. When the teacher sequences the material within a larger context, adolescents' questions and comments evolve organically. Let's look at the same book in different curricula. If you teach Kafka's *The Metamorphosis* in a Great Books class, it may not fit with anything else. However, placing *Metamorphosis* in a unit about family will lead to questions about how family reacts to a change in one family member. In a psychology course, students might ask if Gregor is depressed, bipolar, or anorexic. A history class might ask whether the time of writing influenced the story.

How the teacher arranges the curriculum will determine how students approach the material, because multiple texts deal with the same issues. For example, in Abby's course, The Family in Literature, students read the fairy tale "Sleeping Beauty" and discussed how and why different families react to change. They tried to figure out if family history produced these reactions. When the class read *The Metamorphosis*, students built on previous reading to create connections and notice patterns. One student noted: "Gregor's family sprang into action, while the whole kingdom shut down when the Princess was stricken." From previous discussions, they anticipated the next question: "Why?"

The readings and the discussions provided a context for thinking about the content of the texts and the meanings of their own lives. The discussions led to a writing assignment that asked students to take a pattern in *The Metamorphosis* and apply it to their own lives. Students wrote about cousins joining cults, sudden dementia, menstruation, or alcoholism. Students wrote statements like, "Unlike Gregor's family, my own family came to the rescue of a member after extreme change," or "Families develop patterns of responses. It's not random. Maybe we can predict how families will respond by what happened before."

In a unit about prisons, taught in an English course called Individuals and Institutions, Abby focuses on writings about prisoners such as Aleksandr Solzhenitsyn's novel, *One Day in the Life of Ivan Denisovitch*. The course goal is to examine how those whose freedom has been seriously restricted respond to authority, as opposed to how the students handle authority in schools. Students asked to hear the perspective of the guards and those who believe in the efficacy of prisons. When students could not find anyone to speak to the class, they asked the question they had been taught to ask: "Why?"

A discussion may shape curricular choices. Abby taught *This Beautiful Life*, a modern novel about the consequences on a whole family of sexting by the teenage son. A class discussion uncovered students' perception that the contemporary novel seemed superficial. So Abby asked herself, "What novel deals in depth with the consequence on a whole family system of sexual misconduct?" She told the class that the opening chapter in *Anna Karenina* shows a household in total disarray because of infidelity. Students asked to read the chapter to compare it to the contemporary novel. Those students who might have been discouraged by the length of the Russian novel came to class overflowing with observations about the characters and comparisons to the modern novel. The flatness of the American best-seller whetted the students' appetite, which was sated by the more difficult Russian novel. Rather than the teacher's dictates, the materials and the class discussions directed the students' thoughts about what should be read next. In a science class, a student may show enthusiasm for a topic that the whole class does not have time to pursue, but the teacher may suggest additional resources. Outside reading, even in mandated curriculum, provides opportunity for additional inquiry when discussion sparks interest.

At the beginning of any course, we found that creating a context (sometimes called core or essential questions) is critical. Even when we teach generic courses, like American Literature, we find it helpful to focus the course on a central concept, like resilience or identity or the outsider or disillusionment or loneliness or friendship— all real concerns for the adolescent. We try to find a way into the material that starts with student interests.

While we often must cover a great deal of material, we can still focus on one or two key events or ideas for detailed instruction. If students understand how geography and land patterns affected a particular war, they can be asked to extrapolate to other wars. In science, if students understand how new discoveries lead to new ethical questions, they may speculate about a future scientific discovery and resulting ethical questions.

Sequencing Questions for a Class Discussion

Margaret's early classes felt jumpy as she moved from topic to topic, following her carefully prepared list of discussion questions. Some students did not speak at all and some spoke too much. Other students were so determined to be right that they wouldn't take any intellectual risks.

One year, we taught different sections of the same class. We prepared by reading the material (new to us), and having adult discussions about each short story or essay. We noted what questions we asked and in what order. Although in class we tended to ask informational questions, in our late-night discussions, after quickly clarifying any misunderstandings about the text, we discussed open-ended, challenging questions raised by the text.

From this experience, we developed a generic order of questions that seems to work well in generating energy and challenge in a classroom. We decided that most days we would use this particular order: We begin with a question about the day's topic that any student could answer, even the ones who did not complete the homework. Second, we ask opinion questions, which can have no wrong answers. For example, "What did you like best, or find most confusing, or think was most significant in yesterday's reading?" Third, to create the context for an authentic discussion, we select or construct questions we would discuss with a friend. We avoid teacher-questions that check on facts (e.g., "Name five examples of irony in the story," or "Who are four generals in the Civil War?"). We would never start a conversation with friends with a demand for facts, like samples of irony or names of generals. Instead, as we observed in our own conversations, interesting conversations result from open-ended questions. For example, we might ask: "Does the author make the motivation for suicide clear?" "How do Americans seem to define white masculinity versus black masculinity?" "Can education mitigate violence like Colombine?" "How can the slow law ever catch up with fast technology?" We tried to fit our questions to the larger goal of the course core questions.

When sequencing questions we move from feelings (where no one can be wrong), to opinions, to more abstract questions. Each question should be more challenging than the last. Finally, we ask questions that require a reexamination of the material, additional research, definition of terms, or new meaning constructed from what has been learned. To evaluate their mastery of the material, we ask students to apply what they have learned from one situation or topic to another situation or topic. When we taught students how to read Shakespeare, the exam gave students a passage from a play that had not been discussed.

In the early weeks of a course, when we are establishing good discussion behavior, we end most discussions with a quick assessment of the day's conversation: Which questions moved the discussion forward? What digression turned out to be useful?

What ideas were left dangling? What question would you ask next? What information do you need? What did we learn from this discussion that would improve our next conversation? The class improves at discussion by noticing and reflecting on its own process. Although students may resist the teacher's suggestions for group improvement, students usually pay attention to their peers' suggestions.

Conclusion

Although we have made many mistakes over the years with classroom conversation, we still believe in the glory of a discussion where the class creates new meaning by listening and reacting to each other's ideas. Without discussions, the teacher's information, ideas, and reality flatten the class. No matter how brilliant the teacher is, a teacher-dominated class is limited to one person's perspective. A full class, collectively, will have more and better ideas than any one person, including the teacher. In a social studies discussion about WWII, for example, students discovered that one grandparent had fought on the American side, one had been liberated from the camps, another had been a Nazi Youth member, and another had been part of the French resistance. Multiple perspectives transformed the conversation.

Discussion creates, supports, and strengthens thinking. It relies on evidence, argument, clarification, precision, abstract and concrete thinking, and knowing. Ideally, the students' ideas become clearer and more complex after a full class discussion. Discussion encourages respect for others' ideas as students build on each other's words, not just argue with each other. An effective discussion flows without much intervention, creating new insights by the end of the class.

Beyond the subject matter, our deepest goal is for students to understand that we all think differently when engaging with texts within and across disciplines—a goal endorsed by the Common Core standards. A great discussion helps students rethink their own assumptions and even helps them shift their beliefs as they listen to others. As they lean into the group, listening hard to what others think, realizing that there are many ideas that they have not thought of themselves, they learn that no one person has a monopoly on truth, not even the teacher.

Discussions matter. They require and motivate students to return to the text, do close reading, seek information, and read supplemental material. Discussions also encourage students to think about other people's experiences and ideas. Students clarify their thinking by articulating their own positions; they also enlarge their thinking by hearing and incorporating what others think. Discussions empower students to be teachers as well as students and can propel them to additional reading and more thoughtful writing. The best discussions move students from feeling that they are being chauffeured to feeling that they are learning how to drive.

Additional Resources

Burke, Jim. *Illuminating Texts: How to Teach Students to Read the World*. Portsmouth, NH: Heinemann, 2001.

Burke, Jim. *The English Teacher's Companion: A Complete Guide to Classroom, Curriculum, and the Profession*, 3rd edition. Portsmouth, NH: Heinemann, 2007.

Moffett, James, and Betty J. Wagner. *Student-Centered Language Arts, K–12*, 4th edition. Portsmouth, NH: Heinemann, 1991.

Moffett, Lisa. *Teaching the Universe of Discourse*. Portsmouth, NH: Heinemann, 1987.

Sizer, Nancy F., and Theodore Sizer. *The Students are Watching: Schools and the Moral Contract*. Boston: Beacon Press, 2000.

Research in Digital Literacy

Tools to Support Learning Across the Disciplines

JOSHUA FAHEY LAWRENCE, MARK WARSCHAUER,
BINBIN ZHENG, AND DIANA MULLINS

Imagine an innovative, technologically advanced civilization adapting to pervasive changes as a new generation grows up communicating in completely different ways. Intellectual leaders would be concerned about the impact that these new technologies have on how the next generation remembered what the previous one valued, how they remembered the lessons of their forbearers, and how different sections of society communicated with one another. Of course it is not that difficult for us to imagine this situation: it is occurring today with the rapid diffusion of networked digital media. This is not the first time, however, that new communications technology has transformed a society. In Plato's *Phaedrus*, Socrates tells Phaedrus the story of the inventor of writing (a young tech whiz kid named Theuth), and his presentation of this new technology to the king of Egypt. The king, on hearing Theuth's explanation of the benefits of writing, exclaimed,

> Oh most expert Theuth, one man can give birth to the elements of an art, but only another can judge how they can benefit or harm those who will use them and now, since you are the father of writing, your affection for it has made you describe its effects as the opposite of what they really are. In fact, it will introduce forgetfulness into the soul of those who learned: they will not practice using their memory because they will put their trust in writing, which is external independence on science that belong to others, instead of trying to remember from the inside, completely on their own. You have not discovered a potion for remembering, but for reminding; you provide your students with the appearance of wisdom, not with its reality. Your invention will enable them to hear many things without being properly taught, and they will imagine that they have come to know much while for the most part they will know nothing. And they will be difficult to get along with, since they will merely appear to be wise instead of really being so.[1]

As teachers, there are times that we sympathize with Plato's rather doubtful evaluation of the new literacies that fascinate our students. What is the role of a math teacher when students are under the impression that any problem can be solved by voice commands to their WolframAlpha smartphone app? What is the point of reading ancient history if a Wikipedia query can instantly produce a summary of key events? Einstein commented that he never committed to memory anything that could be looked up—*what does this mean for instruction when almost anything can be looked up online?*

For the last decade, our research team has been investigating classroom use of computers and the Internet in K–12 schools. We have found that technology is not a panacea that improves student learning and that use of computers alone will not transform a school. But some teachers have found ways to use technology in ways that are reliable, engaging, and supportive. In this chapter, we summarize what we have learned about the best uses of technology and how they might help in secondary classrooms. We focus on three aspects of content-based literacy in secondary schools: sources, processes, and products.

Widening the Array of Sources

In chapter 10 of this book, Cynthia Shanahan reviews theory and research on using multiple texts. She notes the way extensive research on this topic, especially in the field of history, provides a theoretical framework for understanding the importance of using multiple texts to support reading comprehension and describes some of her research on how scholars use multiple texts in their disciplines. The research we present in this section is aligned with the perspectives that she presents, except that we focus more specifically on what the widened range of *online* sources available to secondary students means for teachers.

Greater Use of Online Materials to Supplement Texts and Other Published Sources

For today's adolescents, reading is primarily a digital activity. Of course, they still read a great deal of traditional printed material for both scholastic purposes and fun, but on average they spend much more time reading digital texts independently than they do reading other forms of content outside of school.[2] Although schools and educational content providers have been criticized for being slow to deliver content through digital formats, today's schools are doing so more than ever, and there is every indication this trend will continue to accelerate.

In the companion website to this book (www.adlitpd.com/book) we share hundreds of links to content-rich websites that we use in our work with teachers and pre-service teacher candidates. We hope that some of these resources will be useful additions to readers' favorites across content areas. But with greater access to content, the question becomes: how do students navigate and evaluate these resources? Online resources are not always carefully vetted or edited by reputable experts, so we need to help our students evaluate texts and their purposes for using them in each content area.

Although increasing attention has been paid to the need for students to have a critical stance toward information presented to them on the Internet, research suggests that this is still difficult for many students. In their study of secondary students, one research team found five typical approaches that students took to evaluating Internet sites.[3] Although there were some "versatile evaluators," most students only used a limited range of evaluation criteria to determine how credible and useful online sources were. Sloppy evaluation of texts can result in default research habits and attitudes that can lead to error and confusion.[4] This is a typical research sequence for many students:

- Searching in Wikipedia or Google
- Browsing quickly through websites for ideas and quotes
- Cutting and pasting information from the Web into one's own writing without providing proper attribution for it
- Viewing information as free, accurate, and trustworthy
- Treating online information as equal to print information

In his case studies of two students and how they used Internet resources to conduct topical research, Clines and Cobb note that they did not consistently use important strategies such as:

- Checking the purpose of the Web site (for example, the extensions .edu, .org, .gov, .com can often indicate the orientation or purpose of the site)
- Locating and considering the author's credentials to establish credibility
- Looking for recent updates to establish currency or relevancy
- Examining the visual elements of the site such as links to establish relationships with other sources of information[5]

One of our goals as content-area teachers is to help students navigate online resources in our discipline and make strategic and informed decisions about which resources to use, and for what purposes. One approach to website evaluation that has been developed by researchers at Michigan State University is the WWWDOT framework.[6] This framework asks students to consider a set of six dimensions:

1. Who wrote this, and what credentials do they have?
2. Why was it written?
3. When was it written and updated?

4. Does this help meet my needs?
5. Organization of website?
6. To do list for the future

We think that there are some important general evaluative strategies that students should use to search online, however, there are also important discipline-specific criteria that will depend on the kind of website being evaluated. For instance, the stance we take toward evaluating primary source documents will be very different from the stance we take toward evaluating scientific reports. Being critical consumers of information requires that we have a disciplinary stance and purpose in selecting and evaluating information. Content-area teachers may need to explicitly describe the kinds of evaluative processes used in their disciplines for evaluating different kinds of primary documents, summative reports, data sets, and mathematical tools.

Greater Use of Online Data Sets, Manipulables, and Applets

We live in the age of "big data." Being able to understand and analyze data sets is critical to a wide range of careers, not to mention civic participation as a fully informed citizen (see the support website for some of the best data resources). Yet in classrooms without technology, students have limited access either to data sets or to the tools needed to analyze them.

This situation potentially changes if we can make good use of technological resources. This was well illustrated by an example from a social studies lesson we observed in an urban middle school in Southern California.[7] The class was taught in a special program for students who were on the verge of dropping out or failing out of school. The teacher sought ways to relate instruction to students' personal lives. During a lesson on social inequality, rather than just presenting data to students from the news, the teacher allowed students to go to websites that she had provided to find their own data about: (1) the demographic composition of schools in their own district, and (2) the academic performance of those schools. The teacher then helped the students to combine the two data sets in various ways so they could visualize the relationship between demographic composition and academic performance in their own district. Today much scholarship in the social sciences is done by looking at large trends with representative data sets, so this activity helps students to think in disciplinary ways as well as understand how these approaches to understanding social phenomena can connect to their lives.

Digital technology also can help students to analyze data that they generate themselves. For example, Cummins, Brown, and Sayers describe the "Strawberry Project," a field research curriculum implemented among students in Oxnard, California.[8] The project took place in an area surrounded by strawberry fields, and almost all of the mostly Latino students had relatives who worked in the fields. Students from two classes and their teachers worked together to develop survey questions, and the students interviewed people in the community about their working hours, conditions, and experiences. Teachers then taught the students to plot the results and the concomitant standards for correlations and graphing. Students completed this project with only a couple of computers, which they took turns using, demonstrating how a minimal use of technology for some specific application (data aggregation and visualization in this case) can be the linchpin for a well-designed class project.

Innovative teachers are also using technology to collect data. For instance, we observed classes using digital devices that either stand alone or connect to computers to measure temperature, voltage, light, force, motion, and chemical composition. These are being used by classes across the country to help teach data gathering, analysis, and experimentation in science instruction.[9]

What, then, are the keys to success in data analysis projects in schools? Some fascinating information on this topic comes from a study of network science projects.[10] The authors use the term *network science* to refer to a curriculum in which students from different locations throughout the country or world gather data in their community and then upload it for collective analysis. For example, classes in many locations may measure the acidity of local streams and upload that data so that other classes around the world can conduct comparative analyses.

Even though Feldman, Konold, and Coulter had been involved in developing network science projects over many years, their study served to illuminate the limitations of these projects. They found that: (1) many students tended to upload data to the Internet without even bothering to download others' data, and (2) even when they did download data, they did not know how to analyze it appropriately. Some network science projects were successful, but only in cases where strong teacher mentoring, guidance, and instruction took place. These findings suggest that we need to plan for a longer gradual release of responsibility to students as they learn to apply their disciplinary skills in a networked world.[11] Students should see how to collect, analyze, interpret, and discuss data before doing so in small groups or scaffolded settings. It is only then that Internet-based communication and resources provide and add value for students who have the skills to navigate these resources without being overwhelmed by them.

The bottom line? Data can be a great resource for students *if* they are trained to analyze and interpret it well. Our role as disciplinary teachers is more important than ever in a networked world.

Greater Use of Reflective Material Based on Students' Own Work

Using technology to reflect on their own learning is one more way in which students can use technology to support and enhance content learning. Prior to the advent of digital technology, it was much more difficult to archive large amounts of student work and use it to reflect on teaching practice. Today, students can use portable digital cameras, camcorders, cellphones, tablets, and laptops to archive, review, edit, or share digital files, magnifying their abilities to capture their learning experiences and reflect on them.

In one foreign language class we observed, students performed and videorecorded three or four skits that incorporated vocabulary and themes they were studying in class. The performers viewed the videos and filled out a reflection sheet on their language use, looking in particular for language structures that were the focus of instruction. As the teacher explained: "They watch themselves. And they write down 'What can you work on next time?'—whether they stood still too much or they kept making mistakes in their words, or they kept forgetting their lines, or, no matter how many times we kept saying it's *pizarra*, they kept on saying *pizarro*. So they had to really do a reflection of their work."[12]

The teacher reported other advantages to the videorecording: (1) it kept the students motivated and engaged; (2) it provided a medium to inform parents of student progress, further motivating students to do well; and (3) recordings could be reviewed again at the end of the year, providing a chance for broader student reflection on their progress.

Videorecording has also been used to support reflection on student engineering work. In one class, students built model bridges out of wood and then videorecorded what took place when they placed a brick on them.[13] If bridges couldn't hold the brick, a frame-by-frame playback showed how and where the bridge collapsed and thus indicated to the students the precise flaws in their design. It was not easy to document work carefully, but doing so ensured that students would take care in preparing their work, reflect on the strengths and weaknesses of their designs, and also participate in the careful documentation of testing that is a mainstay of applied engineering science.

Digital media has also been used to document student's collective work on major projects. For instance, at the King Middle School in Maine, students work together to complete three major interdisciplinary projects each year.[14] Each interdisciplinary project had one group assigned to making a video documentary. Students documented all aspects of the project, including kick-off events, instructions or rules, formations of teams, visits from guest speakers, student fieldwork, research, product creation, and assessment. The videos, which were distributed on CDs, provided a memento for students of a major middle school project, offered a resource for other educators who wished to organize similar projects, and, most importantly, served as a resource for students to reflect on what took place in the project and what its significance was for their learning. This process took a commitment from the school, support from state and local initiatives, and a long-term plan. We do not hold this up as an example of what every school should do, but as an example of what one school achieved with careful planning and commitment to use technology to document student work.

Improving Literacy Processes

Beyond providing a wealth of expanded content to secondary teachers (the *what*), digital networks also provide opportunities for teachers to transform some literacy processes (the *how*). In this section we focus on how digital networks can help students to become more autonomous in their content learning and more collaborative in their writing as they produce more iterations of their work for a wider set of authentic audiences.

Autonomous Learning

The gradual release of responsibility is a key concept for understanding literacy development.[15] We know that children perform better on reading tasks when they are allowed some level of autonomous choice in making their reading selections.[16] Not surprisingly, opportunities for autonomous choice have been integrated into research-based, content-focused reading programs.[17]

In addition to expanding the range of materials that students can access, networked technologies provide opportunities for students to choose texts at a range of reading difficulties or with a range of scaffolds. For example, students can use Google features to find a range of resources at different reading levels (under *search tools*, choose *reading level* and then choose texts rated as basic, intermediate, or advanced). Students can access books designed with Universal Design for Learning (UDL) principles, see for instance http://www.cast.org/learningtools/index.html, and get multimodal support reading grade-level content area texts. Students can also use online tools like ClipRead, produced by LiveInk.com.[18] ClipRead uses a technique called visual-syntactic text formatting to cascade passages in a way that facilitates reading and comprehension for many students (see figure 8.1).

These supports, which can be used by students autonomously, can help them make use of diverse content and thus may facilitate more autonomous project-based learning. Project-based work helps students better grasp material, make connections across disciplines, and engage in deeper learning.[19] Two excellent examples of the use of technology in project-based learning come from a middle school we studied in Maine.[20]

In the first example, to better understand the U.S. Constitution in social studies class, students visited the website of the Bill of Rights Institute (www.billofrights institute.org), where they found information on recent court cases involving key con-

FIGURE 8.1

A sample text converted to visual-syntactic text formatting with ClipRead

> Four score
>   and seven years ago
> our fathers
>   **brought** forth
>   upon this continent
>   a new nation,
> **conceived** in liberty
>   and **dedicated**
>   to the proposion
>   that all men
>   are created equal.

stitutional issues. Students perused the site and selected cases of interest to them, which often involved issues of relevance to youth. For example, some students selected the case involving an atheist's challenge to the Pledge of Allegiance; others chose a case involving a student's use of his camera phone to take and share embarrassing pictures of other students without their knowledge or permission. The students then read both their case and the background information on it, developed an opinion about the case, and wrote an essay of their opinion, which they e-mailed to the teacher. They then shared and debated their opinions in class. The teacher explained that this helped the students to go beyond memorizing facts and information, such as the content of the Constitution and its amendments, to grapple with the meaning of the Constitution and its applicability today. Although some of these readings were quite challenging, students were able to access a range of texts and online supports to help them complete the assignment.

In a second example, students in mathematics classes carried out stock market projects in which they selected and researched companies, simulated investments in stock, developed spreadsheets to track their earnings, and wrote reports incorporating their research and data analysis. This project was based on work that the teacher had done in previous years, but without the technology component, students were unable to complete research on companies, since accurate and up-to-date information simply wasn't available in the school library. Using networked computers, students were able to carry out and incorporate research on companies, track stocks in real time, and investigate the impact of current events on stock prices. Like most of the examples of excellent use of technology that we have seen, this project was based on strong principles and carefully planned to extend work that had proved successful in the past.

Collaborative Writing

Collaborative writing is a valuable skill in today's networked information society.[21] Indeed, studies suggest that 85 percent of the documents produced in offices and universities have at least two authors.[22] Collaborative writing may contribute to an increased complexity in writing, improved grammatical accuracy, and enhanced overall writing quality.[23] Through collaborative conversation, learners could engage in negotiating meaning with each other and in building knowledge about their language. This process could potentially lead to deeper cognitive thinking and awareness of their language output.[24] For example, Higgins, Flower, and Petraglia found that collaborative writing fosters students' reflective thinking, and a significant correlation between the amount of reflective conversation and the quality of students' writing was also detected among college students.[25] In addition, students put more effort into their compositions when they learn that a broader audience will read their texts.[26]

During a collaborative writing process, learners tend to reflect on their own language production when they attempt to create meaning.[27] However, the process of collaborative writing is typically complex, involving role assigning, planning, brainstorming, drafting, reviewing, revising, and editing.[28] Networked technology can help teachers support these tasks. A meta-analysis of twenty-six studies on student writing with computers found that computer-based writing is typically more collaborative, more iterative, and involves more peer editing than writing done with paper and pencil.[29] New and specific technologies, such as wikis, are specifically designed to promote collaborative writing. Wikis are websites that any visitor can contribute to or edit, and this characteristic makes them suitable tools for supporting collaborative writing. Writing on wikis can involve access to specialized sites, but there are also sites that are free for schools (such as http://www.wikispaces.com/).[30] An alternative collaborative writing environment, Google Docs, has become popular due to its association with other popular Google tools, as well as the simplicity of its writing interface. In our ongoing research, we have found that when schools invest time at the school-, department-, and classroom-level to adopt a collaborative writing platform, students report that they are better organized, find it easier to revise and edit, and receive more feedback than they do with traditional writing (figure 8.2).

More Iterative Writing

The last two points mentioned—the amount of feedback and ease of revision and editing—are especially important for writing. Most real-world writing involves numerous drafts over a period of time as a piece of work is refined after further thought,

FIGURE 8.2

Agreement with writing on Google Docs compared to writing on papers/writing on word processing software (scale: -2 strongly disagree, -1 disagree, 0 neutral, 1 agree, 2 strongly agree)

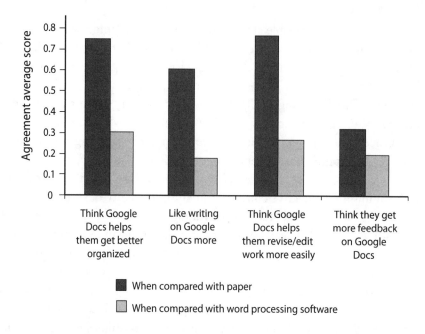

analysis, and feedback from others. This iterative process is much more cumbersome without technology—with use of computers, students often receive better feedback on their work, whether from peers or teachers, who can more easily focus on content when the writing itself is in a legible font (whether online or printed).

Some districts are also using automated writing evaluation (AWE) programs, such as MY Access! (www.myaccesss.com/myaccess/do/log) or WriteToLearn (www.writetolearn.net), both of which provide automated scores and feedback to students.[31] Though the scoring these tools provide is far from perfect and the feedback is not as helpful as that provided by a teacher, classroom research on the use of AWE suggests that it does help teachers manage their classrooms in a way that encourages more revision by students.[32] The software is thus best used to complement teacher feedback, rather than replace it; for example students can submit their early drafts for evaluation by the software, with their final draft evaluated by the teacher. Whether using AWE or other software, there is substantial evidence that students in classrooms with collaborative writing and evaluation technology revise their work more often than classes without it. For example, in our study of the district where students write on Google Docs, we found that students revise each of their papers about four to five times, a number which is undoubtedly much greater than when papers are written by hand.

Writing for an Authentic Audience

Traditionally, secondary students rarely write for an audience other than their teacher.[33] This is changing as teachers use blogs, e-mail, and schoolwide online forums.[34] With these tools, teachers can specify intended audiences precisely.[35] There is an increasing understanding of how writing for different audiences influences the writing process. For instance, one study of ninth- and tenth-grade biology students found that students did significantly better on conceptual questions when they had completed writing-to-learn activities for a peer audience or an audience of younger peers.[36] Similar results of the impact of audience have also been found in students' expository writing in physics, persuasive writing, and other content areas.[37]

Broadening Students' Products

Finally, in addition to broadening the sources and processes of literacy, the use of technology can also dramatically widen the kind of literacy products that students can create in the classroom. This is especially valuable in the English language arts and social studies classrooms, as students can not only write essays but also produce newspapers, magazines, brochures, business letters, reports, and other products.

An excellent example of the value of this was seen in a California English language arts classroom in a low-income Hispanic community, where a seventh-grade teacher had her students work together to produce a literary newspaper based on their reading of *Beowulf*. Though the thousand-year-old epic poem was read in a modernized narrative version, the context, language, and genre of the hundred-page adaptation were all sufficiently unfamiliar to make the poem quite a challenge for the linguistically and ethnically diverse class.[38] Yet, like other students in California, they were expected to read, understand, and interpret it.

The teacher used technology to support many aspects of the reading by providing online resources to help students build background knowledge related the story. She relied on editing software and templates to help students plan, write, and edit the *Beowulf* literary newspaper in small groups. Newspaper sections included the front page, sports, travel, advice column, obituary, comics, and food. Each section was used to summarize and comment on aspects of the *Beowulf* story. For example, in the sports section of one newspaper we analyzed, the main battle between Beowulf and his enemy, Grendel, was repackaged as a boxing match. The travel section described a fall festival that humorously captured the lifestyle of Scandinavia over a thousand years ago. The crossword puzzle provided a playful way for students to select and define challenging vocabulary from the story.

Work on the newspaper actually required two readings. On the one hand, students had to read and reread *Beowulf* to make sure they sufficiently understood the plot and details. After that, they had to consult modern newspapers, available online, to better understand their genre, content, and formatting. They then had to translate the plot, setting, and characters from *Beowulf* into a newspaper format. Old English stories are not typically of great interest to California junior high students. However, by helping students design their own creative modern newspaper on the *Beowulf* theme, the teacher provided an engaging way for students to enter into the world of Old English literature. This project could have been completed without using computers, but it would probably have required much more work on the part of the teacher and possibly generated less enthusiasm from the students, since the product would not have the formatting features that characterize a newspaper.

Of course students can use technology to produce a wide range of multimodal products. This can be highly engaging for students and also help them think about how to reinterpret content meaning across modalities. For example, a teacher in Southern California has her students use software to create an image and brief musical interlude for poems they read, thus requiring the students to move beyond literal understanding. As she explains: "They had to get the emotion, the tone, the climax of the poem. They had to be very thoughtful and think rhetorically. It wasn't a matter of 'This was the answer to the question,' but 'What was the emotion going on in the poem?' They thought more deeply about the poem."[39]

At King Middle School, students use technology to create text-based and multimodal products out of all their interdisciplinary projects. For example, in a science-oriented project, students created a website and CD of endangered species in Maine, which they then distributed to other middle schools around the state. In a social studies–oriented project, students interviewed former civil rights leaders in Maine and then collected the accounts in a book. These kinds of projects require students to synthesize information for diverse products targeted at authentic audiences. Large-scale thematic projects can help bring cross-content teams together, which provides excellent opportunities to think about the way information is presented in different disciplines and the similarities and differences in how mathematicians, social scientists, historians, scientists, and journalists might write about the same topic.

How Do I Turn This Thing On?

We have tried to be careful in describing the examples of innovative technology we have seen, because we are well aware of the limitations and problems with using technology to promote academic literacy. One problem is that if we as educators try to implement too much, too fast, we might end up focusing more on the tools themselves and lose sight of our primary curricular goals. For example, presentation software such as PowerPoint is frequently used in academic and business presentations, and helping students to use this tool well to present their content-area learning in a disciplinary way makes perfect sense if that is one of the goals for a unit. However, in our classroom observations, we have seen teachers and students focus on the mechanics of PowerPoint and underplay its use in presenting content knowledge effectively.[40] Having students simply cut and paste paragraphs from the Internet and plop them into slides with glitzy but confusing transitions does little to enhance the academic literacy or communication skills of students.

Even when clear curricular goals are established and the appropriate tools are used, technical clichés are likely to crop up if sufficient time is not spent establishing routines and working with technologically savvy staff and students. We found that the most effective classrooms had clear *written* guidelines for distributing, collecting, charging, and locking up technology on a daily basis. Students in many of these classrooms were required to use redundant systems to back up work (they uploaded the document to their online portfolio *and* e-mailed it to themselves or saved it to a thumb drive). There were clear guidelines for what kind of academic language students were expected to use online and how they were expected to manage their time. Teachers that worked closely with schoolwide, district, and state initiatives often benefited in unanticipated ways from their access to savvy educators. Even classes that did all of these things encountered difficulties at times; we must expect to encounter rough patches as well as the occasional clear win as we explore content teaching with more technology.

Conclusion

In the real world, scholars and professionals across a wide range of fields have to gather and make use of content from a variety of sources; engage with that content autonomously, iteratively, and collaboratively; and publish material based on that work in a wide variety of genres and modalities for authentic audiences. These are the same types of literacy experiences we need to provide to adolescents if they are going to develop the skills, knowledge, and attitude for success in college and careers.

9

Digital Literacy in Practice
Achieving a Cosmopolitan Orientation

ANN MECHEM ZIERGIEBEL

As secondary school teachers, we are now asking ourselves, "How do we define *new literacies* and how will they be reflected in our teaching?" Today, new literacies evolve out of a constant flow of emerging digital technologies that are changing the way our students read, communicate, and process information. Our new digital orientation shifts some of the focus of learning and engagement from institutional protocols to students' interests and their everyday social and global communication. We must adopt a new stance, perhaps one that connects to the idea of *cosmopolitanism* (derived from the Greek *kosmopolites*, which may be translated as "citizen of the world").[1] Global citizenship has been thrust on our students and on us, challenging us to expand our capacity to be open to the larger world while remaining loyal to local concerns, commitments, and values.[2] Our own teaching, then, becomes an ever-changing response to our and our students' cosmopolitan perspective as we do what we try to do best: engage and motivate our adolescent learners.

Seeking a Cosmopolitan Orientation

Engaging and motivating adolescent learners across content areas requires more attention than ever before as a result of two shifts that we are all experiencing in the field of education: (1) the emergence of Common Core State Standards with a focus on disciplinary literacy and an awareness of new literacies, and (2) the expanding scope of instructional strategies as learning ventures into homes, communities, museums, libraries, and public and unstructured digital spaces. We are already constantly adjusting and tweaking, but perhaps seeking a cosmopolitan orientation encourages us to be responsive, dynamic, and expansive as we engage and motivate our students through their unique intellectual identities. The development of students' intellectual identities requires the daily practices of speaking, listening, and inquiry as they learn to solve problems and build a knowledge base. As we, in our teaching roles, pursue this new orientation while integrating new literacies, we are simultaneously teaching our students how to focus their minds, expand their spirits, and discover how to demonstrate their individual bents to an expanding digital audience.[3]

Bring on the New Literacies

Can we become digitally current enough to stay ahead of our students? Probably not. We are therefore challenged to be open to the new and loyal to the known. In teaching the new literacies, we focus on much more than just the use of digital tools. Integrating digital tools into our classrooms must be combined with an invitation to students to discover, apply, explain, empathize with, and synthesize meaning in a global context. Our backward-design process welcomes new literacies that use the Internet to expand student reading, writing, thinking, communicating, and design. Ito et al., in their summary of findings from the Digital Youth Project, identified four key concepts that characterize the way adolescents live and learn with new media: (1) new media ecology where traditional media such as books, television, and radio intersect with digital media such as online networks and social communication networks (MySpace, Facebook, instant messaging [IM], text messaging); (2) networked publics where mass media converges with online communication; (3) peer-based learning where learning takes place outside of school, primarily in settings of peer-based interaction; and (4) new media literacy where adolescents are developing skills, competencies, and literacy practices through media production and online communication.[4] This study reveals the ways adolescents are developing a wide range of new literacy forms through informal new media practices, including deliberately casual forms of online speech; formats for displaying public connections; and new forms of literacy, such as customizing MySpace profiles, mashups, and remixes.[5]

Mashups and remixes? Do these new digital formats have a place in our classrooms? Well, we must dip our toes into these digital waters because we need to be thoughtfully responding to and researching these changes in adolescent ways of seeing/interacting with the world. We need to be proactive, exploratory, and willing to engage in teens' digital lives. And we need to anticipate the complex and sometimes intense pressures of globalization. Two co-taught interdisciplinary social studies and English language arts classroom units follow, units that encourage the habits of mind that are reflected in all disciplines. Through big ideas and backward design, content knowledge and skills are transferred to new settings, issues, and problems, using the local and global community as the classroom. Several digital tools are introduced that have served to expand this learning community. The following lenses are used to focus on the cultivation of students' intellectual identities while reorienting ourselves and our students with a cosmopolitan perspective: Common Core standards, overarching questions, topical questions, performance tasks, and emerging new literacy technologies.

Unit #1: Place Influences Perspective

In the Gloucester Public School District, eighth-grade social studies commences each year with a review unit on the relationship between Massachusetts geography and history. I review the five themes of geography as history's stage: place, regions, movement, human-environment interaction, and location. ELA begins each fall with an introduction to a yearlong examination of perspective. My ELA co-teacher, Janet Ware, models perspective as being embedded in all teaching and learning. How does place influence individual perspective? We choose this overarching question because it spirals through history, economics, geography, literature, and art. Backward design takes us to topical questions connecting to both social studies and ELA content:

- How does understanding deepen when ideas and subjects are examined from opposite views?
- How does practicing perspective taking in art help us understand and adopt different perspectives in all our disciplines?

These topical questions encourage us to examine our content with energy and precision while remaining open to new student-driven connections. Our math teachers practice perspective taking when analyzing qualitative versus quantitative data, while our science department adds perspective taking to the hypothesis section of scientific method reporting. Although our ELA and social studies content is established by our school district, the Common Core standards guide us in analyzing different points of view (RL8.6) while using domain-specific vocabulary (WHST8.2).[6] We heighten students' engagement by bringing them into their community through a local library in search of local authors (www.sawyerfreelibrary.org), a historical museum in search of local artists (www.capeannhistoricalmuseum.org), and outdoor sites to locally explore themes of geography. These types of resources are available in every district and are uncovered by students as they make inquiries around their *big idea.*[7]

Big ideas that matter get us through the school day. They are exciting. Our big idea—place influences perspective—is the building material of understanding while our daily lessons tackle topical questions. Art is a wonderful gateway to perspective. In Gloucester, as in most communities, artists have painted local scenes that capture their unique perspective. We discovered that the paintings of Fitz Henry Lane, a renowned local artist from the mid-1800s, are a powerful entry into our big idea. Our students can view Lane's original paintings and then visit two sites along Gloucester Harbor where Lane's opposite harbor perspectives (looking in—*Gloucester Harbor*

FIGURE 9.1

"Looking in": Gloucester Harbor from Rocky Neck

Fitz Henry Lane (oil on canvas). Reproduced by permission of the Cape Ann Museum, Gloucester, Massachusetts.

from Rocky Neck—and looking out—*Ten Pound Island from Pavilion Beach*) painted (see figures 9.1 and 9.2, respectively). Lane's shifts of perspective become visual maps of interpretation and observation. Domain-specific vocabulary in geography of relative and absolute location, physical and human characteristics, environment, movement, and regions can connect with the art concepts of *luminism*, *realism*, *perspective*, and *vanishing point*. Student sketches recorded on site become artifacts that can be exhibited as student perspectives are valued, revised, and critiqued.

Using a local artist like Lane and embedding his work in our unit motivates students to research content with perspective as a lens. Reproductions of local artists' work—as simple as postcards, calendar reprints, and poster enlargements—hanging in hallways, bathrooms, closets, and classrooms, establish the enduring value of art in a learning community. Mingle student art (an example is shown in figure 9.3) with the professional pieces, and the importance of student art making is emphasized. Exhibitions of debates, newspapers, journals, stories, reenactments, and artwork displayed in physical public spaces where students congregate (e.g., coffee shops, movie theaters, city halls, post offices, and YMCAs) can be complemented by digital exhibitions. Our local newspaper, *The Beacon*, conducts workshops with our students,

FIGURE 9.2

"Looking out": Ten Pound Island from Pavilion Beach

Fitz Henry Lane (oil on canvas). Reproduced by permission of the Cape Ann Museum, Gloucester, Massachusetts.

FIGURE 9.3

"Looking out": Student watercolor

By Matilda Grow, Janet Ware's eighth-grade ELA class. Reproduced by permission of the Cape Ann Museum, Gloucester, Massachusetts.

involves them in every phase of publication, and circulates one page of student work in the paper, seasonally, reaching over thirty thousand residents in one daily newspaper drop. Content is displayed while perspective is revealed.

Researching content with a perspective lens starts with student acknowledgement that one's unique "place" creates a bias. However, dropping students in the exact places where Fitz Henry Lane sat and asking them to sketch what he sketched can create some squirming and anxious artists. Many students are initially stymied by a blank piece of sketch paper with the heading, "Looking in" and another with the heading, "Looking out." Some usual responses include "I can't draw," "My boat looks too stupid," and even "When's lunch?" Yet noisy resistance turns into a palpable stillness once these scenes draw students in. Then, the rich content of geography's five themes embraces our student artists without text or lecture. Consider the implications of "in" and "out" across all disciplines:

- Apply the perspective of looking "in" and "out" to diverse situations.
- Explain a well-developed theory of "in" as evidenced in your work.
- Empathize with another worldview from someone who is "out."
- Synthesize from diverse elements to form new meanings of "in" and "out."
- Evaluate and make judgments about the value of "in" and "out" perspectives.

Bring on those new literacies to showcase perspective. Perspectives are naturally expressed through exhibition and performance. Connecting exhibitions to new literacies allows students to read and create texts that contain artwork, words, photos, video, and information graphics. A powerful vehicle for digital exhibition of student perspectives is The Sketchbook Project, a traveling library of sketchbooks created by anyone across the globe who registers and submits at http://www.sketchbookproject.com/. Upon registration and payment of a small fee, students receive a blank sketchbook to be returned to The Sketchbook Project after it is filled. Book content can vary and often includes travelogues, memoirs, narratives, atlases, almanacs, chronicles, sketches, documentations, and photo logs. The Sketchbook Project drives sketchbooks across North America for "on tour" viewing before they become permanently archived in the Brooklyn Art Library (New York). Sketchbooks are also digitized and can be experienced by anyone with an Internet connection.

A traveling library of student work, connecting to their understandings of how place influences perspective, can engage the world and motivate learning. One click on the Sketchbook Project website connects each student to his or her sketchbook on its digital trip around the world. As Liz Robbins describes it in the *New York Times*, "For six years, the Sketchbook Project has been offering intimate glimpses into the imaginations of its worldwide contributors."[8] Kwane Anthony Appiah captures the spirit of our students' imaginations, perspectives, and cosmopolitan orientation when he states, "We can learn from each other's stories only if we share both human capacities and a single world."[9] Our human capacity to think, to sketch, to learn, to listen, to speak, and to tell stories helps us to appreciate differences in perspective.

Extensions

Below are some online resources that can enrich students' experience of "place":

- GoogleEarth (free download at http://www.google.com/earth/index.html) allows students to develop their own personal maps of any place, including bookmarking sites, adding images and information and then publishing the maps for others to view.
- Historic Maps of New England (http://docs.unh.edu/nhtopos/nhtopos.htm) and the National USGS Collection (http://nationalmap.gov/historical/) provide maps of most areas in the United States.
- The Rumsey Collection (http://www.davidrumsey.com) and the Library of Congress (http://lcweb2.loc.gov/ammem/gmdhtml/gmdhome.html) are cartographic treasures of cultural, political, historical and economic movements and trends.

Unit #2: Perspective Shapes Your American Dream

As the eighth-grade year at O'Maley Middle School heads into its second trimester, our social studies overarching question shifts from *place influencing perspective to uncovering how perspective shapes each student's American Dream.* Our widening curriculum lens includes themes and content spiraling through American literature, American history, American historical documents, and personal narrative. Topical questions connecting to our enduring understanding of how perspective shapes this American Dream include:

- What events and people shape your perspective?
- What is your unique American Dream?

Exploring an American Dream can involve social studies and ELA content ranging from the Declaration of Independence, to the "all-school-reads" novel *Alice Bliss*,[10] to the upcoming January issue of *Time* magazine featuring the "Person of the Year." District standards for social studies, along with Common Core standards in English language arts, promote writing for specific purposes: writing arguments (W8.1), writing informative/explanatory texts (W8.2), writing narratives (W8.3), and using technology to produce and publish individual or shared writing products (W8.6). Domain-specific vocabulary from historical content, such as *revolution, unalienable, pursuit, life, liberty,* and *happiness* can drive the writing purposes. Disciplinary literacy initiatives focus on applying these writing purposes across all disciplines. Arguments and explanations become integrated literacy practices in the instruction of each discipline as teachers are inviting their students to expand their identities to include academic and specific disciplinary identities. Thus, these new literacy demands on students are unique and discipline-specific.[11] However, consider the throughlines that all disciplines share:

- Vocabulary load that promotes discourse in each discipline
- Assumed knowledge that promotes inferring and investigation
- Academic language that promotes conciseness and compression of complex ideas into few words
- Digital literacy that merges technology, pedagogy, and content
- Perspective making that allows for divergent interpretations

Our big idea—perspective shapes your American Dream—leads our students to examine their points of view, choices, role models, and imaginings. Our teacher stance of openness and purpose encourages students to expand their brainstorming around influences that shape their perspective to include people in their lives, in history, and in literature who inspire them through their writing, art making, life choices, passion, or profession. An event as powerful as the crafting and signing of the Declaration of Independence, a historical figure as controversial as Frederick Douglass, or a fictional character from *Alice Bliss*—these singularly American events and people shape our students' lives.

The idea that students' lives are shaped by "certain unalienable rights, among them life, liberty, and the pursuit of happiness," promotes discourse across all disciplines. Articles in any current newspapers, magazines, research journals, and nonfiction texts provide content and perspectives on the presence and impact of these three rights. Frederick Douglass, who shaped the national debate around the complex issue of slavery, stated in 1857, "If there is no struggle, there is no progress," dreaming of an America where race and color would not matter. He was committed to social reforms that would address problems of inequality for all Americans.

Laura Harrington, playwright, lyricist, teacher, and author of the powerful novel *Alice Bliss*, contributes to conversations around the plight of the less than 1 percent of our American population fighting in wars during this decade and the impact of military service on their families. She creates a captivating portrait of a family and a town infused with unexpressed grief from losses in war, conveyed with precision through Alice's own adolescent perspective. When Alice's father and role model, Matt Bliss, is deployed to Iraq, Alice, her younger sister, and mother, feel left behind, while Matt embodies another perspective—that of leaving behind. Alice, at age fifteen, finds a shoebox in the rafters of Matt's meticulous workshop containing letters for her, each one with a different title: her graduation from high school, her first love affair, her first broken heart, her wedding day, and the birth of her first child. Matt knows he may be leaving behind these precious moments with Alice.[12]

Just as Alice's perspective is shaped by her father's deployment, students' perspectives and the perspectives of their role models are shaped by the content of their lives. Creating a robust interdisciplinary publication, with student perspectives on events, people and literary characters who have shaped their lives, connects to the Common Core writing practices of arguments, explanations, and narratives. Our students at O'Maley Middle School showcase their choices of role models through the challenging layout of *Time* magazine, a digital and hard copy periodical that can be written, edited, and circulated by students. The current managing editor of *Time*, Richard Stengel, encourages students to publish and digitalize their own issues of *Time*. Every November, our students actually send Mr. Stengel their persuasive letters to the editor, nominating their Person of the Year—a person who has dramatically influenced their life. Students always receive a response to their submissions, although they've yet to score an actual cover for the magazine's official January issue. However, our in-house publication—complete with Person of the Year cover images, layout, arguments, explanations, and narratives—can convey the depth of student connection to their shaping influences. In establishing their criteria for Person of the Year, students are honoring their own cosmopolitan perspective, one of hope and possibility. Their researching and wrestling with events and people who have shaped their perspective allows students to envision an American dream. They can become change agents in their class, community, and the world's transformation, a cosmopolitan view that honors every creative act on the part of an individual or community.[13]

Alice Bliss, Frederick Douglass, or—who knows?—someone's great-aunt Peggy as their *Time* Person of the Year? Perhaps. The *Time* class project requires the individual students to create their own publication using multiple genres to showcase their choice. Common Core ELA standards speak to story comprehension and creating: determine a theme or central idea of a text and analyze its development over the course of the text (RL8.2), determine the meaning of words and phrases as they are used in a text, including figurative and connotative meanings (RL8.4), produce clear and coherent writing in which the development, organization, and style are appropriate to task, purpose, and audience (W8.4), and develop and strengthen writing as needed by planning, revising, editing, rewriting, or trying a new approach (W8.5). Reading standards for literacy in history/social studies stress viewpoint and purpose: identify aspects of a text that reveal author's point of view or purpose (RH8.6) and determine the meaning of words and phrases, including vocabulary specific to domains related to history/social studies (RH8.4). Domain-specific vocabulary that makes meaning of texts and stories includes: primary source, secondary source, figurative, connotative, fact, and inference. Public library digital links, such as eBooks, Ebsco Middle Search Plus, NoveList, and News Bank can engage students through primary and secondary sources while they research their Person of the Year. Trying new approaches to research can include out-of-school story collection with digital tools such as flipcams and video recorders that motivate even our reluctant learners.

Stories are at the heart of student engagement and motivation. New technologies provide a perfect opportunity to explore ways in which new literacies can enhance traditional strategies of story comprehension and creation. Jenn Bogard and Mary McMackin augment time-honored literacy strategies, such as graphic organizers, storyboards, conferencing, and pen and paper drafts, with new literacies tools, including the Smartpen, video editing, audiorecording, and software applications to expand the story-writing process.[14] Building literacy practices and disciplinary literacy instructional programs along with literacy strategies leads to understanding. Reading and writing stories reinforces content knowledge and connect understanding to personal experiences. Whether stories are read or written in school or out of school, students become engaged and motivated by just a turn of a phrase, a voice, an image, or a character, conflict, setting, or theme.

Telling their own stories, perspectives, and American Dreams allows students to actively engage themselves and others in their unique place in history. Digital storytelling can support an open orientation to expand a student's audience beyond home, school, and community to across the globe. Flipcams can capture the essence of place while blogs can expand journaling to include text, video, and photos that convey perspective and demonstrate voice. Pinterest, a photo-sharing network, allows users to "pin" photos and videos that support their content and convey their story line onto virtual pinboards. Animoto and Xtranormal are additional digital tools that extend and enhance student stories with music and advanced editing capacities. As virtual audiences grow, students can generate feedback, friendships, and formal critique while demonstrating digital literacy. Reflecting new literacies in our teaching practice is our fresh orientation, combining traditional and new, embracing the local and extending to the global, while engaging and motivating one student at a time.

Extensions

Below are some online resources that expand students' exposure to inspirational lives:

- TIME (http://search.time.com/ and search for "person of the year" covers, or use http://tinyurl.com/personoftheyearcovers) introduces students to "Person of the Year" covers from 1927 to 2011.
- TED (http://www.ted.com/) provides students with profiles of courage, innovation, and heroism.

- ThinkQuest (http://library.thinkquest.org/C001515/heroism/herodb.php) introduces students to biographies of heroes and heroines of the twentieth century.
- Google Docs (http://drive.google.com) or a wiki like PBWorks (http://pbworks.com/) allow students to have accounts, post, and share documents.
- SurveyMonkey (http://www.surveymonkey.com/) promotes input for students by asking peers to "vote" for the person that best fulfills the criteria they've developed.
- StoryCorps presentations (http://storycorps.org/) are vocal testimonials of meaningful relationships and role models.
- Voicethread (http://voicethread.com/products/k12/) provides teachers with the opportunity to offer students a safe and easy-to-use site on which to record their own reactions or interactions to images, photographs, or events.

Future Ready

Engaging and motivating one student at a time is the essence of our job. So, back to our original challenges: defining the new literacies and figuring out their place in our classrooms in the twenty-first century; or, to use a term I find more positive than "literate in the twenty-first century," to help our students to be *future ready*. My school district, like so many others, experiences shifts in administration, new department configurations, technology budget shortfalls, and a wonderful population of diverse learners with a range of resources. But against this backdrop, becoming future ready—comfortable with new literacies and having available a wide range of digital technologies—can be a challenge. Meeting this challenge is a balancing act I suspect I share with many other teachers—as I strive to be open to the new, I am becoming increasingly loyal to the known.

Yet, the two shifts in our teaching practice, the new Common Core standards focusing on disciplinary literacy with an awareness of new literacies, and the new public online spaces where learning is expanding, do provide new directions and exciting opportunities. Student work can travel around the globe, literally and virtually, through The Sketchbook Project. The Person of the Year project, which involves producing and posting online student publications showcasing their artwork, arguments, explanations, and narratives, expands our students' audience and promotes student discourse. Remember the power of student work in the local newspaper—thirty thousand readers with one paper delivery. Empowering, engaging, and motivating one student at a time through the integration of new literacies, both in and out of school, celebrates a cosmopolitan perspective of loyalty and openness.

10

Research in Multiple Texts and Text Support

CYNTHIA SHANAHAN

In this chapter, I make a case for multiple text use in middle and high school classrooms, discuss the theory and research behind multiple text use, and describe the issues that teachers will face in bringing multiple texts into the classroom. Before I begin, I want to say something about my use of the term *text*. When I refer to texts in this chapter, I am referring to a rather broad conception of that word, in that I refer to graphical or pictorial representations of ideas and spoken discourse as texts. Often, these representations may seem more accessible than written discourse but are deceptively abstruse. Yet, even as I refer to these other kinds of texts, the main treatment of them in this chapter is as items in sets of documents that always include written text, recognizing the primacy of written texts in schools and the importance of understanding them.

The Case for Multiple Texts

Worldwide, the easy availability of text information on the Internet and in other media sources makes learning from text increasingly complex and often contradictory. Consider, for example, the number of texts encountered as we decide for whom we will vote. We read newspaper accounts from any number of newspapers on the Web, editorials, website biographies, and tweets. We can tune in to countless talk shows where the host and his or her guests engage in endless speculation and commentary, we see campaign ads and so on, and we can do this anywhere and anytime using devices such as smartphones and iPads. Across and within each of these venues, we get different perspectives, depending on the political viewpoints of the author, the audience the author is addressing, and at times, how various issues are misrepresented. Yet, when Election Day comes, we are expected to base our decisions on our reading of these texts—texts that are incomplete, biased, contradictory, and confusing—about which we know there is no "truth." Such is the nature of much of the reading tasks we encounter in our daily lives.

But what about reading in school? Although individuals have always read more than one text about topics that capture their interest, today texts are far more easily accessed. If I wanted to read about the Little Rock Nine, the nine adolescent African American students who integrated Central High School in Little Rock, Arkansas, a Google search immediately finds thousands of resource materials, including documentaries, memoirs, photographs, transcripts of interviews, newspaper reports, high school publications, court records, legislation, letters, telegrams, and textbook-like summaries. There are over three hundred YouTube videos on the topic! The challenge of choosing which sites to visit, determining how credible they are, and making sense of both corroborated and contradictory information is daunting.

Multiple versions of information, however, do provide an educational opportunity. Using the topic of the Little Rock Nine, for example, I can help my students comprehend the nature of historical interpretation: that there isn't *a* story of history but *many*, depending on the perspective of the storyteller; that what happened in the past can never be fully reconstructed, so that versions of history are never the whole truth; that paying attention to who wrote something is an important tool in determining the trustworthiness of information, and so on.

Multiple texts are not just fodder for history learning. Whether we are learning about a time in history or a process in science, what we learn depends on the time period in which it was written, who wrote it for what audience, and many other factors. For example, an article from a newspaper about a topic in science will have a different level of detail and different vocabulary than the article in the science journal from which it was derived, and a scientific finding in 1953 could be contradicted by a science finding in 2011. Smoking was once considered to offer health benefits, but we now understand that it carries significant health risks. A pronouncement about the environment by an activist group such as Greenpeace risks being more biased than a scientist's report of environmental data over a period of time. Readers are required to make sense *across a number of texts*, weighing evidence and trustworthiness and confronting contradictions, if they are to know how to vote, what to buy, how to stay healthy, or what the most up-to-date scientific explanation is.

Students get a sense of what it means to engage the ideas in a particular discipline when they read from multiple sources. They often have naive ideas about the way in which knowledge is created, shared, and evaluated within a discipline. To use a history example again, they may never have considered that what they are reading in their history textbook is not the incontrovertible truth, but an author's *creation* of history, based on that author's interpretation of primary (e.g., artifacts), secondary (e.g., trade books by historians), and tertiary (e.g., textbooks) documents. There may be nothing in that textbook that even hints at that notion because of its narrative style. It is only when students are confronted with two or more conflicting accounts of the same event and asked to reflect on the similarities and differences of those accounts that they begin to realize what the study of history really is—an exercise in the interpretation of multiple texts. Similarly, students who read their science texts may never have considered that what they are reading is based on a large compendium of corroborated data, and that even these data may be subject to reinterpretation as scientists develop more precise observation and measurement tools, as new theories are developed and tested, and as ways of reimagining the structure of nature are created. It is only when students are confronted with multiple texts that show scientists' differing interpretations of data or changes in scientific thinking across time that they begin to understand the nature of scientific inquiry and the importance of corroboration of data across studies.

Prior to the past decade, reading comprehension research and practice was focused on the reading of single texts. Elementary and middle school students were asked to read for details, make inferences, draw conclusions, and perhaps apply what they learned. In some cases, they were taught to master the elements of Bloom's taxonomy (knowledge, comprehension, application, analysis, synthesis, evaluation), but with only one text at a time. Students learned strategies such as KWL (thinking about what you *k*now, what you *w*ant to know, and what you *l*earned) or feature analysis (e.g., comparing the features of characters in a piece of literature), but with only one text. Students were still unskilled in the use of multiple sources of information by the time they got to high school. Any instruction in high school was usually truncated into instruction focused on the writing of term papers, but this instruction was inadequate—high school teachers often assuming that students knew how to read and write across texts and needed help only on the structure of a term paper and the way to properly cite sources, but finding out that their difficulties were much deeper. This chapter focuses, then, on the concept of teaching from multiple texts, considering the need for and paucity of this kind of instruction in the past.

Multiple Texts and the Common Core Standards

Especially relevant to the current state of reading education and multiple texts are the Common Core State Standards that have been, at this writing, adopted in all but five states.[1] The English Language Arts standards, including the English Language Arts Standards for History/Social Studies and Science and Technical Subjects, call for students to be able to read across a number of texts and text types, to engage in comparison/contrast, and to think critically about the information they read from multiple sources. A review of these standards reveals that multiple texts are referred to more than eighty times across grade levels. They are evident in all major emphases (literature, informational texts, history/social studies, science/technical subjects, and writing for English and the two subject matter areas).

Standards focusing on multiple texts are most prevalent in three sections of the standards—*craft and structure*, *integration of knowledge*, and *research to build and present knowledge*. There is a steady progression in expectations for reading multiple texts that moves from general comparisons of texts (e.g., comparisons of genre or style) to comparisons of structure (e.g., chronology, comparison, cause-effect, or problem-solution), to specific arguments in texts (e.g., claims, counterclaims, and evidence), to evaluations of credibility and usefulness. Also, the standards specify aspects of texts that may vary across multiple texts: genre (letter, textbook explanation, and fiction/nonfiction), modality (picture, print, graphic, numerical, auditory), authorship (reading same and different authors), and audience (reading texts aimed at different audiences).

This focus on text comparisons means that teaching students how to read multiple texts in English, history/social studies, and science/technical subjects will be a major part of instruction requiring careful attention to a movement from less- to more-complex tasks. To give a sense of the way in which the Common Core standards highlight multiple text use, table 10.1 presents some examples from sixth through eighth and eleventh through twelfth grades.

Theory and Research with Multiple Texts

While comprehending a single text is vitally important, many reading educators and researchers no longer think this is enough. Studies on expert readers provided one impetus for the shift. In 1991, Wineburg conducted a study comparing the reading practices of expert historians with that of high school students as they read multiple texts about a single event in history. He found dramatic differences. The high school students, who had already studied the event, read each text as if it were to stand on its own. They focused on learning the facts. The historians, who had little knowledge of the event, learned the facts but also engaged in what Wineburg referred to as sourcing, contextualization, and corroboration. That is, they paid attention to who wrote the text (to determine their perspective, knowledge, purpose), during what time and under what circumstances the text was written (contextualization), and how well the information in the text was substantiated by other texts (corroboration). Their purpose was to come up with an integrated and nuanced interpretation of the event as a whole that spanned all of the texts they read. In addition, they approached these texts as arguments (even though they were written in narrative form), and not as a compendium of facts.[2]

Since Wineburg's study, other studies have confirmed that, without instruction, most students approach multiple texts as if they were a group of unconnected stand-alone texts, rarely comparing and contrasting information across texts and rarely developing the kind of nuanced understanding of events that experts see as beneficial.[3] For example, Stahl et al. found that students stopped adding to their knowledge of the Tonkin Gulf incident after reading a second text, and failed to notice that subsequent texts contradicted each other. Researchers have also confirmed that expert readers in various fields (particularly studying those in history and science) seek and critique knowledge that is quite purposefully integrated across sources.[4] Bazerman, for instance, studied the way in which physicists explicitly made connections between sources of relevant knowledge both when they read to learn information and when they were engaging in critique. Even the mathematicians studied by Shanahan and Shanahan talked about integrating what they were reading with the knowledge they already knew.[5]

It is within the past decade or so that theory and research regarding multiple text use has blossomed, and this is mostly within the discipline of history, perhaps in part due to the widely shared Wineburg study discussed above.[6]

Theories of Multiple Text Use

There are several theoretical frames with which to view multiple text reading. *Cognitive flexibility theory*, for example, posits that, especially in ill-structured domains (domains in which information is highly variable, such as in history), individuals understand complex information better if they are confronted with multiple representations of that information.[7] Each new representation of the information adds to the mental scaffolding necessary to develop complex understandings and to think in novel ways about it. With multiple representations, learners compare and contrast information across perspectives and think about different aspects of the problem space. Regarding the topic of the Little Rock Nine, for example, this theory would suggest that students arrive at a much more nuanced understanding about the integration of Central High School during an era of segregation if they read different perspectives; analyze the political, social, and legal aspects of the event; and read the memoirs of those who both opposed and were in favor of that integration.

Within literary theory, there is the idea of *intertextuality*.[8] Intertextuality has to do with the linking of texts, whether or not those texts include words and nonword symbols; and whether or not they are tangible, such as those located on a written page, or intangible, such as experiences or memories.[9] Engaged readers negotiate textual understandings by linking information both within and outside of the texts they are reading. Hartmann studied eight advanced-level high school students as they

TABLE 10.1
The Common Core State Standards and multiple texts

Common Core standards	Grades 6–8	Grades 11–12
Literature		
Craft and Structure	Compare and contrast the structure of two or more texts and analyze how the differing structure of each text contributes to its meaning and style.	
Integration of Knowledge	Compare and contrast a written story, drama, or poem to its audio, filmed, staged, or multimedia version, analyzing the effects of techniques unique to each medium (e.g., lighting, sound, color, or camera focus and angles in a film).	Analyze multiple interpretations of a story, drama, or poem (e.g., recorded or live production of a play or recorded novel or poetry), evaluating how each version interprets the source text. (Include at least one play by Shakespeare and one play by an American dramatist.)
Listening and Speaking: Comprehension and Collaboration	Analyze the purpose of information presented in diverse media and formats (e.g., visually, quantitatively, orally) and evaluate the motives (e.g., social, commercial, political) behind its presentation.	Integrate multiple sources of information presented in diverse formats and media (e.g., visually, quantitatively, orally) in order to make informed decisions and solve problems, evaluating the credibility and accuracy of each source and noting any discrepancies between the data.
Informational Texts		
Integration of Knowledge	Analyze how two or more authors writing about the same topic shape their presentations of key information by emphasizing different evidence or advancing different interpretations of facts.	Delineate and evaluate the reasoning in seminal U.S. texts, including the application of constitutional principles and use of legal reasoning (e.g., in U.S. Supreme Court majority opinions and dissents) and the premises, purposes, and arguments in works of public advocacy (e.g., *The Federalist*, presidential addresses).
Writing		
Writing: Research to Build and Present Knowledge	Gather relevant information from multiple print and digital sources, using search terms effectively; assess the credibility and accuracy of each source; and quote or paraphrase the data and conclusions of others while avoiding plagiarism and following a standard format for citation.	Gather relevant information from multiple authoritative print and digital sources, using advanced searches effectively; assess the strengths and limitations of each source in terms of the task, purpose, and audience; integrate information into the text selectively to maintain the flow of ideas, avoiding plagiarism and overreliance on any one source and following a standard format for citation.

History/Social Studies

Craft and Structure	Compare the point of view of two or more authors for how they treat the same or similar topics, including which details they include and emphasize in their respective accounts.	Evaluate authors' differing points of view on the same historical event or issue by assessing the authors' claims, reasoning, and evidence.
Integration of knowledge	Analyze the relationship between a primary and secondary source on the same topic.	Integrate information from diverse sources, both primary and secondary, into a coherent understanding of an idea or event, noting discrepancies among sources.

Science/Technical Subjects

Integration of Knowledge and Ideas	Compare and contrast the information gained from experiments, simulations, video, or multimedia sources with that gained from reading a text on the same topic	Synthesize information from a range of sources (e.g., texts, experiments, simulations) into a coherent understanding of a process, phenomenon, or concept, resolving conflicting information when possible.

Writing in History/Social Studies and Science/Technical Subjects

Writing: Research to Build and Present Knowledge	Gather relevant information from multiple print and digital sources, using search terms effectively; assess the credibility and accuracy of each source; and quote or paraphrase the data and conclusions of others while avoiding plagiarism and following a standard format for citation.	Gather relevant information from multiple authoritative print and digital sources, using advanced searches effectively; assess the strengths and limitations of each source in terms of the specific task, purpose, and audience; integrate information into the text selectively to maintain the flow of ideas, avoiding plagiarism and overreliance on any one source and following a standard format for citation.

Source: *Common Core State Standards for English Language Arts and Literacy in History, Social Studies, Science, and Technical Subjects* (Washington, D.C.: National Governors Association Center for Best Practices and the Council of Chief State School Officers, 2010).

read five historical passages that provided a rich intertextual environment. To create meaning, these students, when asked to do so, were capable of making links to their personal experiences or knowledge, links to related information in the same text, and links to related information across multiple texts. However, even though the students were prompted to create links across the text, the data showed that they made fewer of these links than they did links to their prior knowledge and experience and links within a single text. This body of research adds to idea that students need explicit teaching if they are to benefit from multiple text reading.

Another theory of multiple text use from cognitive psychology is the *documents* model derived from Kintsch, which posits that interpretation of text depends on a number of elements: (1) the surface level features of text (words and sentences), (2) the internal meaning of the text (the *textbase*), (3) the interpretation of that meaning by the reader (*situations model*), and (4) the genre of the text (e.g., newspaper article, memoir).[10] Others have added an additional layer when multiple texts are involved— an *intertext* model.[11] Readers use an intertext model in understanding the relations between sources and the integration of information across sources. An individual reads each document for information about the (1) date, (2) publisher, (3) author, author's intent, perspective, and intended audience, and (4) the document's characteristics and content. These understandings are compared and contrasted with those in other documents to develop a coherent mental interpretation about the information of focus. In this model, each source contributes to "global representation of the situation."[12]

When students read multiple texts on topics using a particular disciplinary lens, the intertext model becomes even more complicated. As noted in the Wineburg study and in studies of experts in other disciplines (e.g., mathematics, physics, and chemistry), expert readers bring to the task a discipline-specific set of understandings that include beliefs about the discipline itself (epistemologies), knowledge of the different interpretive frameworks used within the discipline and of the scope and breadth of study, knowledge of the different kinds of documents that are used in the discipline to answer particular disciplinary questions, and a knowledge of an array of linguistic moves that are typically used to communicate knowledge. In other words, they have disciplinary knowledge.

In a recent study of expertise in reading in the disciplines, the experts we studied informed us about the practices of their discipline that impinged on the way they approached texts.[13] For example, the historians we worked with explained that, because they use selections of documents and artifacts from the past, they are limited in the extent to which they are able to accurately portray that past. Maybe their choices of documents left out key pieces of evidence or the documents were biased in a particular direction. Maybe the documents could not be corroborated. Thus, they knew that historical knowledge is always interpretive and contestable. That belief represented a core epistemological stance.

These historians also had a sense of the depth and breadth of historical study and the different frameworks used to study it, even though they were only interested in a part of it (one was interested in the social history of South Africa, for example, but he was certainly aware that there were Civil War historians and that some of those might be interested in studying the great men of the Civil War or be particularly interested in its economic, political, or religious causes and effects). They knew that history focused on change over time, thus involving chronology, and that they must interpret the way events were related—whether they are causative or coincidental, significant or unimportant.

Central to historical inquiry was these experts' reliance on multiple sources, including not only documents and artifacts (primary sources), but also secondary and possibly even tertiary sources (accounts that use primary sources as evidence and accounts that use secondary sources as evidence, respectively). They knew, too, that, when they wrote an historical account, even though they were writing a *narrative*, they were making an implicit argument for their interpretation. Further, they knew they must be wary of any interpretation that casts history simplistically—as an unexamined story of progression and improvement or a story or decline. These aspects of *disciplinary knowledge* guided the ways in which they approached reading and *creating* historical accounts.[14]

The scientists we studied explained that scientists build understandings of the physical world through experimentation and systematic observation. These understandings are constructed incrementally over time, subject to changes in technology and theory building, and are steered somewhat by cultural norms and expectations. One chemist, for example, said that he paid special attention to the date of the articles he read. A scientific finding from a journal in 1980 had the potential to be contradicted by later findings, and he knew he would have to corroborate the information he read with newer information.

However, these scientists had more confidence in their findings from research than did the historians. The historians said that they tried to construct cohesive and plausible accounts of the past using evidence they selected through research. However, they could not predict what would happen in the future based on what happened in the past, and they regarded as a fallacy the commonly held belief that those who do not know history's mistakes are doomed to repeat them. Unlike the historians, scientists can test their interpretations of the physical world through experimentation, and the scientists we talked to had more confidence in their findings because of their predictive power. That is, the scientists could determine a level of probability that a certain phenomena would occur in the future under similar conditions—a level of confidence that the historians could not claim. This belief in the power of sound empirical data represented a key epistemological stance. Objectivity was important to them, and was controlled through strict adherence to systematic methods. They explained, for example, that scientists ask scientific questions, then design experiments that limit the extent to which extraneous factors will influence the results, including their own biases. The conditions for a significant outcome are determined ahead of time, and the results, whether they are expected or are a disappointment, are interpreted in light of that a priori determination.

Further, like the historians, even though they were interested in a very limited set of phenomena, these scientists understood that there were different branches of science and that, even within their own branch, there were different foci and methods of inquiry. Their texts consisted of lab reports, journal articles, research proposals, trade journals, trade books, chapters, etc., but key to all of these was that the science concepts in all the texts were represented in multiple ways—through prose, diagrams, models, equations, tables, etc.—and the scientists explained that a full understanding of a scientific concept wasn't possible unless these multiple representations were understood. They communicated scientific knowledge primarily through explanation and argument, and within this communication, they always tried to signal the degree of precision, certainty, and generalizability of statements of that knowledge—they frowned on overgeneralization. Accuracy mattered.

The chemists we studied differentiated their reading according to their level of knowledge.[15] (Bazerman found the same kind of differentiated reading in physicists.[16]) If the chemists didn't know much about a topic, their reading proceeded in a fairly uncritical way for the purpose of understanding. If they knew a lot about a topic, their reading proceeded in a more critical way—that is, they paid attention to the source of information and its time frame, critiqued the methods used, compared the information to other sources, and so on. When asked how students should be reading in middle and high school, they said that students should be allowed to read on the same differentiated levels, explaining that understanding the science that is already corroborated is hard enough without interjecting the need to critique everything that is read.

When looking at students' textbooks and other reading materials, they noted that technical language was highly prevalent. According to functional linguists, science texts have more technical words than in any other field, and sentences often include nominalization (the turning of a verb into a noun; for example, *distill* to *distillation*).[17] This move essentially changes a particular instance of an action into a generalized concept. Both nominalization and passive voice allow the scientist to portray a sense of objectivity. Thus, the scientists' use of language illustrates how a field's epistemologies are embodied in the way its experts communicate. The scientists we studied used their disciplinary knowledge as a lens that guided how they read.

Taking into account these aspects of disciplinary knowledge, perhaps a caveat concerning the intertext model is necessary. This caveat is that knowledge across documents is not merely assimilated into an integrated model of an event in an individual's mind, but that a reader's level of disciplinary knowledge in many ways determines the way each document is approached and whether or not particular aspects of a document will become part of that intertext model. Because of that, experts in a discipline will be likely to construct a more nuanced intertext model than nonexperts because they look for particular kinds of information to integrate, such as the author's perspective in history or the sophistication of measurement tools in science.

There is some research evidence that factors in disciplinary knowledge such as epistemology are important to multiple text comprehension. Bråten and Strømsø, for example, found that, without instruction, only college students who had sophisticated epistemological beliefs were able to adequately understand multiple, partly conflicting texts.[18] Jacobson and Spiro found that only students who preferred working with complex knowledge in multiple ways and valued active learner construction of knowledge were able to profit from the reading of multiple texts.[19] In that study, personal epistemology was found to moderate the effect of multiple-text reading on deeper understanding but not memory for facts. Rukavina and Daneman found that students holding more sophisticated beliefs about the complexity of knowledge were better equipped to integrate across two texts presenting conflicting information about a scientific topic.[20] More recently, Bråten, Strømsø, and Samuelstuen examined the effect of dimensions of topic-specific personal epistemology on the understanding of multiple texts about a scientific issue, finding that viewing knowledge as complex positively affected multiple-text understanding.[21]

These theories—cognitive flexibility, intertextuality, and the intertext model—help explain an individual's processes in reading multiple texts. Of course, individuals never act in a vacuum, and sociocognitive and sociocultural theories consider the role of more knowledgeable others and the role of discussion and interaction with peers in coming to more nuanced understandings of information.[22] Taken holistically, these theories suggest that students who struggle with text meaning together and with scaffolds are more likely to be motivated and develop deeper understandings than students who struggle with text meaning without the models and scaffolds that others provide. Of course, there are nuances to these theories that aren't captured in this short statement.

In addition, it isn't a given that group work will automatically be beneficial to learning. For example, Hynd, McWhorter, Phares, and Suttles found that high school students with misconceptions about projectile motion who saw a physics demonstration, talked in a group about it, and then read an explanation, did less well on a knowledge test than students who did not engage in group talk.[23] Analysis of the talk within the groups revealed that the talk served to reify the misconception rather than the scientific principle. Thus, it is unclear whether peer collaboration is helpful for creating an integrated understanding across texts. In the physics study, the goal was for students to adopt a scientific rather than intuitive understanding of projectile motion. It may be that collaboration to build cross-text understandings better serves activities in which the goal is more open-ended, such as learning about multiple solutions to a problem; or it could be that collaborations when misconceptions are involved need to be more carefully scaffolded.

Research with Multiple Texts in History

There is a growing body of research in history supporting the idea that instruction with multiple texts facilitates students' ability to learn information, think critically about it, and communicate thinking to others. For example, research suggests that readers can be taught to attend to sourcing, corroboration, and contextualization while reading historical accounts, and they can learn to read across sources to achieve more complex views of the an event.[24] Even students as young as eight years old can be taught to recognize similarities and differences across texts or to coordinate multiple mental representations to achieve a coherent but complex conception of the ideas expressed in multiple texts.[25]

In one study, college students enrolled in a reading/studying improvement course were asked to read multiple, sometimes conflicting texts about the controversial Tonkin Gulf incident as they studied the Vietnam conflict.[26] Students were taught how to read history (i.e., to source, contextualize, and corroborate) and they completed a comparison/contrast chart on a set of partially conflicting key documents regarding text evidence about three questions: What happened? Did the United States intentionally provoke the North Vietnamese? Did President Johnson manipulate Congress to get the Tonkin Gulf Resolution passed? The document authors' perspectives and positions on these issues varied, making it necessary for readers to evaluate the credibility of the various documents.

The researchers interviewed the thirteen students before and after they had read the documents, asking them what historians did, how they determined credibility, and what their strategies were for understanding the texts. Over the course of the unit, twelve of the thirteen students changed their ideas about what historians did, altered their notions of textual representations of "truth," and changed their approach to strategy use. During the first round of interviews, students portrayed historians as (1) *documenters*, who wrote down what happened; (2) *synthesizers*, who used multiple sources of evidence to determine what happened; and, rarely, as (3) *arbiters*, who sifted through conflicting evidence to decide truth. By the end of the unit, those who had initially stated that historians were documenters described them as synthesizers or arbiters, and students who had initially described historians as synthesizers and arbiters described them as either arbiters or affected by their own biases. Students who mentioned bias said that historians were not completely objective, and that their own biases could affect their selection and interpretation of documents. As one of the students expressed:

> I guess it is a tough task for historians to do. I think historians, even though they try to be as neutral as possible, there's some bias that is there as a human being. I guess you could try [to remain unbiased], but it's hard. When historians research a topic, that topic interests historians to begin with, and that interest comes from their parents, maybe. They're unaware of it . . . Not even having good solid reason, you automatically have some stance. And I guess that influences partially what they research on and the stance they take. I don't think there's 100 percent neutrality. That's impossible.[27]

Although these students did not initially engage in the complex thinking required to understand multiple documents in history, the shifts that took place in their thinking uncovered their ultimate ability to do so. These shifts occurred within instruction using multiple, conflicting texts in which students were (1) given the responsibility for making decisions about their own interpretations, (2) taught how historians read, (3) provided with instructional tools or strategies for evaluating the texts, and (4) required to explain their thinking.

Other studies have also found that teaching history students to use multiple texts is beneficial. Nokes, Dole, and Hacker taught students in eight high school history classrooms history content in several ways.[28] They found that, after three weeks, students who read multiple texts scored higher on tests of history content and used sourcing and corroboration more than students who used a traditional textbook only. They concluded that multiple text reading is necessary if high school students are to engage in reading like historians.

Most recently, Reisman studied the effect of history reading instruction on 236 eleventh-grade students in five San Francisco high schools. The six-month intervention involved a number of document lessons that required students to "interrogate, then reconcile" historical accounts from multiple texts.[29] Analysis revealed that students who received the instruction in history reading did significantly better on measures of historical thinking, were significantly more likely to transfer historical thinking strategies to contemporary issues, did significantly better on tests of factual knowledge, and even scored higher on tests of general reading comprehension.

These and other studies provide evidence that even young students and poor readers can be taught to interpret textual evidence approximating the way that historians engage in interpretation. They also provide evidence that students who discuss the activities of historians and engage in the interpretation of multiple texts can develop more mature epistemological stances about historical evidence, adopt more sophisticated reading strategies, and enjoy greater engagement in learning about historical events.

Although research results are too preliminary to be published at this time, Project READi (Reading, Evidence, and Argumentation in Disciplinary Instruction), an IES-funded project, will provide more insight into teaching history with multiple texts. Project READi is focusing on what it means to teach argument to history, science, and English students in middle and high school who read multiple texts. Those of us on the history team are following middle and high school teachers as they teach argumentation using multiple texts. This year, the teachers are focusing instruction with multiple texts on six elements. These elements are:

1. *Epistemology:* The beliefs and principles of historians that guide reading
2. *Close reading:* The dispositions and expectations for digging into texts to carefully consider and reflect on meaning
3. *Sourcing/contextualization:* Thinking about the time period and other contextual factors and their relationship with an author's perspective, motivations, audience, word choices, etc.
4. *Understanding the relationship between events:* Determining chronology and interpreting causality, coincidence, change over time and the various factors that determine change (political, social, economic, etc.)
5. *Understanding claim and evidence relationships:* Recognizing and using documentary evidence to support historical claims or conjectures
6. *Making sense across texts:* Comparison, contrast, synthesis, and analysis.

These elements are the focus of explicit instruction, and the idea is that, over time and with repeated instruction, students will be able to understand and make nuanced, complex arguments—both implicit (in historical accounts) and explicit (in historical arguments) after reading multiple texts about particular events. We came to these elements after spending time working with teachers in middle and high schools in modules of instruction in history—one module on the Black Hills of South Dakota and the conflict between the Lakota Tribe and the United States government, another module on the Little Rock Nine.

Our preliminary analysis of data suggests that focusing on multiple texts and reading like a historian was motivating and that historical thinking was fostered, but students, especially those in middle school, were not used to really digging into a reading passage or comparing one passage with another and needed a great deal of scaffolding. Issues of text complexity loomed large—the middle grade students struggled with reading even a portion of a treaty, for example, and they sometimes lacked the necessary contextual knowledge to make sense of the topic. Some middle grade students, even after the third day of instruction in the Black Hills module, had not sorted out who the Lakota were. The teachers essentially stopped their regular instruction to teach the modules, and found that the three weeks we had allotted turned into four and five weeks of instruction. Like Reisman, we are now looking for ways to incorporate multiple text reading into teachers' existing units—and so the focus on instructional activities within lessons rather than complete modules.[30] As these lessons are carried out with the central teachers in our project, we plan to work with a second group of teachers in a teacher network as they infuse the most successful aspects of instruction into their own units. We expect that this model will provide the necessary scaffolding for teachers needed to ensure that instruction is of high quality.

Research in Multiple Texts in Science

There has not been as much research on multiple text use in science as there has been in history, so we have less evidence that instruction in the use of multiple texts in science classes yields the same benefits as it does in history, even though theory suggests that it may. Without instruction, the way multiple texts are processed by science students varies as a function of background knowledge and epistemology. Students who know more about the topic or strategies (e.g., know how to source a document) or students who have more sophisticated epistemological ideas about knowledge are better able to make judgments about the trustworthiness of various science texts than students who don't know much about the topic.[31] In addition, Strømsø, Bråten and Samuelsten found that the mere use of multiple sources of information helped students to understand the intertextual nature of the task of developing a rich understanding of the phenomenon about which they were reading.[32]

Researchers have also studied the role of task. Wiley and Voss and Le Bigot and Rouet found that giving students the task of writing an argument after reading multiple texts fostered deeper and more integrated understandings of multiple texts in science.[33] These researchers concluded that the argument task helped students to integrate and elaborate information rather than to focus on specific pieces of information in a single text. Gil, Bråten, Videl-Abarca, and Strømsø found that summary writing fostered better understanding of multiple texts about global warming than did argument writing, and it fostered students' ability to integrate information across texts.[34]

Two research teams have found that instruction in reading multiple texts in science is beneficial. The Tools Study Group found that having students read a popular science passage paired with a textbook passage and teaching students to translate science information into different forms (e.g., text to diagram) helped them to write better science explanations.[35] Greenleaf and associates taught science teachers to use multiple texts and multiple representations of data. Not only did students improve their ability to integrate information across sources and representations, they also raised their achievement on state language arts, reading comprehension, and biology tests.[36]

Thus there is some promising evidence that teaching students to use multiple texts in science will foster deeper understandings of science content. We are cautiously optimistic that this is so in a generalizable way.

One problem with most of the research mentioned above is that most of the topics studied straddled science and social science. An understanding of global warming and climate change, the topics of some of the science multiple-text research, rests on not only an understanding of the scientific processes involved, but also on an understanding of the political milieu in which arguments about these topics are taking place. Being able to sort out the positions of various scientists and other sources forming arguments about the causes and solutions of global warming is crucial. Would the same benefit be found if students read multiple texts about mitochondria or the process of distillation?

A further hurdle to evaluating the effect of multiple text reading in science is that science teachers often eschew the use of any text at all. Because students have difficulty reading science texts, teachers find other ways to convey information to them, such as through overhead and PowerPoint notes and lectures, film, and hands-on-activities. This practice makes it unlikely that even single texts will be used, much less multiple texts, and, because of this, there may be a paucity of naturalistic research. Fortunately, educational researchers are currently studying what it means to read multiple texts in science. For example, in Project READi, researchers are helping teachers understand the importance of reading in science inquiry and helping them to teach students to use multiple texts in their classrooms.

In sum, even though we know less about multiple text reading in science than we do in history, there is evidence that having students read multiple texts and representations of concepts improves students' learning.

Multiple Texts in Other Subject Areas

I would be remiss if I did not mention myriad opportunities for students in English, the arts, mathematics, and other subject areas to encounter multiple texts. Teachers in these subject areas may already incorporate multiple texts into instruction. For example, it isn't rare that students in an English class read two novels in succession with the same themes and engage in comparisons and contrasts across the two books. English students can be asked to read history texts that provide a context for a particular piece of historical fiction, or they can be asked to read critiques of literature or a series of informational texts on topics that will be the fodder for their persuasive essays. Mathematics students can read several texts that provide somewhat different ways of solving a problem or several explanations of a mathematical concept. They can read the way in which mathematics is applied to various societal problems in journals and newspapers (e.g., statistical analyses of political polls or population growth and decline) and relate that to the explanations of those same kinds of analyses in their textbooks.

The issue in each of these instances of multiple text use is the role of explicit instruction, however. We know from research in history and science reading that, except for those with the most background knowledge or the most mature epistemologies, students aren't likely to gain much from reading multiple texts on their own. Students need tools. In history, these tools are the strategies that historians use (such as sourcing, contextualization, and corroboration), scaffolds (such as comparison/contrast or evidence charts), and tasks that foster reading *across* texts as well as *within* texts (such as synthesis tasks or argument tasks). Students need to have guiding questions that lead them to think about topics from alternate perspectives. Furthermore, students need to understand the purposes for reading within their disciplines—the kinds of questions that are asked, the norms for communicating information, the ways in which knowledge is created, shared, and evaluated. Understanding what the discipline does and how it determines quality will help students understand what they need to be doing when they read from multiple sources.

In teaching students to read multiple texts, teachers will grapple with text and task selections. One of the most difficult aspects of teaching students to read multiple texts is selecting the right materials to read. Rather than relying on single texts to help students learn or think about ideas in a discipline, teachers must now choose text *sets* that, taken together, provide a complex yet cohesive learning experience. Does each text in the set have a unique voice? Does each text include essential information that, when put together with information in other texts, affords a more complete understanding of the topic? Is each text representative of a disciplinary genre? Does each text have enough information about it to help the reader determine perspective, audience, tone, and trustworthiness? Does the set represent an appropriate range of difficulty? Are there some texts that should be read first, so that they can act as scaffolds for later, more difficult texts? Do the texts, taken together, offer sufficient opportunity for teaching vocabulary and discipline-specific reading and writing strategies? These and other questions need to be asked by teachers as they construct multiple-text instruction, and such questions are quite challenging to answer.

Furthermore, how teachers frame the task is important. For example, asking students to take a stand on an issue in which authors disagree is quite different from asking students to synthesize important information across texts and write an expla-nation or an account that integrates the various sources. In addition, helping stu-dents to understand that an *evidence-based argument* is not a mere opinion piece is important, so that when students are asked to write an argument, they know what the task is.

Finally, students need scaffolding to help them make sense of multiple texts. For example, in the current work of Project READI, students are taught to annotate their texts, provided with various note-taking charts that require comparison and contrast of various texts, and provided with modeling, practice, and feedback in discipline-based reading and writing strategies. They are encouraged to dig into text and grap-ple with meaning. They have explicit discussions about a discipline's norms, and they use these scaffolds to approximate the reading of historians, scientists, and literary scholars.

In sum, Project READi expects that the initiative, when complete, will extend the findings of studies described in previous sections, in that they will know more about the effect of instruction in multiple text reading in science, history, and literature; have models of teaching that support learning in the disciplines through multiple texts; have a clearer notion of the way argumentation differs across disciplines; and know more about the ways in which students develop arguments after reading mul-tiple texts.

I can only say that because of projects like these and the emphasis of multiple texts in the Common Core standards, teaching and learning are positioned for immense change. Teachers across the nation are rethinking the ways they are covering con-tent—they are becoming more conscious of the discourse practices of their discipline, and they are much more likely to be providing time for reading and grappling with multiple texts within the school day.

Conclusion

We live in a complex world, one that requires us to make connections across multiple perspectives to fully understand and act in it. Yet in school, we teach students to live in a simplistic world, where questions are answered in a single text and complexity is eschewed. Whereas I can understand the need to dig into a single text to understand it, as a teacher I want students, especially by the time they leave high school, to be able to do that *and* develop richer, more nuanced mental models that come from dealing with multiple texts. Success in doing this will depend on the extent to which we can equip students with the necessary understanding of disciplinary approaches to multiple texts, provide them with appropriate models and tools, and structure tasks with increasing complexity. Teachers using multiple texts will surely struggle with issues of text difficulty and the time-consuming task of selecting appropriate texts to illustrate the instructional points they wish to make. They will be constantly straddling the line between teaching students to understand what is inside a text and what is outside a text. Students will struggle with the lack of certainty that is part and parcel of studying a topic from more than one perspective. But in the end, research suggests that students engaging with multiple texts will be better at reading about, understanding, and communicating complex issues, which in turn will better equip them for the living successfully in the world.

11

Multiple Texts in Practice

Fostering Accessibility, Engagement, and Comprehension

JOANNA LIEBERMAN AND JANET LOONEY

In chapter 10, Cynthia Shanahan makes a compelling case for using multiple texts in the secondary classroom to promote the growth and development of adolescent readers, writers, and thinkers. As teachers and literacy coaches with decades of experience in elementary and secondary schools, we concur with her assertions. When selected wisely and deployed carefully, multiple texts become a powerful and efficient pedagogical tool for strengthening the literacy development of adolescents.

As educators, many of us have long incorporated multiple texts in our classroom practice. We may have chosen a variety of novels for students to read in book groups. Or we may have paired primary source documents with a textbook selection in a social studies class. However, with the introduction of the Common Core State Standards, teaching with and having students navigate their way through multiple texts is now essentially a requirement in our classrooms. These newly developed standards assert that for students to be prepared successfully for college and work in the twenty-first century, they must "actively seek the wide, deep, and thoughtful engagement with high-quality literary and informational texts that builds knowledge, enlarges experience and broadens worldviews."[1] We can accomplish this goal only if we know why multiple texts matter, how to gather texts purposefully, and how to use them effectively with our students. When selected wisely and deployed carefully, multiple texts become a powerful and efficient pedagogical tool for strengthening the literacy development of adolescents.

In this chapter, we outline three main purposes for using multiple texts in the classroom: readability and accessibility, student motivation and engagement, and comprehension. For each purpose, we offer several examples of how an educator might work with multiple texts in both an English language arts classroom as well as a classroom in another discipline. Throughout the classroom portraits, we offer guidelines to consider when gathering texts in the secondary classroom. There are many online resources that educators can use to learn about and select high quality texts for the classroom. Appendix A is a collection of useful websites to help teachers as they begin to assemble text sets.

Multiple Texts in the Secondary Classroom: Definition and Purposes

The phrase *multiple texts* refers to the presence of more than a single common teaching text in the classroom. In content-area classes like history, a teacher might supplement textbook material with primary sources such as political cartoons, paintings, photographs, and video and other digital media. The presence of these texts enhances students' abilities to understand various perspectives and biases and deepens their knowledge of the content they are studying.[2] Multiple texts can also signify a means of grouping texts on a particular theme or topic. Some of us refer to this practice as assembling text sets. For the purposes of this chapter, we use the terms *multiple texts* and *text sets* synonymously. The examples in this chapter demonstrate how teachers across all content areas might ground their teaching in more than one central text.

As teachers and literacy coaches in secondary schools, we recognize that using multiple texts in our teaching repertoire serves a variety of important purposes. Essential to promoting the literacy success of our middle and high school classrooms is recognizing and working with the reality of our readers. In any given secondary classroom, we have students reading significantly above grade level, significantly below grade level, and everywhere in between. Using multiple texts enables us to acknowledge students' strengths and successes as readers and to match them to texts that offer appropriate supports and challenges. At the same time, educators can use multiple texts to promote access to reading material at the high end of the grade-level complexity bands as required in the Common Core standards. Another purpose for using multiple text sets is to promote student engagement, a critical component for success with secondary school students. By using multiple texts, we honor adolescents' need for choice as well as promote a sense of inquiry and independence in the classroom. Achieving optimal literacy development also requires focus on critical skills, such as analysis, synthesis, and critique. These skills help students become competent and complex thinkers across multiple disciplines. If our goal as teachers of history, science, English, and mathematics is to apprentice our students to our disciplines, then we must support them in the work of integrating and interpreting information from a variety of sources.

Readability and Accessibility

Secondary schools often require students to read and analyze core discipline-specific texts. However, even when provided with significant supports, many of these texts are too difficult for and thus inaccessible to a large number of students. We understand the challenge of providing instruction to a class of students whose reading levels often span several grades. Finding appropriate and accessible texts requires considerable time, effort, and knowledge about the many factors that influence the readability and difficulty level of a text. Fortunately, many resources, including leveled book websites, are available to assist teachers as they gather a wide range of texts to support and challenge their readers (see appendix B for a list of leveled book websites that teachers can use when assembling text sets).

The Common Core standards require students to read "increasingly complex texts" with a focus on high-level comprehension.[3] This by no means implies that all students at a particular grade will readily navigate texts at the same complexity level, nor does it mean that we should limit students' access to highly sophisticated texts.[4] If students receive explicit instruction along with ample time to read and practice higher-level comprehension skills, their ability to interpret more complex reading material will increase. We want our students to do the higher-level thinking and close reading required in the Common Core standards; therefore, we must make purposeful teaching decisions to help them get there. We need to know our students as readers, provide a pathway of instructional scaffolds to strengthen their reading abilities, and supply them with a rich collection of texts and resources that are both immediately accessible and highly sophisticated. Creating text sets that reflect the variable needs of readers in our classes is one way to ensure equity and accessibility and to promote higher order thinking skills.

Readability and Accessibility in English Language Arts Classrooms

In English language arts classrooms, text sets are typically organized around genre, theme, author, craft element, or text structure. Let's consider preparing a text set for a genre study. First, we compile several quality texts that are matched to curriculum standards, unit objectives, and the range of readers in the class. The set should reflect the diversity of the students and include subgenres that vary in content, theme, and format. Being cognizant of students' reading levels, strengths, and interests will ensure an entry point or "way in" for all readers.

As literacy coaches, we have assisted middle school teachers in assembling texts for units of study. For a sixth-grade short story reading unit, we selected various texts from the Fountas and Pinnell text gradient, knowing that the levels and complexity of texts had to reflect the current needs and ultimate goals of readers in the classroom (levels R–Z) (see figure 11.1). Fountas and Pinnell have developed a system for classifying texts along a continuum of complexity from A to Z+, with A being the least complex texts suited to the skills of our earliest readers and Z+ being the texts well matched to our most competent and sophisticated adolescent readers.[5] While

FIGURE 11.1

Sixth-grade short story text set

This set includes only a handful of sample texts that could be included in a sixth-grade short story collection. A complete text set would include several short stories or collections at each level and a larger picture-book collection.

Possible short stories/collections	
Text/Author	Level
Every Living Thing, Cynthia Rylant	R
Hey World, Here I Am, Jean Little	S
Throwing Shadows, E.L. Konigsburg	T
Baseball in April and Other Short Stories, Gary Soto	U
Seedfolks, Paul Fleischman	W
What Do Fish Have to Do with Anything?, Avi	W
Tales of Mystery and Imagination, Edgar Allen Poe (retold by Margaret Naudi)	Y
Free? Stories About Human Rights, Amnesty International	Y
"Shoes for Hector" from *El Bronx Remembered*, Nicholasa Mohr	Z
Possible picture books	
Title/Author	Genre
Your Move, Eve Bunting	Realistic fiction
Mississippi Morning, Ruth Vander Zee	Historical fiction
Wings, Christopher Myers	Fantasy
Read-aloud/mentor texts	
Title/Author	Genre
"The Goodness of Matt Kaizer," from *What Do Fish Have to Do with Anything?*, Avi	Realistic fiction
Pink and Say, Patricia Polacco	Historical fiction
"Eleven," from *Woman Hollering Creek and Other Stories*, Sandra Cisneros	Realistic fiction

we acknowledge that text leveling is only one pedagogical tool in an educator's repertoire, we assert that it offers teachers guidance as they consider their complex, adolescent readers.

To begin the unit, the teacher reads short stories aloud, stopping to model thinking, provide focused teaching, and engage students in a conversation around literary elements, genre, structure, and craft of each story. Read-alouds are intentionally selected that would pose significant challenge to many students in the class if they were to read them on their own without supports or explicit instruction. Through interactive read-alouds and shared readings, the teacher models the close reading techniques an expert reader activates to make meaning of a literary text.[6] Following the read-aloud, students read a mixture of complex and more accessible short stories independently or in small instructional groups, recording observations and thinking and practicing the close reading modeled in mini-lessons around the mentor text.

By reading texts at their independent level, students tackle the teaching principles presented in the mini-lessons. They practice and apply new learning, doing the "same work repeatedly, in books that are appropriately complex for them to read."[7] If the text is too challenging, struggling readers will spend most of the time trying to decode and comprehend the literal meaning, rather than attending to the critical thinking and analysis required in the Common Core standards. As students increase the volume of reading, they should be encouraged to select and read more challenging and increasingly complex texts.

Readability and Accessibility in Social Studies and History Classrooms

Reading for content often poses different challenges for readers. In middle and high school social studies and history classes, textbooks are the primary means of delivering information. We understand their value and purpose. Textbooks are organized around major topics of study, include key pieces of information, and provide common language and experiences. Moreover, textbooks are often used in college courses, so secondary teachers do students a service by teaching them how to navigate and learn from textbooks. On the other hand, textbooks often lack in-depth or critical study of topics, usually include only one perspective on a concept or issue, and fail to offer enough supports for struggling readers or challenges for above-level readers. To provide learners with equitable access to the same content at different levels of challenge, we suggest that teachers consider supplementing the traditional textbook. This can be accomplished through the use of multiple texts.

In social studies and history classrooms, to complement the central teaching text, text sets can be organized around major topics of study and include texts at different complexity levels and from various perspectives. When assembling collections, select diverse high-interest texts that vary in genre, length, and format. Be purposeful; match texts with your readers. Try to include a wide range of reading levels (juvenile, young adult, and adult books) in the collection. In addition to informational texts, consider: primary source materials, magazine and newspaper articles, picture books, literary nonfiction, historical recounts, biographies, poetry, hybrid texts, historical fiction, and nontraditional texts, such as charts, graphs, maps, and digital media. To meet the critical reading required in the Common Core standards, students should read increasingly challenging texts that offer diverse perspectives and multiple viewpoints on a topic. Middle and high school history textbooks may devote only a few pages (or few paragraphs!) to a topic, so we must provide students with alternative texts on alternative perspectives.

To illustrate a social studies text set, we designed a multigenre collection to support an in-depth study of the civil rights movement (see figure 11.2). Included in the collection are picture books as well as complex expository texts, providing several options for students to obtain information about this topic. We selected a range of texts that the teacher could read aloud to build students' background knowledge around the causes, significant people, and important events of the civil rights movement. Even though this set was designed for middle school, high school teachers might craft something similar, still including read-alouds and texts students can navigate independently. The shared readings may also serve as mentors when teaching students how to process key ideas and critically analyze texts. As they read a variety of material independently, students practice strategic close reading.

For students to become proficient at processing challenging informational texts across content areas in secondary school and beyond, they need to read regularly and widely across genres, formats, and structures. As with literature, students can handle increasingly complex nonfiction as they learn to think critically and read with sophistication.

Student Engagement

Over the last two decades, research and practice have drawn increased attention to the roles of motivation, engagement, and choice in adolescent literacy.[8] The more engaged and motivated our students, the more likely they are to succeed as literacy learners. Those of us who have taught adolescents recognize this reality. When we offer choice in the texts our students read and we design learning opportunities that promote their sense of independence and agency, they rise to meet the challenges before them. Once again, multiple texts in our secondary classrooms can help us foster these attributes.

FIGURE 11.2

Social studies text set: Civil rights movement

Title	Author	Genre
Intermediate (grades 4–6)		
When Marian Sang: The True Recital of Marian Anderson, The Voice of a Century	Pam Muñoz Ryan	Biography
Rosa	Nikki Giovanni	Biography
M.L.K.: Journey of a King	Tonya Bolden	Biography
Remember Little Rock: The Time, the People, the Stories	Paul Robert Walker	Expository
Malcolm X: A Fire Burning Brightly	Walter Dean Myers	Biography
Remember: The Journey to School Integration	Toni Morrison	Hybrid
Through My Eyes	Ruby Bridges	Memoir
Freedom Walkers: The Story of the Montgomery Bus Boycott	Russell Freedman	Literary nonfiction
Young adult (grades 6–10)		
Marching for Freedom: Walk Together, Children, and You Don't Grow Weary	Elizabeth Partridge	Literary nonfiction
Freedom Riders: John Lewis and Jim Zwerg on the Front Lines of the Civil Rights Movement	Ann Bausum	Biography
Birmingham Sunday	Larry Dane Brimner	Expository
Malcolm X: By Any Means Necessary	Walter Dean Myers	Biography
A Dream of Freedom: The Civil Rights Movement from 1954 to 1968	Diane McWhorter	Expository
The Power of One: Daisy Bates and the Little Rock Nine	Judith Bloom Fradin and Dennis Brindell Fradin	Biography
Today the World Is Watching You: The Little Rock Nine and the Fight for School Integration, 1957	Kekla Magoon	Expository
The Voice That Challenged a Nation: Marian Anderson and the Struggle for Equal Rights	Russell Freedman	Biography
To the Mountaintop: My Journey Through the Civil Rights Movement	Charlayne Hunter-Gault	Memoir
Spies of Mississippi: The True Story of the Spy Network That Tried to Destroy the Civil Rights Movement	Rick Bowers	Expository
Digital Archive (The Martin Luther King, Jr. Center for Nonviolent Social Change)	http://www.thekingcenter.org/archive	Hybrid
Adult (grade 8 and up)		
Warriors Don't Cry: A Searing Memoir of the Battle to Integrate Little Rock's Central High	Melba Pattillo Beals	Memoir
The Autobiography of Malcolm X	Malcolm X and Alex Haley	Autobiography
Walking with the Wind: A Memoir of the Movement	John Lewis with Michael D'Orso	Memoir

Since the publication of the first edition of *In the Middle* in 1987, Nancie Atwell has argued that students need time to read the texts that matter to them.[9] For over twenty years, she has shared portraits of her classroom where students regularly read, write about, and discuss more than thirty books a year. Atwell uses the pedagogical frame of a reader's workshop. Students choose the texts they want to read, with guidance from peers and Atwell herself, and they are given ample time to read in class. As part of their reading work, they regularly confer with their teacher and discuss their thinking and interpretations of their chosen texts. They write extended reflections and analyses of those texts, thereby engaging in ongoing literary conversation with their teacher and peers. By the end of their eighth-grade year, students have read passionately across authors, genres, and themes and explored books they may never have otherwise encountered without the supportive frame of the workshop. According to Atwell, "The only surefire way to induce a love of books is to invite students to select their own."[10] Finding ample instructional time for students to select their own texts is a challenge. Realistically, we know that students cannot choose their own material all the time, particularly in content-area classes, but having *some* choice some of the time is a reasonable goal. As Atwell and those of us who have followed her lead can attest, students' ability to choose really does matter.

In addition to choice, motivation is another factor that promotes increased literacy achievement for adolescents. Moje, Overby, Tysvaer, and Morris argue that educators must attend to the needs of adolescents when crafting opportunities for literacy learning.[11] They debunk the myth that many adolescents, particularly those in urban schools, do not willingly engage in reading and writing activities outside of school—in fact, they do. However, the authors point out that adolescents do not necessarily choose texts recommended or valued by adults. Moreover, students in their study place a premium on using reading and writing to sustain and nurture their social networks. The authors imply that attending to adolescents' levels of engagement and their social arenas may translate into more powerful literacy learning experiences. The themes outlined by Atwell and Moje et al. emerge in the following portraits of an English language arts class as well as science and math classes.

Engagement in English Language Arts Classrooms

Many secondary teachers incorporate book groups (sometimes known as literature circles or book clubs) into their classroom practice. In a book group, small clusters of students (as few as three or as many as six) gather to read and discuss a shared text. Careful consideration about the selection of texts, the structure of the groups, and the guidelines for conversation enables the teacher to maximize engagement and independence.

We often organize book groups around author studies, genre, or even thematic explorations. This way, the entire class can engage in a course of study, but students have input into the texts they read. For example, we have helped teachers assemble a book club unit on the novels of Jerry Spinelli. Spinelli, a prolific writer of intermediate and young adult fiction, regularly crafts intriguing protagonists who teach readers the value of individuality in the face of conformity. In this particular unit, the teacher selects five Spinelli novels for the class to explore.[12] Students can have input into the novel they will read, while the teacher reserves the right to make final decisions about which students are matched with each particular text.

During the unit, teachers use the mini-lesson portion of the workshop to teach students how to work productively in a book club and how to analyze literature through a lens of character and theme. Mini-lessons on "process" include a range of topics such as: designing a reading schedule, asking and responding to open-ended discussion questions, learning to cede the floor so all members participate, and supporting assertions with evidence from the text. In the more analytical lessons, the teacher may demonstrate how book club participants can use their conversations to: analyze the unique nature of Spinelli's characters, explore the moral and ethical dilemmas those characters face, critique the nature of the book as a whole, and explore the resonance of the themes in their own lives.

But middle school is not the only place for book groups; they have an important role in high school instruction as well. We have taught units on the literature of the Holocaust, a period in human history that merits attention not only in social studies but in literature classes as well. During one particular course of study, we used Elie Wiesel's memoir *Night* as a shared class text. Depending on the needs of the class, we have used this as either a read-aloud text or a whole-class book study. Wiesel's work lays thematic groundwork for emotionally and morally challenging literary texts. In the later phases of the unit, students participate in book groups focused on some of the other powerful texts to emerge from this historical legacy. In selecting possible titles for book groups, we have used the graphic novel *Maus I: A Survivor's Tale: My Father Bleeds History* by Art Spiegelman; *I Never Saw Another Butterfly*, the collection of poetry from the camps at Terezin edited by Hana Volavkova; the novel *The Book Thief* by Markus Zusak; and Anne Frank's *The Diary of a Young Girl*. By offering a wide range of genres, points of view, and levels of complexity, students can gravitate toward the text that most speaks to them while deepening their understanding of the literary implications of the era.

Adolescents need to choose their reading material, and book groups allow for that scaffolded and purposeful choice. In addition, the social nature of a book group honors the premium adolescents place on interaction with peers, creating authentic engagement with texts.

Engagement in Science and Mathematics Classrooms

Meaningful engagement with texts does not reside solely in the domain of English language arts. The Common Core standards require broad and deep interactions with texts in all content areas. Fortunately, many teachers of science, social studies, and even mathematics can adeptly weave meaningful text work into their classes.

Consider a middle school science unit on evolution. While the teacher must create ample time to explore the fundamental scientific tenets of evolution, there will always be far more content to examine than any one teacher could possibly cover. Often in these cases, a teacher may assign a research project to extend students' knowledge of the subject. Perhaps the teacher wants his or her students to explore how theories of evolution have changed over time or the nature of the most current debate in the field. She or he may want students to trace the evolutionary history of a particular organism or to research the impact of humans on the evolutionary process. To deepen their understanding of a particular topic, students must interact with a variety of texts. They can make reading selections from journal articles, popular magazines, websites, nonfiction trade books, and of course, textbooks.

A teacher might even guide his or her students through a multidimensional look at the evolutionary scientist Charles Darwin. Imagine a book club unit in a science class where students read, in genres of their choosing, accounts of the life of Charles Darwin (see figure 11.3). The texts may range from historical fiction to standard biography to picture book to literary nonfiction, thereby supporting the Common Core goal of reading broadly. In addition to meeting in clubs around the same book, students can also gather to talk across texts, growing their understanding of the complexities and resonance of a figure like Darwin. By encouraging our students to read widely and inviting multiple texts into our disciplines when possible, we increase the likelihood that our adolescents remain engaged.

But what about mathematics? Bringing multiple texts into our mathematics classrooms is certainly challenging, but not impossible. In one of the secondary schools in our district, a literacy coach colleague, together with a team of teachers, has instituted a "wide reading" component across the entire school program.[13] Each term, one content-area teacher engages his or her students in independent reading relevant to the discipline. For example, in the fall quarter, students have wide reading in science class. Next, the program moves to mathematics. Over the course of four terms, students engage in wide reading in all the disciplines. Some teachers choose a topic (e.g., evolution, as discussed above), while others leave the text choice up to the students themselves.

In a model like this one, we can envision high school students choosing texts with mathematical underpinnings such as nonfiction pieces like *Moneyball* by Michael Lewis; *Bringing Down the House: The Inside Story of Six M.I.T. Students Who Took*

FIGURE 11.3

Text Set on Charles Darwin and evolution

Title	Author	Genre
The Tree of Life: Charles Darwin	Peter Sís	Nonfiction picture book
The Evolution of Calpurnia Tate	Jacqueline Kelly	Historical fiction
Charles and Emma: The Darwins' Leap of Faith	Deborah Heiligman	Biography
What Darwin Saw: The Journey That Changed the World	Rosalyn Schanzer	Graphic biography
Charles Darwin	Kathleen Krull	Biography (humor)

Vegas for Millions by Ben Mezrich; and *Freakonomics: A Rogue Economist Explores the Hidden Side of Everything* by Steven D. Levitt and Stephen J. Dubner. They might also read fiction such as the novel *Flatland: A Romance of Many Dimensions* by Edwin Abbott. Students may even pursue periodicals (such as the *Wall Street Journal* or *The Economist*) that ask them to blend mathematical thinking into their reading lives. High school students have ever-broadening views of the world around them. Such forays in reading undoubtedly will support a deeper understanding of the role mathematics has in their everyday lives. Anecdotally, our colleagues who designed this model have reported increased engagement across all disciplines and a renewed interest in texts each time the wide reading program moves to another class. These examples from the content areas represent just a few of the promising possibilities for using multiple texts to increase independence and engagement.

Comprehension

To make meaning of a text, readers activate decoding, fluency, and comprehension skills.[14] In the earliest stages of development, young readers work hard to master the decoding skills that enable them to process increasingly difficult texts with flexibility and fluency. Reading instruction in the elementary grades often emphasizes phonics, decoding, and fluency in addition to comprehension as students solidify their relationship with grade-level texts. By the time they reach middle school, however, reading instruction focuses more on comprehension and less on decoding and fluency. While secondary educators will continue to encounter students who need support with decoding and especially fluency, the majority of adolescents benefit from increasingly sophisticated and nuanced instruction in comprehension. In other words, most adolescents have a comfortable mastery of decoding and fluency, but successful navigation of the texts they will encounter in middle school, high school, and beyond requires ongoing work in comprehension. [15]

Calkins, Ehrenworth, and Lehman argue that the Common Core standards place great "emphasis on high-level comprehension skills." They write, "In order for students to do Common Core reading work, they'll need explicit instruction in the skills and strategies of high-level comprehension."[16] In other words, adolescents need explicit instruction as they learn to synthesize, analyze, and critique texts in both English language arts and other disciplines. In addition, they need opportunities to apply this instruction to a range of texts in our classrooms. If our goal is to apprentice students to our disciplines, we must support them in the work of integrating and interpreting information from a variety of sources. In the examples that follow, we demonstrate how using multiple texts supports the instructional goals of higher-level comprehension.

English Language Arts

For students to analyze and critique a wide range of increasingly challenging texts in English language arts, we must provide them with opportunities to examine and study high-quality fiction and nonfiction. Typically, English language arts teachers gravitate toward literature, poetry, and drama. As former ELA teachers, we appreciate the sense of story, and we willingly share that with our students. Throughout this chapter, we have offered many examples of units of study that focus on fictional texts. We can readily envision the high leverage comprehension work students will do to navigate such texts. And yet the Common Core standards require that secondary students read "literary nonfiction of steadily increasing sophistication" and "complex informational texts with independence and confidence because the vast majority of reading in college and workforce training will be sophisticated nonfiction."[17] This mandate requires that we guide our students as they develop sophisticated strategies for understanding literary nonfiction as well.

Fortunately, excellent young adult literary nonfiction abounds. We have designed a middle school unit of study on interpreting and evaluating literary nonfiction. Our unit focuses on texts with a similar topic, the history of medicine or forensic science. However a literary nonfiction unit need not center on a particular subject. One can just as easily gather high-quality texts on a variety of subjects and allow students to make personal reading choices. Our unit begins by reading aloud a text such as *Phineas Gage: A Gruesome but True Story About Brain Science* by John Fleischman. As the teacher reads aloud and models his or her thinking, the class devises a working definition of the nature of literary nonfiction and how it differs from more traditional nonfiction. Students then choose a text for independent reading to which they will apply their learned analytical skills.

Once the read-aloud is complete, the mini-lessons in the reading workshop focus on how to read literary nonfiction deeply and thoughtfully. The teacher may demonstrate the importance of summary skills and how readers must revise their thinking when they encounter new information in a text. In addition, the teacher can teach students that literary nonfiction has parallels to more traditional fiction. These texts frequently have story elements, like protagonists, that make the texts resemble novels. Literary nonfiction texts often leave the reader with lingering themes, as do conventional fiction texts. However, thoughtful nonfiction readers recognize that authors ground their writing in extensive, careful research and bring a particular point of view or perspective that has an impact on the reader's experience.

By teaching students how to read literary nonfiction with an eye on how it approaches and diverges from literature, we are addressing the Common Core standards and broadening our students' abilities to think deeply across a wide range of texts. In our unit, students must analyze the subgenre of literary nonfiction not only to research a topic or to familiarize themselves with a subject that intrigues them, but also to learn how to interpret these texts and to incorporate them into their regular reading lives. Throughout the unit, students write, reflect, and discuss their reading experiences as they develop their comprehension skills. And they gain analytical tools to prepare them for the wealth of nonfiction they will encounter in high school and beyond.

Social Studies

Although the standards assume that teachers of English will primarily focus attention on literary nonfiction, the expectation is clear that English language arts and content teachers collaborate and share responsibility in teaching students how to successfully navigate and comprehend informational texts. If we expect students to analyze and think deeply across nonfiction genres, then we must provide them with the necessary texts to do this work.

In order to implement an effective study that builds students' comprehension, students must have access to many varied texts in which to practice developing skills. Once teachers have selected the focus for the unit of study, the next step is to intentionally choose texts that contain strong examples of authors' point of view and purpose and those that offer different interpretations. The diversity of material allows teachers to demonstrate and model how successful readers analyze, critique, and interpret texts for deeper understanding.

Let's return to our civil rights movement text set (figure 11.2). The unit begins with students spending several days immersed in self-selected texts around this topic. To ensure that students acquire an in-depth understanding and exposure to divergent accounts of this historical time period, the collection should be supplemented with several primary source and digital texts, including speeches, newspaper articles, and personal accounts.

Throughout the unit, spend a portion of each class leading the students in a shared reading activity. For example, the teacher may share a September 1957 *New York Times* article about the integration of Central High in Little Rock, a personal account such as *Warriors Don't Cry* by Melba Pattillo Beals, or an excerpt from the biography *The Power of One: Daisy Bates and the Little Rock Nine*, pushing students to notice how language and tone reveal perspective. He or she models gathering textual evidence to support each author's stance. For the next several days, students read and analyze additional texts, making observations about author's purpose, and how the inclusion or exclusion of details and examples indicate bias.

Providing a range of genres and text structures for students to practice new understandings not only builds awareness of how texts are written with specific views, but also deepens content knowledge. The Common Core standards require that middle and high school students compare texts with similar perspectives, contrast those with opposing viewpoints, and interpret contradictory accounts. To accomplish this task, students must integrate a large amount of information, connect ideas from one text to another, and assess reliability of sources. If we want students to analyze and critique arguments, perspectives, and ideas rather than just to read and accrue facts, then they must engage in significant amounts of discipline-specific informational reading.

Conclusion

As teachers and coaches, we recognize the challenges secondary teachers face as they work to simultaneously meet the content-area goals in their discipline and nurture the literacy development of their adolescent learners. Limits on instructional time, resources, and support can easily derail efforts to open our curriculum and pedagogy to multiple texts. However, we believe that teaching with multiple texts better equips us to address three issues critical to adolescent literacy development: readability and accessibility, motivation and engagement, and comprehension. The examples provided in this chapter offer viable models for experimenting with more than one core text in the classroom and for supporting adolescent students' literacy development across content areas.

Additional Resources

Buehl, Doug. *Developing Readers in the Academic Disciplines.* Newark, DE: International Reading Association, 2011.

Fountas, Irene, and Gay Su Pinnell. *Genre Study: Teaching with Fiction and Nonfiction Books.* Portsmouth, NH: Heinemann, 2012.

APPENDIX A
Websites for Finding Texts

Amazon.com (reviews)	http://www.amazon.com/Childrens-Books/
Common Sense (book reviews and ratings)	http://www.commonsensemedia.org/
ALA Young Adult Book Awards	http://www.ala.org/yalsa/booklistsawards/booklistsbook
Titlewave	http://www.titlewave.com/
NoveList	http://www.ebscohost.com/novelist/
Goodreads	http://www.goodreads.com/
Horn Book Online (subscription required)	http://www.hornbookguide.com
Library Book Lists	http://librarybooklists.org
Notable Social Studies Trade Books for Young People	http://www.socialstudies.org/notable
National Science Teachers Association (NSTA): Outstanding Science Trade Books	http://www.nsta.org/publications/ostb/
NCTE Orbis Pictus Award for Outstanding Nonfiction for Children	http://www.ncte.org/awards/orbispictus
Radical Math	http://radicalmath.org
Mathematical Fiction List	http://kasmana.people.cofc.edu/MATHFICT/

APPENDIX B
Websites for Leveling Texts

Website	Description (What does this site offer/)	Leveling factors (How are levels determined?)
Fountas and Pinnell Leveled Books K–8 http://www.fandp leveledbooks.com	This subscription-based site searches books by title, author, level, and genre. The frequently updated database contains over 40,000 books. Each book is assigned a guided reading level from A (kindergarten) to Z+ (high school).	Each text is reviewed and leveled by Irene Fountas and Gay Su Pinnell in conjunction with their team of levelers using the *F&P Text Level Gradient,* a continuum of characteristics related to the supports and challenges a reader encounters during reading. Texts are analyzed using ten characteristics: genre, text structure, content, themes and ideas, language and literary features, sentence complexity, vocabulary, word difficulty, illustrations, and book and print features.
The Lexile Framework for Reading http://www.lexile.com/	This site searches books by title or author. Advanced search finds books that match additional criteria, such as publisher and keyword. The site provides a level that represents a text's difficulty on the Lexile scale, ranging from below 200L for beginning readers to above 1300L for advanced adolescent readers.	A text is analyzed by *MetaMetrics* using a software program that evaluates its readability. It measures a text's complexity by using characteristics such as word frequency and sentence length.
OKAPI Readability Tool http://www.lefthand logic.com/htmdocs/ tools/okapi/okapi.php	This site uses OKAPI, an Internet application that allows you to submit up to 200 words of a text sample. Through readability analysis, a grade-level reading score is computed.	Using the Spache or Dale-Chall Readability Formulas (average number of words per sentence and number of words not found on the Spache or Dale familiar word lists) a readability grade level is determined for the sample text.
Readability Consensus Calculator http://www.readability formulas.com/ free-readability-formula-tests.php	This site uses a readability calculator to determine reading and grade level using seven readability formulas. Between 100 and 600 words of text may be submitted for analysis.	Number of sentences, words, syllables, and characters in the passage are analyzed and reading level, grade level, and text difficulty are determined using each of the seven readability formulas.

Website	Description (What does this site offer/)	Leveling factors (How are levels determined?)
Scholastic Book Expert Online http://src.scholastic. com/bookexpert/	This site searches the Scholastic Reading Counts library by title, author, or keyword. Advanced search finds books that match additional criteria. This site also supplies information about a book's content, awards, interest level, reading level, guided reading level (GRL), and Lexile level.	Reading levels are taken from the publisher when available. Otherwise, texts are assessed using readability formulas. A team of librarians and teachers reviews the reading levels, making adjustments when necessary.

12

Research in Writing

The Rightful Place of Writing-to-Learn in Content Teaching

VICKI A. JACOBS

Writing-to-learn? Haven't we done that already? Isn't it the same thing as writing across the curriculum? We've had in-service on it—all about journals and reflection, right? I do a lot of that already. Now, you know, the talk is all about Common Core and the need to teach argument; so I have started to use debate and am assigning more research projects and essays. Since I am not a writing teacher, I count on the English department to teach my students how to write essays. Honestly? I would do more to teach writing; but with testing and the push to cover material, I'm pretty maxed out. I just don't think I can do more than I already am.[1]

This quotation is a composite of comments I received when I asked twelve high-school English, science, math, and history teachers what they would appreciate learning from a book chapter on theory and research related to writing-to-learn. I have worked closely with these teachers over the years in my role as a former English teacher and in my current roles in teacher and literacy education. Some of these teachers are veteran and some not. All are skilled professionals whose practice I deeply respect. As a group, they maintain a reflective stance about their teaching and their students' learning and are dedicated to building their practice in response to their students' needs.

Today, teachers, researchers, and school leaders alike are very familiar with the adolescent "literacy crisis" and the "writing crisis," in particular.[2] Similarly, my teaching colleagues' comments demonstrate their awareness of recommendations made by national reports to address those crises.[3] For example, they have attempted to integrate principles of the writing process into their content instruction and have given students time to practice answering the short- and long-answer questions that are typical of today's tests. Those familiar with the general tenets of *writing-to-learn* (which is a subset of *writing across the curriculum* but often used synonymously with it) have asked their students to question the content they are learning and then investigate those questions by keeping reflection journals, taking notes, and using graphic organizers.

Yet some of these teachers have confided that they have maintained, at best, a guarded relationship with the notion of writing-to-learn. They do not question that writing is an important part of teaching and learning content; rather, they are concerned about how to support students' writing when they do not see themselves are writers. ("I went into math to avoid writing!") They worry that spending more time on the writing process might cost them time for content instruction. ("We have an extended day. Maybe writing instruction belongs there?") A few are honest enough to confess that they just do not "get" what to do with writing. ("Honestly? If someone would just tell me what to do, I would certainly do my best to do it!") In short, these teachers are ready and willing to promote writing in their content instruction, but they seriously doubt they have the time or the expertise to do so.

The purpose of this chapter is to address my colleagues' concerns about the rightful place of writing—and particularly of writing-to-learn—in their content instruction. To do so, this chapter summarizes some of the key issues and contentions that writing research and theory have examined in an effort to define what writing-to-learn can accomplish and what it cannot.

Defining Writing-to-Learn: Origins

The notion that writing and thinking are inextricably related has enjoyed a long history in the literatures of both literacy and cognition. However, ideas about how to use writing instructionally to support student learning have struggled to take root. This section examines the theoretical and instructional traditions from which writing-to-learn has evolved and the current challenges to its implementation.

Defining Writing as Skill Development

Before the mid-1960s, although a few educational psychologists had examined writing as the development of ideas, the theory, research, and practice of writing focused primarily on sentence-level structures and skills (e.g., grammar, sentence-structure [syntax], conventions, handwriting, and fluency).[4] Learning to write well meant mastering a set of sequentially learned, discrete skills required to produce well-constructed sentences, then paragraphs, and finally extended pieces. The responsibility for teaching skills and forms of writing resided squarely on English teachers' shoulders. In other disciplines, teachers used writing primarily to assess students' content knowledge.[5] The assumption was that, once students had "learned" the requisite skills and forms that they needed to write "correctly," they would be able to apply those skills appropriately to any writing assignment.

Beginning in the 1960s, research began to question the common assumption that the study of grammar (particularly at the sentence level) improved composition.[6] In response, writing instruction began to shift from the deconstruction of already well-formed sentences (e.g., through parsing or diagramming) to the construction of meaning through the manipulation of sentence-level structures (e.g., through sentence combining—a way for students to construct meaning while connecting thoughts in increasingly sophisticated and "mature" ways).[7] This early focus on constructing *meaning* in writing—if only at the sentence level—was a harbinger of a much larger shift from thinking of writing as a matter of discrete skill development to thinking of writing as a meaning-making process—the matter of cognition.

Defining Writing as Thinking

Early research on the role of thinking in composing drew heavily from the work of Vygotsky, who described the act of writing as a means by which writers could make systematic connections between ideas, deliberately structuring a "web of meaning" through analysis and synthesis that they could use for further learning.[8] In the 1970s, for example, researchers examined what students were thinking (e.g., about the choices they were making concerning form and content) as they drafted. They found that the act of writing was not only a "unique language process" but an equally "unique mode of learning" that promoted abstract thinking in younger as well as older children.[9] In short, research began to define "good" writing as more than the sum of specific skills; "good" writing also involved a problem-solving process through which writers could compose their thoughts.

Early models of the composing process all included at least two requisite modes of writing.[10] The first could be called *writer-based* prose.[11] Such writing could be characterized as exploratory and tentative as well as associative, narrative, and reflective of writers' thought processes.[12] The audiences for writer-based prose are generally the writers themselves or others close to the writer; thus writer-based prose does not have to account for the needs of readers who might be uninformed about the psychological and situational contexts necessary to understand a piece of writing fully.[13]

Journal writing quickly became, if not synonymous with writer-based prose, a means to engage students in academic or personal exploration.[14] Using principles of freewriting, students could use journals to commit tentative thinking to paper, which they could review and synthesize at a later time.[15] Through journal writing, students could draw on their personal perspectives (influenced by their background knowledge and experience) to explore new concepts and information.[16] In this way, journal writing could help secondary students overcome the "essentially neurotic activity of writing" by providing them with "frequent, inescapable opportunities" to think—that is to compose their thoughts.[17]

The second mode of writing could be called *reader-based* prose.[18] Reader-based prose requires writers to take a less egocentric stance than writer-based prose by anticipating the needs of an unknown, uninformed audience.[19] If the process of writer-based prose is about the generation, investigation, and clarification of ideas for the writer's benefit, then the process of reader-based prose is about writers ensuring that readers will have appropriate access to their ideas through purposeful use of language (e.g., appropriate use of sentence structures, vocabulary, and conventions) and form (required, for example, by argument, exposition, or persuasion). While the responsibility for teaching the language and forms of reader-based prose generally remained the purview of the English teacher, the potential for applying principles of writer-based prose to support students' exploration and learning of content seemed quite promising.

Defining Writing as Thinking Across the Curriculum

A foundational principal of the writing across the curriculum movement was that writing, as a thinking (i.e., cognitive) activity, could support students' learning of content both within and beyond the English classroom.[20] The movement focused on how writing could engage students actively in learning—learning that involved constructing meaning about content and about themselves as learners and writers in particular academic disciplines. As such, the movement strove to increase students' ownership of and investment in what and how they wrote across subject matter while achieving teachers' instructional purposes.[21]

The following sections investigate further how the purposes, principles, and practices of writing-to-learn can serve varied instructional purposes for teaching content.

Instructional Purposes for Writing-to-Learn

Having students write for the sake of writing might help develop students' fluency with the written word, but it is not the same as using writing for the purpose of learning about content. Similarly, the simple act of assigning an essay is not as much about using writing as a way to explore content as much as it is about using writing as a means for students to demonstrate what they have already learned about content (or forms of writing). In other words, for a writing strategy to qualify as a writing-to-learn strategy, the act of writing must be used to as a means for students to achieve the instructional purposes we have established *for* their learning.

As teachers, we can use writing to achieve a variety of instructional purposes. Most broadly, the act of writing can serve to focus students' attention and engage them in thinking about a particular topic—for short-term purposes (e.g., to brainstorm in preparation for class discussion, use graphic organizers to anticipate text, or take notes to prepare for a quiz) or long-term purposes (as a record of thought that students can revisit and revise to prepare a draft of an essay).

Research has found that having students write about what they read can improve reading comprehension, fluency, and word meaning.[22] In addition, writing can engage students in:

- Academic processes (e.g., questioning, evaluating, hypothesizing, analyzing)
- Inquiry (e.g., close reading, formulating hypotheses, generalizing, and synthesizing)
- Deep understanding of content (e.g., of concepts as well as one's own learning)
- Collaborative inquiry
- The analysis of their attitudes about and habits of learning[23]

In these ways, writing-to-learn fosters "the ability to question; create problems (as well as solutions); wonder; and think for oneself while working with others."[24]

Not all kinds of writing activities serve all instructional goals equally well. The effectiveness of any particular writing strategy—including writing-to-learn strategies—depends on how well it serves the kind of learning that an instructional goal requires. In other words, how we choose to use writing to support learning depends on how we define what it *means* to learn.

How Writing-to-Learn Supports Different Kinds of Learning

Taxonomies have long described the cognitive process of learning as a continuum.[25] At the most concrete level, learning is about memorization and recall of *what* (e.g., facts, dates, names, details, definitions, steps in processes). At this level, learning is a transaction through which teachers relay information or explain processes and students memorize them. Assessments of this kind of learning often ask students to perform steps (e.g., prepare a microscope slide, solve an equation algorithmically); list, outline, or describe facts (e.g., the chronology of historical events, the elements of short story, qualities of a geographic area); define (e.g., content-specific terms, an axiom, the eight parts of speech); or recite (e.g., how to conduct a geometric proof, steps in the scientific method, the rhyme scheme of an Italian sonnet). Teachers can support memory and recall by asking students to organize information in writing (e.g., using time lines, webs, outlines); maintain a notebook of content-specific definitions of common academic terms (e.g., *analyze, argue, compare, contrast*) and concepts (e.g., exposition, photosynthesis, supplemental angles, colonialism); or engage in strategic study (e.g., taking notes or using study plans such as SQ3R [survey, question, read, recite, review]).

On the other end of the learning continuum, learning is a matter of constructing abstract, conceptual understanding about what we know or can do and using that understanding to compose ideas. This kind of learning is a problem-solving process through which students investigate a genuine (that is, open-ended) question or dilemma through guided instruction.[26] For example, beyond learning that the Pythagorean theorem is, $a^2 + b^2 = c^2$, students might investigate how the theorem was originally developed to understand why. Beyond memorizing the definition of alliteration, students might compare two poets' use of it to reinforce the meaning and style of their works. In addition to noting the sequence of Civil War battles on a time line, students might explore the connection between the outcome of a particular battle and the onset of another. In addition to listing reasons for global warming, students might explore the possible effects the continued use of different kinds of fuel might have on its progression.

To achieve instructional purposes that are more about deep understanding than rote memory, the teacher's role becomes less about "telling" and more about facilitating students' construction of meaning. Teachers can use principles and strategies of writing-to-learn to scaffold students' learning at each stage of this process.[27] In other words, teachers can purposefully select strategies (including writing strategies) that serve not only as means to achieve a particular *kind* of learning but also serve as means to achieve each stage *of* that learning.

How Writing-to-Learn Can Support Different Stages of Learning

To understand how writing can support different stages of learning, we need to define the purposes and processes of each stage. Theories about stages of learning have drawn heavily on research on the interrelationship of neurology (the brain), language, and learning disabilities to describe the processes—or stages—of learning as the "comprehension" of ideas.[28] This section investigates how one such model—*schema theory*—defines learning as a three-stage, problem-solving process during which teachers provide means (e.g., bridges or scaffolds) to enable students to (1) prepare to learn (2) engage in guided (or strategic) learning, and (3) consolidate their learning.

During the first, preparatory stage of learning, teachers provide students with strategies that activate their background knowledge and experience (the *given*—stored in memory in networks called *schemata*) that will be relevant to a lesson's goals. Then teachers provide strategies that allow students to organize the given in anticipation of what is to be learned (the *new*) and to extend students' background knowledge, as necessary, before they encounter the new. Also during this preparatory stage, teachers can:

- Provide students with explicit purposes for learning/reading
- Problematize content by introducing it as a means to investigate an open question, an authentic dilemma, or essential question
- Preview a lesson's vocabulary, central concepts, and text organization

- Promote students' engagement/motivation by providing means by which they can develop preliminary questions or hypotheses about content/text

In the graduate courses I have taught on learning, teaching, and adolescent literacy development—as well as in the workshops I have conducted with middle and secondary educators over the years—I have demonstrated how purposes of the various stages of learning can be accomplished through writing. One practical example I have used to illustrate the connection between learning and writing involves a ninth-grade social studies teacher, with whom I had worked, who was ready to embark on a unit on U.S.-Russian relations.[29] Ultimately, the teacher wanted to assign an essay that would examine how similarities and differences between the United States and Russia have had an influence on their relationship during an important world event. The first chapter of the textbook that the teacher used focused on facts about Russia's demographics as they related to its geography and about Russia's capital, Moscow. Thus, during her first lesson, the teacher wanted students to investigate how demographics and geography are interrelated and to begin to hypothesize about the similarities and differences between the United States and Russia though the lens of that relationship.

To serve the purposes of the lesson *and* of pre-learning, we agreed that we needed to determine how we would activate and organize the relevant background knowledge and experience students were likely to bring to the text (that is, their points of entry into learning). The teacher knew her students were not likely to know much about Russia or Moscow, so we decided to construct an activity through which students could activate and organize what they already knew about something more familiar—the United States and Washington, D.C. The exercise would provide students with a schematic, based on what they already knew, that they could then apply to something new (Moscow) and thus begin to construct their understanding of the relationship between the United States and Russia.

During the lesson, we had each student brainstorm a list of his or her simple associations with Washington, D.C. (e.g., the Vietnam Veterans Memorial, the White House, cherry blossoms, Congress, museums, restaurants). We had students write their lists because we wanted them to be able to refer to their initial thoughts during class discussion and later, when drafting their final essays. After students completed their individual brainstorms, the teacher assigned them to small groups in which they compiled their individual lists (thus acknowledging and using each student's thoughts), organized the master list into kinship groups, and then labeled those groups (e.g., national landmarks, governmental/political structures, tourist activities, museums). Then the teacher shared with the class that Moscow was the capital of Russia, showing them where Russia and Moscow were on a map and asking them to hypothesize and question how their associations with Washington, D.C., might or might not be relevant to Moscow (e.g., What national landmarks, memorials, and/ or and museums would a tourist in Moscow see? Is spring in Russia warm enough for cherry blossoms? Did Russia have a White House or president? If not, what did it have? Would a tourist find fast-food chains in Moscow?).

By having students record their associations and questions regarding Moscow and its relation to Washington, D.C., the teacher used writing to help her students *learn*. Specifically, students recorded and organized their background knowledge and experience (their given) in anticipation of information about Russia (the new)—all in light of the lesson's instructional goals. Further, the teacher planned to have students use their initial hypotheses and questions to probe their assigned homework reading for further connections between the United States and Russia.

The first day's lesson prepared students to engage with the second stage of learning: guided learning. During guided learning, we needed to provide students with strategic means by which they could integrate the given (which they had activated and organized during pre-learning) with the new information they encountered in their reading assignment. Through this integration of given and new, students could begin to achieve a deepening understanding of content—enriching, broadening, and/or restructuring their existent schemata (or constructing new ones). The teacher and I also discussed additional opportunities that guided learning provided to students for:

- Practicing new skills or trying new models of thinking
- Investigating *how* they learned through metacognitive activities
- Returning to their initial questions to address or revise them and/or pose new ones
- Beginning to make tentative generalizations/assertions about what they were learning

While the number of strategies available to teachers to achieve purposes of guided learning is legion, the teacher and I needed to select only those strategies that would help students to accomplish the specific goals of the lesson and purposes of guided learning. Some of the writing-to-learn strategies we could have used to accomplish both included:

- Focused freewriting (non-edited, reflective thinking about a dilemma, problem, issue, or question)
- Attitudinal writing (which examines how students feel about a concept and how they think about their strengths and difficulties with learning)
- Metacognitive writing (which allows students to describe their learning behaviors, analyze their effectiveness, and think about how to strengthen them)
- Summarizing and paraphrasing (e.g., what is most meaningful in class or a reading)
- Making tentative assertions[30]

We chose to use a multiple-entry (or dialectical) notebook to probe the relationship between the United States and Russia more deeply (see figure 12.1).[31] We had each student divide a piece of paper into four columns. As illustrated in the figure, in the first column, students identified ideas from the assigned reading that seemed particularly problematic or powerful to them. In the second column, students recorded their thoughts about those ideas, using what they already knew from their background knowledge and experience, their notes from the previous lesson, and the homework reading. In the third column, students summarized their thoughts or questions about the idea. Then the teacher paired students to further the investigation of each other's ideas (thereby informing each other's thinking while broadening each student's personal understanding or schemata). Finally, in the fourth column, students noted the takeaways from their pair-share discussion—as well as questions that remained. Each pair then reported out to the entire class their takeaways and questions, which the teacher used for whole-class discussion.

The multiple-entry notebook served as a writing-to-learn activity because it provided students with means to achieve the lesson's goal (of gaining a deeper understanding of how the United States and Russia are alike or different). It also served the purposes of guided learning (allowing students to integrate their given with the new, to question and revise questions, and to practice a new skill—questioning text), and it provided students with a chronological record of their thinking for later use (e.g., during whole-class discussion and as data to support the argument of their culminating essay).

During the third stage of learning, we needed to provide students with strategic means by which they could consolidate their learning *before* demonstrating what they had learned in their compare-and-contrast essay. In terms of schema theory, our consolidation activity would have to provide students with the opportunity to organize what they had learned so that they could store it in long-term memory as extended, amended, revised, or new schemata. In addition, we could use our consolidation activity to provide students with the opportunity to:

- Assert tentative solutions to dilemmas or answers to questions
- Test the validity of their assertions and refine them based on that investigation
- Become self- (or meta-) aware about what they learned and/or how they learned

To consolidate learning, we gave students an exit ticket at the end of the second class that asked them to write (1) two facts they had learned about the relationship between the United States and Russia and why they thought those facts were important to know and (2) a statement about how the multiple-entry notebook affected how they learned and why.

FIGURE 12.1

Example of a multiple-entry notebook

Idea that is particularly powerful, meaningful, or problematic	Your thoughts about this idea	Summary thoughts and questions	Takeaway and questions from your pair-share
The reading said that the majority (three-fourths) of Russians live in or near Moscow and that Moscow is west of the Urals.	The majority of us in the United States don't live in or near Washington, D.C., although we do seem to live mostly in or near cities. When I looked at the map, I noticed that most of our big cities are on coasts or near water. There aren't many cities in the middle of the United States. Well, there are state capitals. I know there are a lot of farms in the middle of the United States. Where are Russia's farms?	Why would so many Russians live in/near just one city and what is so important about the cities being mostly west of the Urals? Where are the farms in Russia?	We talked about the fact that Russia has so much more land than the United States. But the reading said that Russia has about half the population. We think that maybe there is less livable land east of the Urals, so that is why most Russians live west of the mountains. And, if the land isn't very livable, then the farms must be west of the Urals, too, which means there doesn't seem to be a lot of farmland. We also talked about how the book said White Russians were the largest ethnicity west of the Urals and how we can't really say something like that about the United States.

The exit ticket was a writing-to-learn strategy. To explain why they thought particular facts were important, students would have to synthesize and apply what they had learned. By reflecting on the utility of the multiple-entry notebook, students would have to develop some awareness of themselves as learners.

During the third class, we decided to continue to help students consolidate their learning by having them choose one of their exit-ticket assertions (e.g., "Where cities are depends on whether or not there is some kind of water nearby") and then write a statement of belief about it ("I believe my assertion that 'where cities are depends on whether or not there is some kind of water nearby' because most major cities in Russia are on rivers and most cities in the United States are either on rivers, oceans, or lakes"). Students then wrote a statement of doubt ("I doubt my assertion that 'where cities are depends on whether or not there is some kind of water nearby' may be true because mountains also seem to determine where they are").[32] Students had to substantiate each of their statements with evidence from their class notes, the textbook, maps, and handouts.

Next, we assigned students to small groups of four. The first student shared his or her assertion. Then everyone in the group wrote and shared a belief statement for that assertion—and then wrote a shared a statement of doubt (again using class materials for evidence).

Through this activity, students generated further questions (e.g., "Why isn't there much water east of the Urals?") that they could use to probe additional ideas and facts they would encounter as the unit progresses. Because students wrote their beliefs and doubts, they would be able to trace the development of their thinking about U.S.-Russian relationships when they would begin to prepare to draft the culminating essay.

The Role of Writing-to-Learn In Reading Comprehension and Composition

In addition to playing a powerful role in facilitating students' understanding of content, writing-to-learn also facilitates students' ability to comprehend what they read and serves as a means for students to compose their thoughts before they begin to compose a piece of writing.

The Role of Writing-to-Learn in Reading Comprehension

A sizeable number of studies over the past thirty years have investigated and confirmed the symbiotic relationship between reading and writing.[33] In fact, reading researchers and theorists have used such cognitive models of learning as schema theory to describe the reading comprehension process as a thinking, meaning-making process.[34]

Not surprisingly, then, many of the strategies that research and textbooks recommend for reading across the curriculum are similar to, if not the same as those recommended for student learning in general. Both capitalize on purposes for preparing students to learn, engaging them in strategic learning, and consolidating and testing the validity of what they have learned. For example, the popular study scheme, SQ3R, asks students to prepare to learn/read through surveying and questioning the new. After reading, students recite (facts) and review (to memorize or synthesize) what they have read to consolidate their learning. Another popular study scheme, KWL, prepares students to learn/comprehend by asking them to think about what they already know and what they want to know.[35] During guided reading, students reassess what they know and want to know further. During consolidation, students reflect about what they have learned.

Further, the effectiveness of most study schemes can be enhanced by capitalizing on the general advantages of writing and the specific advantages of writing-to-learn. For example, during SQ3R, by recording their questions, students can revisit them during review; during KWL, students can use writing to reassess what they would like to know (e.g., using "starters" such as "I wonder . . . "; "I am surprised that : . . ."; "I don't understand . . . "; "This reminds me of . . . ").[36]

The Role of Writing-to-Learn in the Composing Process

Composing is a reflective, thinking process.[37] A synthesis of quantitative studies that examined the effect of various writing strategies on the improvement of composition found that the focus of writing that had the greatest positive effect on the improvement of composition was "inquiry."[38] This process is strikingly similar to the one described above—a three-stage process of learning as understanding and comprehension. As Hillock describes it:[39]

> Inquiry focuses the attention of students on strategies for dealing with sets of data, strategies which will be used in writing. For example, treatments that categorized as inquiry might involve students in the following: finding and stating specific details which convey personal experience vividly [i.e., pre-learning], examining sets of data to develop and support explanatory generalizations, or analyzing situations which present problems of various kinds [i.e., guided learning] and developing arguments about those situations [i.e., consolidation].

In this view, inquiry is a process through which students can engage in the kind of problem solving and critical thinking required to understand something well enough to organize, then present that thought in writing. In other words, inquiry is a process through which students literally compose their thoughts before they begin to draft them into writing.

Twenty years after Hillocks's research, Graham and Perin completed a similar meta-analysis of research into the effectiveness of a variety of instructional practices (*interventions*) on improvement in writing.[40] Their study found that, while inquiry (as well as pre-writing activities and the process-writing approach) still had positive effects on composition, these effects were much weaker than the effects of other processes (e.g., summarization, peer assistance, and explicit goal setting [for products]).[41] The results of these two hallmark studies reflect the ongoing tension between the relative importance of cognitive processes and of the skills necessary to produce successfully written products (described at the beginning of this chapter). While content teachers might embrace the use of writing as a means to help students construct meaning related to their instructional goals, they remain resolute that English teachers should be responsible for teaching skills. Thus, the debate about whose responsibility it is to "teach" writing is kept very much alive.[42]

Conclusion: The Rightful Place of Writing-to-Learn

Using the basic assertions this chapter has made about writing-to-learn, we can better understand the reasons behind the statements my teaching colleagues have made about using writing-to-learn (presented in the opening of this chapter), as well as the responses I gave to them.

Writing-to-learn? Haven't we done that already? Isn't it the same thing as writing across the curriculum? We've had in-service on it—all about journals and reflection, right? I do a lot of that already.

In this case, teachers are correct in noting a relationship between writing-to-learn and writing across the curriculum; and their use of journals as a reflective activity is commendable toward both ends. I would add, however, that the worth of any instructional strategy (such as journals) depends on how well we use it to expedite students' achievement of our explicit learning goals, to engage them in the kinds of learning those goals require, and to help them achieve the purposes of a particular stage of learning. Thus, our implementation of a designated list of writing strategies or our simply assigning more writing may not necessarily be effective uses of writing-to-learn. If not in service of instructional goals, writing activities such as journals can, in fact, rob content instruction of time; and students who might not understand the purposefulness of such writing activities are likely to disengage from them or complete them perfunctorily.

Now, you know, the talk is all about Common Core and the need to teach argument; so I have also started to use debate and am assigning more research projects and essays.

The Anchor Standards for Writing in the Common Core State Standards focus on production (e.g., of text types written over a concentrated or long period of time) and skills (e.g., those necessary for the production of "clear and coherent writing in which the development, organization, and style are appropriate to task, purposes, and audience").[43] As written, the Common Core standards focus on "results rather than means":[44]

> By emphasizing required achievements, the Standards leave room for teachers, curriculum developers, and states to determine how those goals should be reached and what additional topics should be addressed. Thus, the Standards do not mandate such things as a particular writing process or the full range of metacognitive strategies that students may need to monitor and direct their thinking and learning. Teachers are thus free to provide students with whatever tools and knowledge their professional judgment and experience identify as most helpful for meeting the goals set out in the Standards.[45]

To choose the most appropriate means (or strategies) to achieve the standards' outcomes, teachers need to develop an acute self-awareness of their instructional purposes and the kind of learning required to achieve those purposes; and they need to choose strategies that will help students to achieve those purposes most expeditiously. In a conversation I had with the teacher in this example, he explained that he had chosen debate purposefully to scaffold students' understanding of content and to practice using some of the elements of argument that they would need to write convincing essays. The teacher was also pleasantly surprised to realize that his use of debate also engaged students in pre-drafting (by helping them compose the argument and ideas they would later use in their essays). In other words, in addition to his assigning "more research projects and essays," he was also supporting his students' ability to write them.

Since I am not a writing teacher, I count on the English department to teach my students how to write the essays.

The debate about English teachers' and others' responsibility for "teaching" writing has deep historical roots.[46] What the field generally agrees on, however, is that every academic discipline, including English, has its own accepted and specialized concepts, language (e.g., vocabulary, sentence-structures, argumentative structures), and interpretive habits of mind. Thus, while English teachers might be expected to teach generalizable principles and skills of composition, they are not generally apprised of the rules of reasoning required by other disciplines and thus required of other disciplines' writing.[47] For students to produce effective writing in each discipline, we need to teach students explicitly about a discipline's habit of mind and its expectations about how to apply those habits of mind while composing their thoughts in writing. By doing so, we develop students' understanding of what it means to think and thus be a member of an academic discipline.

Honestly? I would do more to teach writing; but with testing and the push to cover material, I'm pretty maxed out. I just don't think I can do more than I already am.

My colleagues' concern about coverage is thoroughly valid in today's test-driven climate. Whether we teach for breadth (e.g., by lecturing about facts or concepts) or depth (e.g., by engaging students in inquiry-based activities that scaffold deeper understanding about facts and concepts), the assessments we use must measure what we have expected students to learn. If the final assessment is to be an essay, then we certainly need to ensure that we have provided students with sufficient instructional support in developing the ideas they will need to draft; in addition, however, we need to ensure that students have the skills to meet the requirements of the particular kind of writing we expect them to compose. The teacher described above, who used debate to scaffold students' understanding of content and of argument, did just that.

A Final Thought

Every teacher is *not* meant to be a teacher of writing; however, I would argue that all teachers have the responsibility to ensure that the writing they use or assign serves their instructional goals and the kind of learning those goals require—at each stage of that learning. They must ensure that their assessments, written or not, measure what they have in fact taught; and they must be explicit with students about not only what they need to do and how they need to do it—but also *why*, if we are to develop students' meta-awareness of their own learning.[48]

Because using writing-to-learn requires thoughtful teaching, we need to provide teachers with time to think about its place in their instruction.[49] Teachers deserve time to come to consensus about the purposes of teaching and learning in general—and for teaching their disciplines in particular. They need time to examine why and how particular modes of writing can serve those purposes and time to determine the relative value of various writing-to-learn strategies as scaffolds for students' achievement of specific instructional purposes. Teachers deserve this time in order to make instructional decisions about writing-to-learn purposefully. In turn, administrators, researchers, and policy makers alike need to listen carefully to their conversations. As I have found throughout my career as a teacher and researcher, conversations about what is best for our students' educational growth are at best incomplete—and at worst misguided—unless they include the voices of teachers, those who are burdened with the responsibility of translating theory, research, and policy into effective practice.

Writing in Practice

Strategies for Use Across the Disciplines

CAROL BOOTH OLSON AND CATHERINE D'AOUST

The Common Core State Standards define the cross-disciplinary literacy expectations that today's students must meet in order to be college and career ready and emphasize the shared responsibility for developing students' literacy among teachers in all content areas.[1] Perhaps because of NCLB's strong emphasis on reading skills, content-area teachers may already be familiar and even comfortable with the anchor standards for reading.[2] But the call for teachers to "routinely" engage students in writing over short time frames for a range of discipline-specific tasks, audiences, and purposes as well as having them write frequently over extended time frames about complex discipline-specific topics and texts, including time for revision and reflection, may cause some consternation. After all, teaching writing is the province of the English teacher. Or is it? In a recent large-scale study, Applebee and Langer found that although students write more for their English classes than they do for any other core subject, they write more for their other subjects combined than they do for English.[3] However, they also discovered that while students are writing more in all subjects than they were thirty years ago, that writing often consists of fill-in-the-blank or short answer exercises, for which there is a presumed "right" answer. These types of writing assignments do not provide students with "opportunities to use composing as a way to think through the issues, to show the depth or breadth of their knowledge, or to go beyond what they know in making connections or raising new issues."[4] In other words, students are not *routinely* engaging in the kind of writing promoted in the Common Core standards.

So what's in it for content-area teachers when they add to their already overloaded teaching agenda by incorporating more writing in the curriculum? The answer is simple. Students will learn and retain their content better while also developing as strategic thinkers. A report from the Carnegie Corporation confirms that students' reading skills and comprehension of discipline-specific content improves when students: (1) write about the texts they read, including writing personal responses, analyses and interpretations, summaries, notes or annotations, and written responses to questions; (2) learn the writing skills, processes, and text structures they need to create their own texts; and (3) increase the amount of time spent on writing.[5]

Clearly, writing is a powerful tool for learning. Let's look at some strategies for integrating writing-to-learn in the content areas.

Expressive Writing Strategies to Help Students Interact with Content

As the director and codirector, respectively, of a site of the National Writing Project at the University of California, Irvine, for over thirty years, we have worked with thousands of teachers on expanding their toolkit of pedagogical strategies to foster writing-to-learn across disciplines and have found them to be especially receptive to integrating expressive writing into their classroom instruction. In his book, *Holding On to Good Ideas in a Time of Bad Ones*, Newkirk identifies expressive writing as "maybe the best idea of all" because rather than focusing on writing to show what they've already learned, expressive writing allows students to think out loud on paper, explore ideas, draw conclusions, and form interpretations.[6] It fulfills the call for routine writing under short time frames for a range of tasks, purposes, and audiences in the Common Core standards, and because it is intended for the students' own use as a draft of their evolving ideas, it does not necessarily have to be evaluated by the teacher.

Say, Mean, Matter

One expressive writing strategy that advances students' comprehension and helps them to meet the Common Core standard that calls for students to determine what the text says explicitly and then to make logical inferences from it is *Say, Mean, Matter*. This strategy can be used in virtually any subject area to facilitate students' construction of meaning. It is effective for all grade levels and students—from English language learners to honors students—and can be applied to interpret academic texts, fiction, and nonverbal material as well. It also is a powerful prewriting strategy for text-based analytical writing.

The Say, Mean, Matter strategy is designed to focus students' reading and/or examination of a text first on literally what the text *says*, followed by what is important about the text or what it *means*, and then on why the passage or visual is significant within the text as a whole and/or beyond the context of the text itself—in other words, why it *matters*. Generally, students use this strategy with a trifold graphic organizer that allows them to plot their interpretations of the text and see the levels of meaning it provides.

Say

The Say column includes important quotations or unclear passages, sentences, or phrases from the reading. A teacher who wants to assess students' literal comprehension of a text passage would have students write the quotation *and* paraphrase it in this column; this is particularly important when the vocabulary and/or syntax of the passage are difficult. Otherwise, the quotation alone can be written in the Say column. The selection of the passage or quotation is very important. Initially, as students learn to use this strategy, the teacher provides the text passage. Later, as students continue analyzing this or other texts, they choose passages or visuals that stand out for them or confuse them. The students' analysis of what is important provides the teacher with formative assessment on comprehension. The Say column addresses any of these questions:

- What does the text say? (quote and/or paraphrase)
- What happened?
- Who is speaking to whom?

For example, figure 13.1 presents the Say column for an analysis of Lincoln's *Gettysburg Address*.

Mean

The Mean column requires students to read between the lines, going beyond the literal analysis of what the text is saying. Students must consider first what the text says and then determine what meaning it has for the reader or viewer. This requires some abstraction, as the reader is encouraged to *step into the text* to address what it means. The Mean column addresses any of these questions:

- What does the text mean?
- What does the text say between the lines?
- What does the author mean?

Figure 13.2 demonstrates how in the Mean column, the student analyzes author's craft to form an interpretation about what the text of the *Gettysburg Address* means.

Matter

The Matter column is the most abstract and difficult for students. Students reflect on the text to determine the significance of the quotation to the whole of the text, to themselves, to others, and/or to other texts beyond this one. This interpretation is easiest when students explain the significance to their own lives. With practice, students can move beyond a personal interpretation and consider how the text relates

FIGURE 13.1

Say, Mean, Matter (U.S. history): Say

Text: *Gettysburg Address*   Author: Abraham Lincoln

Say
"Four score and seven years ago our fathers brought forth on this continent a new nation, conceived in liberty, and dedicated to the proposition that all men are created equal." (November 19, 1863)

FIGURE 13.2

Say, Mean, Matter (U.S. history): Mean

Text: *Gettysburg Address*   Author: Abraham Lincoln

Say	Mean
"Four score and seven years ago our fathers brought forth on this continent a new nation, conceived in liberty, and dedicated to the proposition that all men are created equal." (November 19, 1863)	Lincoln uses biblical language to reference the Declaration of Independence, signed 87 years before, reminding his audience that the United States was created in the pursuit of liberty for all men—men who are all created equal.

FIGURE 13.3

Say, Mean, Matter (U.S. history): Matter

Text: *Gettysburg Address*   Author: Abraham Lincoln

Say	Mean	Matter
"Four score and seven years ago our fathers brought forth on this continent a new nation, conceived in liberty, and dedicated to the proposition that all men are created equal." (November 19, 1863)	Lincoln uses biblical language to reference the Declaration of Independence, signed 87 years before, reminding his audience that the United States was created in the pursuit of liberty for all men—men who are all created equal.	By referencing both the Bible and the Declaration of Independence, Lincoln is signaling that if his audience trusts the words in those documents, then they should trust his words as well.

to other texts and the world around them. The Matter column addresses any of these questions:

- Why does it matter to me or others?
- Why is this important?
- What is the significance to:
    The text as a whole?
    Me?
    Society?
    The world?

Figure 13.3 illustrates how the student moves to evaluation in determining why the quote by Lincoln should matter to his audience.

Process

The teacher introduces Say, Mean, Matter by modeling how to use the strategy. He or she writes a quotation from the text (if it is a written text) in the Say column. The teacher then reads between the lines of the quotation and writes in the Mean column the significance of this quotation. Finally, the teacher considers why the quotation has meaning beyond the text, how it matters to the world, possibly personalizing the significance to his or her own life. The process for a visual text is similar. For example, if the text were a political cartoon on slavery from 1862, the teacher could project the visual and then describe the cartoon without interpretation in the Say column; explain its importance to the antislavery movement in the Mean column; and finally interpret its significance to the world and slavery today in the Matter column.

Once students have completed the deep reading for this strategy, they can use their notes to structure and write an evidence-based analytical essay. The Say, Mean, Matter graphic organizer keeps track of details from the text and provides practice in interpreting and commenting on the text. Their paper's thesis derives from the Matter column, supported by quotations from the Say column. The Mean column provides commentary and explanation for the quotations.

Note Taking, Note Making, and Exit Slips

Students often read their textbook or listen to a lecture and take notes, writing down facts or information verbatim without actually taking the time to process and think through what they are recording. A double-entry journal prompts students to thoughtfully review and reflect on what they are learning—to puzzle over, sort through, clarify, comment on, or draw conclusions about the task they are engaged in. On the note-taking side of the page, students simply record their notes as they progress through the lesson. On the right-hand side, they record reactions in response to the notes they took. Part of the power of this strategy is that it can be adapted to suit the discipline. For example, in science or mathematics, as students are conducting an experiment or solving a problem, the columns might be labeled "What I Did" and "What I Wondered/Concluded." To facilitate critical thinking, the teacher may want to provide sentence stems such as the ones below for students to use as a point of departure:[7]

- *Tapping prior knowledge:* I already know that . . .
- *Making connections:* This reminds me of . . .
- *Making predictions:* I'll bet that . . .
- *Clarifying:* To understand better, I need to know more about . . .
- *Forming interpretations:* The idea I'm getting is . . .
- *Revising meaning:* At first I thought, but now I . . .
- *Reflecting and relating:* A conclusion I'm drawing is . . .

The note-making column may be cognitive or affective or a mixture of the two. A common rule of thumb is ten minutes of lecture/lab work/problem solving followed by two minutes of processing.

Figure 13.4 contains a student's note-taking/note-making sheet from a coin flip experiment in a middle school math lesson designed by Marie Filardo.[8] Filardo adapted the strategy to enable students to record and reflect on an experiment they were conducting to explore the laws of probability. After each round of the coin flip, Filardo asked students to record the results of their experiment and then to respond to the question, "What observation can you make about this?"

Students have a habit of closing up shop mentally, and sometimes even physically, five to ten minutes before the bell rings. One expressive writing strategy that can keep students productively engaged and help crystallize their learning as well as give the teacher a window into what they have grasped or are struggling with on a given day is an exit slip. Popularized by Bob Tierney, a high school biology teacher, an exit slip is a student's ticket out of the class. For the last five or ten minutes of a class period, students are asked to reflect on what they learned that day and to summarize their understanding, write down a question, explore a puzzlement, or share an Aha! moment. The teacher stands at the door to collect each slip as the students file out of class. Exit slips can offer the teacher an important perspective on and an opportunity to monitor the learning taking place in the class. They can provide the signal to move full steam ahead—or send a teacher back to the drawing board if the students have clearly missed the boat. Exit slips also send a message to students that what they have to say about their own learning matters to the teacher. Here is an exit slip from Marie Filardo's laws of probability lesson. Filardo asked the students: "What theory can you

FIGURE 13.4

Note taking/note making double-entry journal

Note taking	Note making
1. What is the ratio of heads to the total number of flips after the first 25 flips? H/F: 14/25 What is the ratio of tails to flips after 25 flips? T/F: 11/25	What observation can you make about this? 1. Heads seem to fall more often than tails. I had a hunch that would happen. So, it's better to call heads than tails
2. What is the ratio of heads to the total number of flips after the first 50 flips? H/F: 22/50 What is the ratio of tails to the total number of flips after the first 50 flips? T/F: 28/50	2. Now, tails are occurring more often than heads. Maybe my prediction was wrong. I need to keep flipping.
3. What is the ratio of heads to the total number of flips the second 50 flips? H/F: 27/50 What is the ratio of tails to the total number of flops after the second 50 flips? T/F: 23/50	3. The ratio is even closer, although heads came up more often than tails. It's weird that heads came up four times in a row but then things evened out.
4. What is the overall ratio of heads to the total number of flips after 100 flips: H/F:49/100 What is the overall ratio of tails to the total number of flips after 100 flips? T/F: 51/100	4. The more often we flipped the coin, the more even the ratio got. Why is that?
5. What can you predict about future flips?	5. Maybe if we did it again, heads would win. If we continued, though, it would eventually come out 1:2.

Source: Marie Filardo, "The Laws of Probability," in *Thinking/Writing: Fostering Critical Thinking Through Writing*, ed. Carol Booth Olson (New York: Harper Collins, 1992), 354.

conclude from your note taking and note making?" (As yet, she had not introduced the term the laws of probability.): "As the number of flips increases, the ratio of heads and the ratio of tails to the total flips comes closer to being 50 percent for each. This surprised me because at first I was pretty sure that heads would come up more. But it looks like there is a one out of two chance that either side will come up. I can't wait to do the spinner activities with the colors and the dice experiment tomorrow to see if the odds will stay the same."

These are just three examples of a wide array of expressive writing strategies content area teachers can weave into their instruction to enhance content knowledge. While these strategies can be used in short, nonevaluated responses to instruction, they can also be combined in scaffolded instruction leading toward multiple draft process writing and assessed for ideas as well as for style and correctness.

Writing Activities over Extended Time Frames

The Common Core standards not only recommend that students in all content areas write routinely in short time frames (a single sitting, or a day or two) for a range of tasks, purposes, and audiences, but advocate that students also write over extended time frames, including time for research, reflection, and revision. Let's explore two examples of the integration of writing into content-area instruction—one focused on a unit of study that might be accomplished in a week or two and another over several months.

The Hero Paul Revere: Fact or Fiction?

The Common Core standards acknowledge "the time honored place of ELA teachers in developing students' literacy skills" while at the same time recognizing that teachers in other disciplines have a shared responsibility for cultivating students' reading, writing, listening, speaking, and language.[9] Veronica Reinhart, a history teacher, and Katie Stahle and Tina Thomas, English language arts teachers, work at a large urban middle school where 97 percent of the students are Latino and 88 percent are English language learners. They are participating with us in a two-year professional development program designed to prepare ELLs to meet the Common Core standards. They took this message about the shared responsibility for literacy instruction to heart by deciding to team up and develop an interdisciplinary unit of instruction on the Revolutionary War that would engage students in thinking critically about the role of Paul Revere in igniting the American Revolution, assessing his heroic qualities, and comparing the legend of Revere popularized by Henry Wadsworth Longfellow's famous poem, "Paul Revere's Ride" (1861) with the reality behind this historical event described in an article by Justin Ewers entitled "Rewriting the Legend of Paul Revere: Every Schoolchild Knows the Story, but Most of It Is Wrong."[10]

Veronica kicked off the lesson by having students create the K (know) and W (want to know) portions of a classic KWL graphic organizer about the Revolutionary War, using the painting "The Battle of Fort Moultrie" by John Blake White as a point of departure.[11] This painting depicts an important battle that took place just days before the signing of the Declaration of Independence, when a small American force, led by Colonel William Moultrie, withstood a formidable attack by the British fleet. This visual text also celebrates the heroism of Sergeant William Jasper, who risked his life to retrieve the fort's flag, a silver crescent on a blue field, and return it to the fort's rampart.

After activating students' background knowledge and providing additional information on the struggle between the colonists and the British in the Revolutionary War, students listened to Hal Holbrook's rendition of "Paul Revere's Ride."[12] Using visuals and sentence starters they had already been taught in English language arts (see appendix A), students reread the poem silently and made marginal annotations.

Many teachers perceive the domain of history as one that is exclusively focused on informational texts and expository writing, whereas the English class is perceived as the discipline most associated with reading fiction and writing responses to literature. Veronica, Katie, and Tina decided to mix things up. In their history class, students attended to the tone, mood, images, and sensory details in the poem and imagined Paul Revere's thoughts and feelings on this historic ride. After creating a flow map to sequence the events of "Paul Revere's Ride" and selecting adjectives to describe his feelings (*nervous, apprehensive, excited, defiant, determined, relieved*, etc.), students were invited to assume Revere's persona and, speaking in his voice, to reflect on his remarkable journey in a one-page journal entry (see appendix B for the prompt students used to plan their journals). Since these middle school students were ELLs, they were also given sentence stems like those that follow to use as a starting point, if they wished to:

- I just arrived back from . . .
- You wouldn't believe what I did last night.
- When I first saw the signal, I felt . . .
- I was so worried because . . .
- It was important to warn the colonists because . . .
- If I had failed, it would have caused . . .
- I think the colonists and the British will go to war because . . .
- In the future, I think _____ will happen.

A sample student journal entry is included in appendix B.

In English class, Katie and Tina continued this interdisciplinary approach. They introduced the article "Rewriting the Legend of Paul Revere," which reviews the many historical inaccuracies in the poem, such as the fact that there were actually three riders dispatched that night to warn the populace and that Revere himself was captured and interrogated before he even got to Concord.[13] Nevertheless, the article acknowledges the important role Revere played in touching off the Revolution, even if he wasn't the lone hero. To compare and contrast the poem and the article, students created a Venn diagram. Subsequently, they discussed why Longfellow might have chosen to ignore certain facts to make his poem more dramatic and whether or not this was ethical.

Katie and Tina presented their students with the analytical essay prompt (see appendix C) that requires students to reference both the poem and the informational text as they consider why Revere was viewed as a hero by the colonists. To plan and draft their essays, students first completed the L (*learn*) section of their KWL chart, then used an A, B, C strategy (*a*ttack the prompt, *b*rainstorm ideas, and *c*reate an outline) to plan their essays and engaged in peer review prior to revising and editing. A sample student essay is reprinted in appendix C.

Veronica, Katie, and Tina so thoroughly enjoyed their collaboration that they are currently exploring having students work in groups to create a travel brochure advertising the historic route of Paul Revere's ride, complete with an exciting cover page, a map of the region, a brief history of Paul Revere's ride, two pictures or drawings of the area, travel tips (currency, climate, population, other cities of interest, etc.), and a description of life in the area today.

The Multigenre Research Paper

While "The Hero Paul Revere: Fact or Fiction?" example demonstrates how two content-area teachers might integrate extended writing into an interdisciplinary lesson or unit over a week or two, the multigenre paper involves students in a research process that might extend over a matter of months. Multigenre papers are a popular alternative to the traditional research paper. The idea for the multigenre paper came to teachers affiliated with the UCI site of the National Writing Project via Tom Romano.[14] Romano, who gave a day-long workshop on our campus, read a book by Michael Ondaatje called *The Collected Works of Billy the Kid,* in which the author blended genres (songs, thumbnail character sketches, a comic book excerpt, stream of consciousness passages, newspaper articles, photographs, and drawings) to capture both the factual and imaginative world of this famous outlaw.[15] Intrigued by this approach, Romano challenged his students to write research papers in Ondaatje's multigenre style. They rose to the occasion. To prepare students to explore and write about their own topics, Romano suggests giving them an encyclopedia entry about a historical figure (for example, Count Basie) and asking them to write a summary of what they learned. Then he gives them a poem about Count Basie and again has them write about what they learned. Students immediately recognize that the encyclopedia conveys facts, while the poem goes beyond facts to create "a visceral scene" of the man and his art. Romano points out that each genre does different work. Multigenre papers give students the opportunity to look at a topic through different lenses and to "mold the cognitive with the emotional."[16]

Inspired by Romano's workshop at UCI and by his book *Blending Genre, Blending Style: Writing Multigenre Papers*, Lisa Holman, a teacher/consultant from our Writing Project site, implemented the multigenre paper as an annual history project in her sixth-grade class. She began by explaining that students will have several months to investigate an event (9/11 terrorist attacks, the Holocaust, the Great Depression, etc.), a place (Pompeii, the Pyramids, Gettysburg, etc.), or a person (Ghandi, Mother Teresa, Abraham Lincoln, Martin Luther King Jr.) of historical significance and to write about it in multiple genres over an extended period of time. For the final project she required a cover page, a personal research design involving an expanded KL and research questions, a seven-hundred-word traditional research essay, eight genres (which could include visual and multimedia projects), a reflective essay about the process and the product, a works-cited page, and a storage container to house the research project (for example, one student studying submarine warfare in WWII constructed a torpedo to house his project!). She then asked her students to think "outside the box" to brainstorm a variety of genres to write in. Here are just a few:

Advice column	Memoir
Ballad	Newspaper article
Campaign speech	Postcard
Horoscope	Map
Eulogy	Recipe
Fable	Tweet/text message
"I Am" poem	Wanted poster

Lisa had integrated the teaching of these genres into her instruction throughout the year; so many were familiar to the students. But she also took several weeks to introduce new genres. Students progressed on their projects in a workshop style—with time for teacher conferences, peer group sharing, revision, and editing sessions. Each multigenre project contained a big idea or theme statement that the reader could infer from reading the multiple genres. For example, one student decided to investigate the Holocaust and to house her multigenre entries in a photo album illustrated with photographs from Nazi Germany. Her album included a page with pictures from World War II; a "What I Know, Assume, or Imagine" section to introduce her topic; a traditional research paper on the Holocaust; a poem entitled "Tortured," written from the point of view of a Jew on the way to a concentration camp; a recipe entitled "How to Make a German Nazi"; a letter in English and German from a captive in Auschwitz-Birkenau; an obituary for Jewish-American POWs who died in Germany; and a "Wanted" poster for Dr. Joseph Mengele and Adolf Eichmann. This is an example of a student saturating herself in a topic—not regurgitating what happened from other sources, but constructing her own meaning. She was intrigued with the concept of power and how it can corrupt people.

Although the multigenre paper lends itself to the history and English language arts classroom, it can be adapted for other content areas. For instance, Tom Romano has an excellent example of a science multigenre paper from seventh-grader, Jeff, who chose to investigate the allosaurus, a type of dinosaur. His paper includes a character sketch, free-verse poem, stream-of-consciousness piece from the perspective of the allosaurus, two-voice poem, dialogue, newspaper article, encyclopedia article, cartoon, document, list, and diary entry.[17]

Sources for Writing in the Content Areas

To sum up, writing is a tool for learning across the disciplines because it fosters critical thinking. Writing:

- Focuses thought
- Makes thought available for inspection
- Helps make abstract thought more concrete
- Is a building block to more complex thought
- Helps students retain the content they are learning
- Helps students internalize problem solving strategies
- Is a vehicle for discovery as well as a mode of communication

Integrating writing in the content areas routinely over short time frames as well as frequently over extended time frames not only has these cognitive rewards and prepares students to meet the high bar of academic literacy set for them in the Common Core standards, it has affective ones as well. Students are more engaged with their content and, consequently, the learning experience is more memorable.

APPENDIX A
Cognitive Strategies Sentence Starters

Visualizing
As I read, I see in my mind

_____

_____

_____

Forming Interpretations
The big idea I'm getting about Paul Revere is

_____

_____

_____

Evaluation
Paul Revere's ride is important because

_____

_____

_____

Predicting
In the coming war between the colonists and the British, I predict that

_____

_____

_____

APPENDIX B
Sample Journal Entry for "Paul Revere's Ride"

April 19, 1775

Dear Future Generation,

Last night I was waiting for the British to come. I was suspecting that they would come by sea. When I saw the British I lit the lantern and I felt fear, but determination to warn the colonists. I was ready to leave except I need to cross the river first. "How was I ever going to be able to do all this?" I thought to myself. So I finally rode off to warn the colonists. Before I reached Concord, I was captured and interrogated.

As I rode, I was recognizing that this ride may be the most important ride in American history. Without this ride, the British might have killed many colonists with weapons in their house. Without this ride, the British might have kept sending in more soldiers. I was afraid that the colonies will become a place where we have to hide from the red coats. I am so proud of myself for choosing to do the ride.

I think that the battles that went on yesterday will lead to a war. If there is a war, I will gladly help the rebel troops. Hopefully that will come, and we become Free and Independent States.

Sincerely,

Paul

(Bryan Reyes)

Writing Directions:
Imagine that you are Paul Revere, and you have just arrived back at the Wayside Inn from your long ride to Lexington and Concord. Write a one-page (at least three-paragraph) journal entry in which you reflect on your feelings after your long ride. How did you feel when you first saw the signal in the church tower? In your journal entry, explain why it is so important that you stayed up all night going door to door to warn the colonists that the British were coming. Imagine what would have happened if you had not gone on your ride. Make a prediction about the coming war between the colonists and the British. Use sensory details to describe your thoughts, feelings, and experiences.

Your journal entry will be graded on these key traits:

- Ideas
  - Clearly describe Paul Revere's thoughts and feelings in the journal entry.
  - Use details from the poem and article to support your ideas.
- Organization
  - Include a salutation, three body paragraphs, and a closing appropriate to your journal entry.
- Voice and Word Choice
  - Use precise, descriptive language. Make the reader feel as if you truly *are* Paul Revere.
- Writing Conventions
  - Use correct grammar, punctuation, and spelling.
  - Use complete sentences of varied sentence structure.

APPENDIX C
Analytical Essay on "Paul Revere's Ride" and
"Rewriting the Legend of Paul Revere" *

"Listen my children and you shall hear of the midnight ride of Paul Revere."
"Paul Revere's Ride," a poem by Henry Wadsworth Longfellow, and "Rewriting the
Legend of Paul Revere," a nonfiction article by Justin Ewers, both focus on Paul
Revere's famous ride. Even though Longfellow and Ewers use different generes to
write about Revere's actions, they each depict him as being brave and heroic. In
society, heroes are described as a unselfish person who thinks about others.

In the poem and the article, the colonists consider Paul Revere a hero because
he was wide awake and ready to go. The actions of Paul Revere are important
because he was preparing for war. First, he told his friend to make a signal if the
British comes. Also, he rode his horse to warn people. Revere's decision to act is
important because if he wouldn't stay up all night, people would have been killed.

"Paul Revere's Ride" and "Rewriting the Legend of Paul Revere" have some
differences and some things the same. For instance the poem has less facts.
Especially significant according to Ewers is that the poem says "Lonely and
spectral and sombre and still" where in fact he arranged with the help of several
other people to sneak across the Charles River. While Revere's actions show his
bravery, Longfellow uses poetic license to make him seem even more courageous.
For instance, he describes Revere galloping into Concord. But Ewers believes he
never made it that far because he was arrested. Ewer's point is that Longfellow
wanted to make Revere's actions more dramatic.

Even though Longfellow makes Revere seem more heroic than he was in real
life, he still was brave and risked his life to warn others. To sum up, we still need
heroes like Revere today who will stand up for their country.

—Luena Cuenca

*Unedited student work.

Writing Situation:

There are many historical heroes in U.S. history, including Paul Revere. In the poem "Paul Revere's Ride" by Henry Wordsworth Longfellow, a landlord at Boston's Wayside Inn describes what he thinks Paul Revere's ride to Lexington and Concord was like. However, after reading "Rewriting the Legend of Paul Revere," a *U.S. News and World Report* article by Justin Ewers, we learn that not all the events of the poem are historically accurate.

Writing Directions:

Write an essay that shows your knowledge of Paul Revere from "Paul Revere's Ride" by Henry Wordsworth Longfellow and "Rewriting the Legend of Paul Revere" by Justin Ewers. Why do you believe that Paul Revere was a hero to the colonists? In your introduction, explain the characteristics of a hero. Which of these characteristics did Paul Revere have? Be sure to create a thesis statement that expresses why Paul Revere was a hero.

In the body of your essay, be sure to discuss the following:

- Describe the events of Paul Revere's ride from Longfellow's poem. Explain how the events show the importance of Paul Revere's decision.
- Compare and contrast the poem with the article by Ewers. Explain how the structure of the poem is different from the structure of the article. Detail at least two inaccuracies (information that is incorrect) in the poem that did not happen in reality.
- Explain how Paul Revere's actions in the poem revealed aspects of his character (e.g., brave, determined, etc.) How does Longfellow's description of Paul Revere in the poem make him seem more heroic than he was in real life?

Support your ideas with facts, reasons and examples from both the poem and the article.

In your conclusion, explain how Paul Revere's characteristics are still important in modern times. Do we still need heroes like Paul Revere today?

Professional Learning as the Key to Linking Content and Literacy Instruction

JACY IPPOLITO

Much of this book has focused specifically on what educators can do to simultaneously focus on content and literacy goals in secondary classrooms. In our minds, the most important interaction in education is between teachers and students, and this book rightly keeps the focus on improving the quality of those interactions by linking content and literacy instruction to prepare students for twenty-first-century citizenship and careers. However, there is an important component of this work that needs to be addressed in order for the good ideas in this book to be translated into improvements in classroom practices and student achievement. School and district leaders, alongside teachers and teacher leaders, must design and engage in the most effective forms of professional learning in order to adopt research-based instructional practices, meet the demands of the Common Core State Standards, and address students' academic needs. Without explicit attention to professional learning in schools, research has little chance of translating into effective classroom practices.[1] Alternately, administrators and teacher leaders who are aware of the potential and pitfalls of professional learning communities (PLCs) in schools are more likely to help teams translate research and standards into practice.[2]

To help readers make the most of the resources presented in this book, this chapter outlines four critical ways of thinking and working that we (the editors of this volume) rely on when engaging teachers in professional development related to secondary content and literacy instruction. Every time we work in schools, we consider the following:

1. Technical versus adaptive change
2. Professional learning communities
3. Instructional coaching
4. Discussion-based protocols

These topics represent entire bodies of literature related to professional learning. While we understand that there are many factors educators must consider when designing professional learning experiences (e.g., budgets, departmental structures), we have also found that keeping these four constructs in mind helps teachers and leaders to more easily implement the practices described in this book. Below are brief introductions to each critical area related to professional learning, freely available tools to help educators address these areas, and examples of how different forms of professional learning might be adopted and integrated to maximize school resources.

Adaptive Versus Technical Dilemmas and Change

Ronald A. Heifetz and his colleagues have spent nearly two decades talking to leaders across all sectors about the differences between *technical* and *adaptive* dilemmas and organizational responses.[3] The technical/adaptive framework is especially important to consider when introducing and refining disciplinary literacy instructional practices at secondary levels. Because of the large number of individual, group, and organizational changes that must take place for authentic, long-lasting shifts in teaching and learning to occur, the teacher teams we work with appreciate using Heifetz's framework for understanding and addressing instructional dilemmas both large and small.

Heifetz defines technical dilemmas as those that we "know already how to respond to."[4] He adds, "These problems are technical because the necessary knowledge about them already has been digested and put in the form of a legitimized set of known organizational procedures . . . "[5] In other words, technical dilemmas have fairly straightforward answers, even if those answers require a great deal of time, effort, money, and human resources to solve. An example from the field of medicine helps illustrate this idea. A technical dilemma might be a simple infection for which there is a known antibiotic cure. In this case, a patient appropriately relies on a doctor's expertise and the medication's efficacy to solve the problem. From the world of education, an example of a technical dilemma comes from a high school biology teacher lamenting that students are not frequently using new vocabulary from their textbook in lab reports and weekly journal entries. Students' discussions in class and writing are filled with misused terms and nontechnical language. Noticing this behavior, the teacher consults her department chair in search of science-focused vocabulary lists. After a quick conversation, the department chair points the teacher to several online lists of scientific terms for high school students.[6] The department chair recommends that students complete Frayer Model concept maps each week with five words from the online lists and then receive extra credit for using them in their lab reports and weekly journal entries.[7] After a month of experimentation with these practices, the teacher notes a slight increase in students' use of technical scientific language and thanks the department chair for the excellent suggestions.

Notice in this example that both the framing of the dilemma and the solution seem to suggest that the teaching and learning issues at hand are clear and well defined. The teacher views the dilemma as students not being exposed to enough scientific language. She seeks outside expertise (the department chair) and settles quickly on a solution—increasing the number of words students encounter (in the form of lists) and writing science-specific words in graphic organizers and in weekly assignments.

This process of dilemma identification and solution happens every day in schools, and in many cases, technical solutions do result in changes in student behavior. However, the questions a savvy coach or school leader might ask here include: "Though students are using certain words more frequently, are they getting better at reading, writing, and presenting like scientists? Are they remembering the words they're using and applying them flexibly in written work and presentations over time?" After a yearlong experiment with Frayer Models and lists of scientific vocabulary, the frustrated biology teacher might acknowledge that students do not seem to be retaining scientific vocabulary over time and that the overall quality of students' written products and test scores seem relatively unaffected. Perhaps more is going on here?

This is when it becomes important to consider adaptive dilemmas, which have no immediate, clear answers. Heifetz describes adaptive dilemmas as those for which "no adequate response has yet been developed . . . No clear expertise can be found, no single sage has general credibility, no established procedure will suffice."[8] Adaptive dilemmas are often intractable and multifaceted, resistant to single solutions. From the field of medicine, there are many examples of adaptive dilemmas, perhaps most notably how best to treat cancer. While there are many treatment options available, no single best solution has emerged for all patients all of the time, in part because of variability between patients' particular cases. Solving the adolescent literacy crisis is an educational example of an adaptive dilemma for much the same reason.[9] No single program, strategy, or set of texts has proven to unilaterally help all teens read and write proficiently, for much the same reason—variability in students' needs, teachers' preparation, teachers' practices, districts' policies, and schools' organizational structures. Moreover, there is no single authority or expert to whom we can turn.

We (and Heifetz) fully acknowledge that the distinction between adaptive and technical dilemmas is a bit of a false dichotomy. Many education-related dilemmas include both technical and adaptive components and require both technical and adaptive responses. Moreover, we argue that leaders and teachers using this book must consider both technical and adaptive elements of the work. This is the advice we would give to the high school biology teacher in the previous example.

In one sense, the teacher has identified a fairly straightforward technical dilemma (i.e., students are not spending enough time reading and writing scientific vocabulary). This dilemma might be solved with a straightforward technical response (i.e., exposure to lists of scientific vocabulary and practice with classroom-tested strategies such as the Frayer Model). Though this seems like a clear-cut case, larger adaptive dilemmas suddenly become clear as the teacher and her department chair reflect at the end of the year. There are so many new words introduced in high school biology classes—how can students master them all? What if vocabulary lists are not the most effective means for students to acquire new scientific words? Which general academic words in the science textbook also appear in other content-area texts and might cause confusion (e.g., *transform, hypothesize, conduct, determine, solution*)? How do we know if and when students have mastered new vocabulary? What are the best ways for students to acquire and use new words? What are the relationships between learning words and reading, writing, and presenting as scientists? These are questions without simple answers. They challenge our assumptions about how students learn words, which words matter, and even what it means to *know* a word. If the high school biology teacher and her department chair begin asking these questions, they would be considering the larger adaptive dilemmas involved. Their responses might be slower, more collaborative, and more systemic—ultimately shifting the way they (and other teachers) teach vocabulary. Thus what originally seemed like a technical dilemma, easily solved by finding new vocabulary lists and strategies for students, becomes an adaptive dilemma requiring both leaders and teachers to jointly reflect on entrenched habits, mind-sets, and obstacles both logistical and cultural.

An adaptive response to this dilemma might include the biology teacher forming a study group with departmental and cross-departmental colleagues to look at word study across classrooms. The group might collaboratively experiment with different strategies for introducing words and keeping track of the results. The group might visit classrooms to observe vocabulary instruction in action and reflect on various levels of student engagement and resulting written products. Ultimately, the group might adopt and adapt a multipronged framework (much like the one introduced in chapter 5 of this volume) to encourage word learning across classes, constantly refining techniques based on formative assessment data.

Educators who view this only as a technical dilemma requiring new vocabulary lists will almost always be frustrated when results do not match expectations; whereas educators who view it as a combination of technical and adaptive elements will approach solutions collaboratively and iteratively, with the expectation that new patterns will need to be introduced, modeled, tested, revised, and refined. As noted in chapters 4 and 5 of this volume, disciplinary and academic vocabulary instruction is complex and requires a great deal of flexibility and experimentation in order to help students acquire and use new words. Technical responses alone will be unlikely to increase word learning and use.

Heifetz et al. write about a continuum of challenge ranging from purely technical dilemmas, to a mixture of technical and adaptive, to purely adaptive.[10] The more adaptive the challenge, the more learning that individuals and organizations must undertake. In the vocabulary example above, if teachers in the high school have a long history of authentic collaboration and the true dilemma is simply choosing which words to explicitly teach, then perhaps only a small amount of technical learning would be required (i.e., collaboratively identifying science-specific and general academic language vocabulary). If the teachers rarely collaborate in PLCs, then a great deal of learning at both the individual and group levels would need to take place in order to design departmental and cross-departmental vocabulary instruction. Leaders and teachers would need to engage in adaptive learning requiring them to fundamentally change the way they think and work.

Teams of secondary teachers benefit from thinking about adolescents' literacy needs through this technical/adaptive lens because it allows them to move forward strategically and with eyes wide open about which elements of a particular dilemma must be considered technical or adaptive or both. We as educators often make the mistake of addressing adolescents' disciplinary literacy needs primarily through a technical lens. In our eagerness to help students, we naturally look for the new strategy, vocabulary list, reading program, or intervention that will help all of our students, instead of considering the deeper cultural and habitual aspects that will require us to adapt our own ways of thinking and working. Once again we are reminded that there is no single best solution; most of the rich examples provided throughout this book must be adopted and adapted with caution, with full understanding that there is almost always an adaptive element to this work. Real change comes over time, from collaborative experimentation and reflection. Considering instructional dilemmas and responses within the technical/adaptive framework helps save us from our own tendencies to jump to quick conclusions and instead urges us to engage in meaningful professional learning.

Will the Real PLCs Please Stand Up?

Professional learning communities (PLCs) are a second useful construct for readers considering how to use the information in this book. PLCs have been a primary mechanism for adult learning and professional development in the United States for much of the late twentieth century.[11] Now, in the second decade of the twenty-first century, it is rare to find a district that has not dabbled with PLCs in one form or another. It is common to hear district and school leaders describe PLCs as the primary way that teachers engage in professional learning. However, as one of the most widely cited proponents of PLCs, Richard DuFour, notes: "People use this term [PLCs] to describe every imaginable combination of individuals with an interest in education . . . In fact, the term has been used so ubiquitously that it is in danger of losing all meaning."[12] We agree with DuFour and have met many educators inappropriately calling any small gathering of teachers a "PLC," a practice that devalues the work of real professional learning communities: groups of educators who meet regularly over time, learn together by focusing on student learning, and challenge and support one another to improve practice.

Readers who wish to experiment with the ideas in this book in PLCs would do well to focus on the articulated principles of effective PLCs identified across the literature:

- Deprivatization of practice
- Trust and respect
- Openness to improvement
- Reflective dialogue
- Collective focus on student learning
- Collaboration
- Shared norms and values
- Time to meet and talk[13]

Groups who do not embody these practices may not be maximizing their PLC time. Of course, administrative support plays a large role in the efficacy of PLCs. If training in how to facilitate adult learning, time to meet, and clear policies allowing teachers freedom to experiment are not made available, then it is understandable how a supposedly rich professional learning experience quickly turns into an empty activity.

Educators might use Heifetz's technical/adaptive framework as one way of considering the degree to which their PLCs are challenging the status quo and pushing systematically toward more effective instructional practices. Less-effective PLCs may unintentionally focus more on technical dilemmas and rush to technical solutions, while more-effective PLCs may take the time to notice and tackle adaptive dilemmas through an iterative process of analysis, research, experimentation, and reflection. The differences between less- and more-effective PLCs (see figure 14.1) are important for leaders and teachers to consider as they use the content of this book to continually refine content and literacy instructional practices.

Less-effective professional learning communities may have low levels of trust, few shared norms, and cultures that prioritize autonomy and concealing instructional practices (e.g., closing classroom doors, discussing only classroom triumphs and not dilemmas). Such PLCs will tend to focus on the obstacles to teaching and learning

FIGURE 14.1

Less- and more-effective professional learning communities

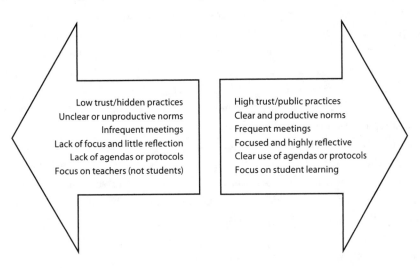

Low trust/hidden practices	High trust/public practices
Unclear or unproductive norms	Clear and productive norms
Infrequent meetings	Frequent meetings
Lack of focus and little reflection	Focused and highly reflective
Lack of agendas or protocols	Clear use of agendas or protocols
Focus on teachers (not students)	Focus on student learning

(e.g., not enough time, poor schedules, large numbers of English language learners, large numbers of students with disabilities) instead of seeking out, trying, and analyzing practices to evaluate which have the greatest effect for different groups of students. Groups that constantly return to issues such as "If only we could find the *right* reading comprehension strategies" or "If only we had ninety-minute blocks of instructional time" might be limiting their growth by focusing exclusively on technical dilemmas and solutions, or issues beyond their control. Monetary and structural obstacles are ever-present in all schools, yet if PLCs focus exclusively on these dilemmas, they run the risk of never fully turning their attention to the efficacy of their own daily interactions with students.

In contrast, effective PLCs focus on surfacing and analyzing patterns in their own instruction and the resulting effects on student learning. Both successful and unsuccessful practices across classrooms are described and shared with colleagues. Dilemmas of practice are front and center. While acknowledging structural and organizational constraints, the focus of the group always returns to: "Given current constraints, how can we work differently to improve student learning?" Members of effective PLCs consider how they spend their time together, how they talk with one another, and how they will get better over time at collaboration. Members of effective PLCs design and rely on explicit norms, clear agendas, and discussion-based protocols to make sure that time is used productively and that conversations stay focused on teaching and learning. Effective PLCs also address technical dilemmas (e.g., adopting a new schedule, strategy, program), but they are always aware of the underlying adaptive dilemmas that require longer, deeper changes in their own thinking and work. Finally, the most effective groups we have worked with clearly articulate questions that focus their energy for a semester or a year, such as "How can we better meet the reading needs of English language learners across our content-area classes?" or "What difference will the explicit teaching of inferencing skills make in high school content-area classes?" To answer these questions, groups of teachers bring student work to their PLC, describe or show video footage of their own instructional practices, read new books and articles together, and collaboratively adopt and adapt new practices that are then reviewed and refined.

Much like Releah Lent argues in her book *Literacy Learning Communities*, we have found that educators focused on improving student learning must pay just as much attention to how adults in schools learn.[14] Highly effective secondary PLCs ask essential questions about literacy (often related to one or more of the six domains—disciplinary literacy, vocabulary, discussion, digital literacy, multiple texts, and writing-to-learn—presented in this book) alongside questions about their own group processes. For example, one team we recently observed asked, "How can we improve accountable talk in our classrooms, while also improving the ways in which we talk with each other?" These essential questions come from a literacy leadership PLC that spent nearly two years considering Common Core standards, evidence-based discussions, and how teachers might better model the language and processes of academic discussions. Most importantly, the team spent a great deal of time considering how they would learn together as a team (e.g., looking at student work, observing classrooms, videotaping their own discussions, and reflecting on them). We completely agree with the team's theory that in order to continually improve classroom instruction that their PLC needed to focus on slower, adaptive, incremental improvements and refinements of core practices like discussion—not the quick-fix technical solutions adopted by less-effective PLCs.

Instructional Coaching as a Complement To PLCs

Sometimes even the most effective PLCs can benefit greatly from outside expertise and support.[15] Where members of PLCs need additional support, instructional coaches can provide objectivity along with content and facilitative expertise. We have found that coaching at middle and high school levels can be productive in helping teachers explore and refine practices related to the six domains in this book; however, coaching is most effective when it is clearly defined and supported by a number of contextual factors.[16]

Mirroring the evolution of PLCs, instructional coaching has spread rapidly in schools over the past two decades. This hurried adoption has produced widespread confusion about what *coach* means from school to school, district to district, and state to state. The opening chapter of McKenna and Walpole's book *The Literacy Coaching Challenge* is particularly helpful for readers considering different coaching models to help promote adult learning around our six domains (see table 14.1 for a summary).[17]

Leaders and teachers considering how instructional coaching might help them make use of this book's resources should consider several factors. First, it is important to match a coaching model with school and teacher team goals. While all coaching models share an end goal of improving student learning and achievement, different coaching models approach that ultimate goal in different ways.

Some models, such as *peer coaching* and *cognitive coaching*, focus on helping individual teachers achieve professional goals they set for themselves. Both mod-

TABLE 14.1

Summary of coaching models

Mentoring new teachers	A senior colleague coaches a novice teacher, typically for the first year or two of that teacher's career. The primary goal of this model is to ensure that new teachers survive and thrive in their new positions.
Cognitive coaching	A designated coach works with a teacher to help her/him develop new ways of thinking, working, and teaching based on the teacher's individual goals. Individual growth (professional and intellectual) is the primary goal of this model.
Peer coaching	Pairs of teachers coach one another by observing each other's practices, listening to each other's challenges, experimenting with new practices together, co-planning, etc. Importantly, the coach is the one who is teaching, and observer is the one who learns from watching and listening to the reflections of the coach. Promoting collaboration and strong partnerships is the primary goal of this model; targeted feedback is not.
Subject-specific coaching	A coach works with one or more groups of teachers within a particular discipline (e.g., literacy, math, science, social studies) to introduce, align, and refine subject-specific instructional practices. One of the primary goals of this model is alignment of best practices across classrooms.
Program-specific coaching	A coach works with one or more groups of teachers across a department or school to introduce and refine practices associated with a specific framework or program. A primary goal of this model is fidelity to a program.
Reform-oriented coaching	Coaches are "directors" and/or "mentors" alternately working to change systems within a school (e.g., schedules, literacy leadership teams) and working with teachers on embracing and refining best practices. Increasing student achievement is the primary goal, but unlike some of the models described above, particular methods (i.e., specific strategies, programs, content) are not dictated.

Source: Adapted from Michael C. McKenna and Sharon Walpole, *The Literacy Coaching Challenge: Models and Methods for Grades K–8* (New York: Guilford Press, 2008), 4–14.

els presume that teachers have a fair bit of autonomy, a clear vision of both their instructional needs and goals, and flexibility in their schedules to collaborate with at least one other colleague (e.g., visiting classrooms, co-planning, reviewing data). These coaching models position teachers as experts with control over their own professional learning. Other models, such as *program-specific* and *subject-specific coaching*, focus on building particular skill sets and capacities in teachers, teams, and entire schools. These forms of coaching nudge and support teachers as they adopt, adapt, and refine specific strategies and programs. An assumption underlying these models is that increases in student achievement come from alignment of practices across classrooms, not just individual teacher growth. Finally, *reform-oriented coaching* (McKenna and Walpole's term) positions coaches as powerful change agents who work with administrators on changing organizational structures and with teachers on changing classroom practices. This last model suggests a patchwork of coaching practices focused on increasing student achievement, a flexible model that changes quickly if results are not satisfactory.

Beyond particular models, a second consideration might be how responsive or directive coaches need to be in their interactions with teachers.[18] In other words, to what degree is a coach responding to teachers' needs and interests (e.g., cognitive coaching or peer coaching) versus directing teachers to enact specific practices or programs (e.g., subject-specific or program-specific coaching)? When asked, coaches reported striving to achieve a balance between these positional stances in order to influence teachers' practice.[19] For readers considering using this book as part of coaching work, we argue that the balance between directive and responsive stances rests partly on the weight of research evidence presented for each of our six domains. In cases where there is a fair bit of research evidence (e.g., discussion, vocabulary, writing-to-learn), coaches might take a more directive approach in suggesting particular practices or ways of thinking and working. In cases where research evidence is still growing (e.g., disciplinary literacy, digital literacies, multiple texts), coaches might take a more responsive approach and listen closely to teachers' disciplinary interests, needs, and questions.

A third consideration related to the responsive/balanced/directive framework focuses on the nature of coaching activities, what Moran calls the *literacy coaching continuum* of professional learning practices.[20] Moran describes a continuum of coaching practices that range from least to most "intrusive." Collaborative resource management (i.e., finding and sharing resources that teachers need) is less intrusive than classroom visits, coplanning, or study groups (similar to PLCs), which themselves are less intrusive than peer coaching and coteaching (the most intrusive end of the continuum). Moran suggests that coaches and teams of teachers consider their goals, the varying levels of trust among different teacher teams, and design a sequence of coaching activities that slowly builds collaborative capacity. Moran suggests that these practices can be engaged in iteratively, moving back and forth between more and less intrusive practices in order to build comfort and trust. We agree wholeheartedly. When combined with the responsive/balanced/directive framework, the continuum of coaching practices becomes a powerful model for considering *how* a coach might work with professional learning communities of teachers at different points in a school year to increase reflection, provide objective feedback, and facilitate challenging conversations about new practices.

Finally, readers should consider whether or not hiring a part- or full-time coach is the best use of a school's resources, given middle and high schools' many competing commitments and whether or not expectations of secondary coaches are realistic.[21] The International Reading Association's 2006 *Standards for Middle and High School Literacy Coaches* outline a daunting list of qualifications for coaches at secondary levels, including leadership standards (being skillful collaborators, job-embedded coaches, and evaluators of literacy needs) and content-area standards (being skillful instructional strategists across content areas).[22] Each of these standards comprises multiple elements, and even seasoned secondary coaches might blanch a bit at all that is expected of them. A similar discomfort might arise if they take the *Self-Assessment for Middle and High School Literacy Coaches*.[23] This twelve-page, somewhat intimidating self-assessment helps secondary coaches consider their own strengths and weaknesses across nine different domains of knowledge and skill related to secondary coaching, from foundations of literacy, to assessment, to classroom coaching and facilitating adult learning. Looking back at this self-assessment, which I played a small part in creating, it seems impossible that a single coach could be masterful in all nine domains! Yet I still believe it is a useful document to guide self-reflection.

There is great power in coaching as a professional learning mechanism, and research has found modest effects of coaching at the secondary level.[24] Recently, Lent has argued that peer coaching models may be one of the cheapest and easiest ways for secondary teachers to engage in coaching activities as part of larger PLCs.[25] We agree. A lone instructional coach is unlikely to introduce and effectively spread the ideas presented in this book, such as Lieberman and Looney's suggestions for using multiple texts, without the support of PLCs engaging in ongoing inquiry. When working alongside teachers meeting in departmental and cross-department PLCs, coaches have greater opportunity to influence classroom instruction and facilitate professional learning. Teachers in a high school history department we observed were much more likely to consider using multiple texts as part of units on World War II and immigration when their coach gave them specific suggestions *after* they had already begun asking questions about text sets in their PLC. In this way, a coach works alongside a PLC to enhance (not dictate) group learning.

Discussion-Based Protocols as Capacity-Building Tools

The reciprocal relationship between coaches and PLCs also allows coaches to easily introduce the fourth construct for consideration in professional learning: discussion-based protocols. By introducing protocols to teams of teachers organized into PLCs, coaches support teachers as they engage in challenging conversations about their own instruction—a practice still uncommon in many schools.[26]

For groups of educators engaging in professional learning around disciplinary literacy, discussion-based protocols are the most inexpensive and effective tools available. Discussion-based protocols have been widely described as essential tools for adult collaboration and professional development in schools.[27] For the purposes of this chapter, *protocol* can be defined as an "agreed upon set of discussion or observation rules that guide coach/teacher/student work, discussion, and interactions."[28] Some protocols are designed primarily to help students adopt particular habits of mind and ways of observing, analyzing, and discussing ideas.[29] Such protocols are quite simple and can be adapted for a wide range of discipline-specific purposes with students or adults. One of our favorites is the "see, think, wonder" protocol that asks groups to first look at a text, piece of art, object, or other artifact and then write and share their descriptions, interpretations, and questions. Ideally, engaging groups of students or adults in these steps helps them to slow their thinking, explicitly describe an artifact before rushing to judgment, and end with questions that might lead to further explorations and connections. Embedded in this simple protocol are the basic habits of mind adopted by scientists, researchers, and artists. It is easy to imagine how such a simple set of guidelines for engaging with new artifacts could be tailored to discipline-specific purposes across grade levels.

More sophisticated protocols, for use with adults in professional learning communities, might be catalogued according to what we call a *continuum of protocols* (see figure 14.2). This is one way that we have introduced protocols to teachers and literacy coaches across districts.[30] The continuum is built on the principle that different levels of trust, familiarity, and collegiality allow for fundamentally different types of conversations in schools. Certain conversations among educators are low stakes and can be entered into easily and with fairly simple protocols for getting to know one another, sharing ideas, and looking at professional texts. Alternately, there are conversations that many educators find challenging if they have not spent a great deal of time to first establish high levels of trust and collegiality (e.g., conversations in which colleagues discuss each other's practices, analyze video footage of one another's instruction, or discuss issues of equity and social justice). We designed the continuum of protocols to guide coaches, teacher leaders, and PLC facilitators as they con-

FIGURE 14.2

Continuum of discussion-based protocols

Protocol category	Purpose for discussion/examples of protocols
Sharing experiences	*Purposes:* Sharing personal connections, breaking the ice, exploring ideas, surfacing assumptions *Examples:* Compass Points, Connections, Chalk Talk, Continuum Dialogue, Block Party, Microlab, Passion Profiles
Text-based discussions	*Purposes:* Exploring text together, revisiting core concepts, learning new concepts, challenging assumptions *Examples:* Three Levels of Text, Text-Rendering, Chalk Talk, Final Word, Four A's, Save the Last Word for Me, Microlab, Text-Based Seminar, Block Party
Looking at student work	*Purposes:* Surfacing and aligning expectations of student work, challenging assumptions, calibrating teacher responses, planning instruction *Examples:* Collaborative Assessment Conference, ATLAS—Looking at Data, Art Shack, Student Work Gallery, The Slice
Tuning	*Purposes:* Improving a piece of writing, improving a unit/lesson/assessment, solving a dilemma of instruction, looking at student work in relationship to an assignment, improving a specific plan or process already in place *Examples:* Tuning Protocol, Tuning a Plan, Constructivist Tuning Protocol, Tuning for Larger Groups
Looking at data	*Purposes:* Designing instruction based on assessment, focusing instructional and intervention efforts, making data-based decisions, aligning instructional reform efforts *Examples:* ATLAS—Looking at Data, Data Driven Dialogue, Data Mining Protocol, The Slice
Planning and observing	*Purposes:* Planning or coplanning instruction, exploring use of physical space, observing teacher/student interactions, observing student responses to instruction *Examples:* Into-/Through-/Beyond- Planning Guide, Lesson-Planning/Observation Guide, Video Camera Court Reporter, Focus Point, Interesting Moments, Observer as Learner, Person Observed as Coach
Dilemmas of practice	*Purposes:* "Defining" problems of practice, expanding thinking about dilemmas, collectively "owning" dilemmas, offering next steps/new ideas *Examples:* Consultancy, Issaquah, Charrette, Back to the Future Protocol
Equity and social justice	*Purposes:* Surfacing assumptions, examining inequities, discussing the "elephant in the room," offering new ideas *Examples:* Equity Protocol, Equity Stances, Looking at Student Work: Equity, Classroom Equity Writing Prompt, Provocative Prompts for Equity Conversations, Tuning for Equity Protocol

Increasing intensity, degree of trust required, and time group has been meeting

Note: Example protocols above are listed roughly in an order in which they might be introduced to new groups. To view the protocols listed, visit www.schoolreforminitiative.org, http://www.nsrfharmony.org/, and http://www.literacycoachingonline.org/tools.html.

sider when and how to introduce structures over time that might help teachers build the capacity to engage in increasingly challenging collaborative work.

The continuum borrows Critical Friends Group tools and traditions, but it sequences classic protocols into an order that teachers and coaches find meaningful and that slowly builds the capacity to enter into riskier conversations.[31] We have grouped and sequenced the protocols as follows:

1. Sharing experiences
2. Text-based discussions
3. Looking at student work
4. Tuning
5. Looking at data
6. Planning and observing
7. Dilemmas of practice
8. Equity and social justice

Online repositories of protocols have grown exponentially over the past decade, and can be freely downloaded from the websites of groups such as the National School Reform Faculty, the School Reform Initiative, and the Literacy Coaching Clearinghouse.[32] Coaches and teachers can use the continuum to group and sequence the ever-growing number of protocols, and perhaps more importantly, can use both existing protocols and the continuum to help design their own discussion structures.

The greatest strength of using protocols with groups of educators is that it establishes clear and consistent habits for describing, interpreting, suggesting, and refining instructional practices. Protocols prevent groups from lapsing into advice-giving modes, jumping to conclusions, misinterpreting one another's practices, or quickly adopting technical solutions. Of course, the strength of protocols partly lies in their rigidity. We often hear teachers ask, "Do we *have* to follow this protocol? Can't we just *talk* with one another?" Teachers may bristle at first when asked to adhere to timed rounds of discussion focused on observation, questioning, and interpreting. However, adhering to the time limits and steps in classic protocols such as the "Consultancy" or "Collaborative Assessment Conference," at least at first, teaches new and nonjudgmental ways of interacting. Over time, groups that have become familiar with a range of protocols might so thoroughly adopt the habits embedded in them (e.g., noticing, questioning, wondering) that they may begin designing effective protocols tailored to their specific team or departmental tasks. Lisa Messina's work with a disciplinary literacy network (see chapter 3 of this volume) is a prime example of an experienced coach and facilitator adapting protocols to meet content-area teachers' specific professional development needs.

Lessons Learned

In conclusion, I present evidence from three of our partner schools to illustrate how, when considered together, the four constructs at the heart of this chapter (technical/adaptive change, PLCs, coaching, and protocols) can have powerful effects on professional learning. Each "lesson learned" below is the result of the commingling of the four constructs and comes directly from our work as researchers and consultants in schools over the past five years. Pseudonyms for schools are used to protect privacy.

Careful Self-Study and Reflection Are the Springboard for Adaptive Change

Conducting a targeted needs assessment, or self-study, focused on adolescent literacy is certainly not a new concept for seasoned secondary teachers and leaders. However, conducting a needs assessment effectively is challenging. When done well, self-study can support collaborative PLCs wishing to engage in both adaptive and technical aspects of improving disciplinary literacy instruction. Data collected from teachers and students can help leaders decide how best to allocate professional development resources and which topics teacher teams must address during cycles of inquiry. Our own thinking about self-study has especially influenced the work of thoughtful teachers and leaders in three schools (one middle and two high schools) across two states in New England.

Literacy leadership teams (comprising administrators, department heads, teachers, and specialists) at the three partner schools we highlight in this section each contacted us (the editors) in search of efficient, effective, and flexible structures for improving disciplinary literacy instruction in their schools. After initial consultations, each leadership team determined that conducting a careful self-study was the first step to designing robust professional learning experiences. Capstone Middle School is a large magnet middle school serving roughly twelve hundred sixth- to eighth-grade students from both urban and rural communities. Boddington High School is a large urban high school serving a diverse population of over seventeen hundred ninth- to twelfth-grade students originating from over seventy-five countries and speaking more than fifty languages. Hillock High School is a midsized rural high school serving over eleven hundred eighth- to twelfth-graders.

While methods of data collection (focus groups, interviews, surveys) and length of self-study (several months, one year) varied, one strong commonality across the schools was their use of the Content-Area Literacy Survey (CALS). The CALS was collaboratively designed by researchers and practitioners affiliated with the Strategic Education Research Partnership.[33] The survey, freely available online, allows administrators and team leaders to survey an entire school faculty, or faculty across an entire district, as well as students. Originally designed for use at the middle school level, the survey has now been successfully piloted at the high school level. The purpose of the survey is to gather descriptive data from teachers about their literacy-related instructional practices, as well as a host of other important factors, including:

- Instructional rewards and challenges
- Professional development experience and needs
- Collective responsibility for literacy instruction
- Teacher views of student reading and writing
- Student literacy practices outside of school

Furthermore, the student survey collects corresponding data about reading and writing habits, classroom experiences, and motivation and engagement. The survey, which includes skip logic to allow participants to talk specifically about particular content-area experiences, takes about twenty minutes to complete on a computer. The results are compiled online in real time, with each new participant's response instantly added to growing tallies. Bar charts are automatically created for each survey item, visually demonstrating results. Results are available to survey administrators, who then may choose when and how to disseminate data to leaders and teacher teams for analysis.

Capstone, Boddington, and Hillock each asked teachers to complete the survey, and Capstone and Hillock also administered the survey to students. Results were compelling and allowed each literacy leadership team to begin asking questions that would lead to both technical and adaptive work. For instance, Hillock's fifteen-member leadership team compared teacher and student data using an adaptation of the Data Driven Dialogue protocol.[34] The team first made predictions about what the data might show, then observed the data and shared purely factual descriptions of what they were seeing, "Some patterns I notice . . . " "I notice that . . . " "I'm surprised to see . . . " After describing the data, the team broke into small groups and engaged in a round of sharing inferences, with members suggesting explanations for patterns they saw in the data, taking great care to phrase their inferences as possibilities and not certainties. Finally, the team came back together as a whole group and shared and compared inferences, ending with a round of suggestions for how to connect the survey data to other information such as state test scores, writing assessments, and SAT and PSAT scores. This work by the leadership team was distilled and presented back to the entire school's faculty and leadership, and the survey data and analysis became a starting point for the leadership team and departmental teams to begin considering some of the largest literacy-related concerns in the schools. Topics such as reading engagement and motivation were found to be a concern among most teachers and students, while other departmental concerns were more specific (e.g., science teachers reporting the need for support in effectively using textbooks).

Importantly, none of these schools' leadership teams used the CALS data in an evaluative or punitive manner or as evidence that technical solutions (e.g., new vocabulary lists or a computer-aided reading intervention) would quickly raise achievement. Instead, the schools used the CALS data to identify areas where adaptive change seemed most promising—where areas of strength and areas of challenge overlapped enough for departmental PLCs to begin cycles of inquiry and experimentation. For example, at Hillock, survey findings revealed that fewer history teachers reported providing vocabulary instruction than English language arts teachers. Instead of taking the history department to task, or quickly purchasing a vocabulary program, the literacy leadership team identified vocabulary instruction as an adaptive challenge worthy of team exploration in the coming year. Teams were encouraged to try new strategies, keep track of student learning, and report back to the larger literacy leadership team. In this model, teams of teachers were supported with time and autonomy to explore best practices over time with colleagues—first steps toward addressing the adaptive challenge of how adolescents can best learn, retain, and use academic and content-area specific words. Without the CALS survey as part of each school's needs assessment process, and without protocol-based discussions analyzing the subsequent data, each of these schools may have fallen into the all-too-common position of quickly adopting technical solutions with little teacher investment and little effect. That is not to say that some technical solutions were not adopted as the result of the CALS work; however, the data allowed the literacy leadership teams to identify topics requiring longer adaptive inquiry cycles (e.g., motivation and engagement, vocabulary) and technical challenges requiring targeted resources (e.g., better Internet access in each classroom).

Identifying Small Teams of Teachers to Be Coached in PLCs

When professional development for large middle and high schools that house traditional content-area departments (much like the size and structure of our partner schools) are being designed, initial questions often center around how to provide high-quality professional development for all teachers at the same time. Secondary school leaders may rightly identify a need for disciplinary literacy professional development, but they may jump too quickly to the decision that professional development budgets would be well spent hiring one or two instructional coaches to consult with teachers a handful of times per year. The theory of action in these cases is that there is something that the faculty doesn't know about adolescent literacy, and if only an expert coach could come into the school a half dozen times and share that missing knowledge (a technical response to an adaptive challenge), teaching and learning will suddenly change. Unfortunately, we know from the literature and from our own experiences in schools (both as teachers and as unwitting coaches) that this model rarely has the intended effect.[35]

While we strongly believe in coaching as a model of professional learning and school change, we have found through our work with dozens of schools that developing and maintaining a core focus is the key to productive instructional coaching. We have found that engaging fewer people over a longer period of time leads to bigger changes in teaching and learning. If coaching efforts are too infrequent or dispersed, little real instructional change is likely to occur as a result. Similarly, at the secondary level, a single coach (whether outside consultant or on staff) may often be expected to work across content areas with dozens of teachers—an unrealistic and unproductive design model. Finally, unless careful attention has been paid to simultaneously building PLCs or connecting coaching work to existing PLCs, instructional changes resulting from coaching will be difficult to sustain over time.[36]

In Capstone Middle School, outside literacy coaches were initially going to be hired to work with all eighty faculty members; however, after the literacy leadership team examined data collected through the CALS and focus groups, it was determined that the English language arts teachers, history teachers, and special educators (about thirty-five teachers altogether) seemed most ready to engage in inquiry cycles around identified topics of student need: reading motivation, habits of mind associated with disciplinary literacy, authentic discussion, and working with complex texts. Two coaches were hired to work over a two-year period with these three groups of teachers, meeting twice per month. As a result of that work, teachers rewrote the major questions guiding their content-area courses, collaboratively designed and implemented academic language vocabulary instruction, collected and constructed new text sets of materials at various reading levels, and reorganized how classroom teachers and special educators shared information.

Part of the successful shift in instructional practices at Capstone Middle School might be attributed to the smaller numbers of teachers being coached. Working with smaller teams of content-area teachers, the coaches were able to balance responsive and directive stances toward the teachers.[37] The coaches carefully alternated between responding to teachers' questions and specific curricular needs while also directing the teachers toward best practices, such as those outlined in the previous chapters of this book. This relationship between coaches and teachers somewhat reflects McKenna and Walpole's *reform-oriented coaching* and allowed teachers to remain experts while simultaneously seeking to improve.

A second successful aspect of the project was the formation of PLCs within the content areas. Previously, teachers had been collaborating primarily in grade-level teams, but there had been little opportunity for content-area teachers across grades to coordinate efforts. Cross-grade PLCs within each content area, including special educators, began meeting and working together as a result of coaching work. Those PLC groups were formed during coaching sessions, and discussion-based protocols were modeled during the sessions. The coaches and teachers used an online bulletin board to share questions, concerns, discoveries, and resources between coaching sessions. Meanwhile, the newly formed PLCs were encouraged to meet between and beyond the coaching sessions, establishing a mechanism for teachers to continue exploring and refining practices.

Similarly, at Boddington High, the literacy leadership team agreed that focusing on coaching several teams of teachers was far better than trying to blanket the entire faculty (nearly 150 teachers). Given Boddington's size, the literacy leadership team was understandably more concerned with how to bring lessons learned in small PLCs to the larger school. As a result, they designed a four-year professional development model, with two two-year cycles of teacher teams working with a pair of coaches. Importantly, content-area teachers were asked to apply as teams to take part in the professional development project, and as part of their application, they needed to elect a coach. The coach would receive partial release time from teaching duties and a small stipend. In exchange, the coaches for each team were required to meet with their team members and other coaches on a weekly basis and communicate regularly with outside consultants to grow their own coaching skill sets. In this model, three teams were selected to participate in the first two years of professional development (a subset of English, history, and world language teachers), while other teacher teams were encouraged to participate in the final two years of the four-year project. The three teams participating in the first two years of the project participated in a week-long summer institute outlining the ideas presented in this volume, introducing discussion-based protocols, and helping teams develop and refine initial questions that would form the basis of cycles of inquiry during the school year. The focus of the first year of work was piloting new instruction, with the second year's focus being the scaling up of effective practices to the larger departmental level. While the project is still in its first two years, we have already seen teachers immediately implementing new practices—focusing on vocabulary instruction, designing text sets, engaging students in close reading to highlight disciplinary habits of mind—and reflecting deeply on their instruction in weekly PLC meetings, on an online bulletin board, and during quarterly meetings where the three teams share findings.

These designs for professional learning are powerful because they focus simultaneously on adult professional learning and student learning. Teachers in these schools are working in small teams toward collaboratively defined goals, measuring their success at regular intervals by collectively reflecting on changes in student achievement.

Part of the nature of engaging in adaptive change processes, such as improving adolescents' disciplinary reading and writing skills, is that few simple, clear answers exist. Yet as educators, we must return to the classroom each day and do our best to help students acquire the disciplinary reading, writing, and presentation skills they will need for college and the workplace. Understanding that tension, the literacy leadership teams at these schools have chosen to invest in building intentional professional learning communities that can carefully consider ideas such as those presented in this book and respond by experimenting with new practices and reflecting on the results of those experiments as part of inquiry cycles. These leadership teams understand that in order to improve student learning, we must simultaneously focus on improving adult learning.

Final Thoughts

It is common to hear platitudes about professional development these days—that it needs to be job-embedded, ongoing, data driven, linked to student achievement, etc. While there are grains of truth in these statements, we have not found such advice to be very helpful when sitting down with literacy leadership teams to design professional learning experiences. On the other hand, we have found that focusing on the four constructs outlined in this chapter (technical/adaptive change, PLCs, coaching, and discussion-based protocols) has allowed our partner schools to engage teachers in meaningful professional learning that both introduces new ideas (e.g., teaching disciplinary literacy habits of mind) and responds to long-standing dilemmas (e.g., how do we help our students engage in more authentic discussion?). Focusing on these four constructs allows for the formation of collective goals and movement toward shared practices, while still honoring the needs of individuals. Budgets, schedules, and district policies regarding professional development will always be a consideration. Yet if schools are going to meet the adaptive challenge of improving adolescents' disciplinary literacy skills, then we as educators must begin taking as much care with the design of our systems of professional learning as we do with designing classroom instruction.

Meeting the Challenge
of the
Common Core State Standards

JACY IPPOLITO AND COLLEEN ZALLER

Throughout this book, authors have referred both directly and indirectly to the Common Core State Standards, and as editors we would be remiss not to spend several pages explicitly connecting the ideas of this volume to these landmark standards.[1] Adoption of the Common Core State Standards by forty-five states and three territories by early 2013 represents a major shift in the history of U.S. education. By adopting common standards for instruction in literacy and mathematics K–12, states are ushering in a new era of collaboration and curricular alignment. This level of alignment across states, and frankly across districts within those states, is unparalleled in the history of education in the United States. While many nations throughout the world long ago adopted national standards for instruction across academic disciplines and grade levels, the United States has held fast to its historical origins, with decisions about what students must learn and how they learn it determined initially by individual teachers in each one-room schoolhouse, then by leaders in each school and district, and eventually by policy makers in each state. In the relatively short history of education in the United States, widespread adoption of common standards across states seems like the next logical step toward producing a national education system able to prepare citizens to compete in a global economy.

From our perspective as researchers, teachers, and writers focused primarily on connections between literacy and content knowledge and instructional practices, the Common Core standards are both a reinforcement of evidence-based practices already embedded in excellent classrooms and a gentle push toward increasing the depth and rigor of instruction K–12. For readers keeping close track of the implementation of Common Core standards across states, discussion of the *six major shifts* in literacy instruction prompted by the standards is perhaps quite familiar. In this chapter we discuss those six shifts briefly, but more importantly for readers using this book in university and professional development settings, we connect those shifts explicitly with the six major domains of instruction explored in this book.[2] We highlight the overlap and the gaps between the Common Core standards and the research, arguments, and information contained in this book. Finally, we provide resources for readers wishing to explore additional topics, beyond our six domains, that receive limited attention both in the Common Core standards and in this book—including fluency instruction, motivation and engagement, and the particular needs of English language learners (ELLs) and students with special instructional needs. Neither the Common Core standards nor this book can address *all* aspects of literacy-related instruction in secondary settings; however, this chapter extends the reach of both by providing clear connections and additional resources.

Of Shifts and Domains: Connecting This Book to the Common Core

One of the perennial tensions in education is how we as educators divide and accept responsibility for teaching different skills and knowledge. The Common Core State Standards address this tension directly. Secondary content-area instruction in the United States is currently divided (distinct classes in history, math, science, English language arts, foreign languages, etc., each with their own particular subdomains) partly due to differences in the habits of mind required by different disciplines and partly due to historical trends. Traditionally, explicit instruction in reading, writing, and presenting has been perceived as the purview of English language arts (ELA) teachers at the middle and high school levels, with less widespread adoption of literacy-related instructional practices in non-ELA content area classrooms.[3] This makes the recent adoption of Common Core literacy-focused standards across states exciting and challenging, for different states have traditionally divided teaching responsibilities in various ways—some integrating reading, writing, and presentation skills more thoroughly into the content areas, with others relegating this work mainly to ELA classes.

The Common Core standards tackle this tension about division of skill and knowledge instruction over time by encouraging six major shifts in literacy-related instruction across the content areas. The standards ask all secondary content-area teachers to:

- Provide students with a balance of informational and literary text
- Share responsibility for teaching discipline-specific reading, writing, and presenting skills
- Encourage reading of complex texts that increase in challenge over time as part of a staircase of complexity
- Answer text-based questions in class tasks and discussions

- Require text-based evidence in students' written opinions and arguments
- Focus on students' acquisition of academic vocabulary[4]

Some readers may review this list of shifts and scoff, "*What* shifts? We've been giving students complex fiction and nonfiction for years! And we always teach academic vocabulary and require students to cite the text when answering questions orally and in writing. The Common Core is nothing but common sense!" While this may be a fair response from some teachers who indeed have been following these guidelines for years, we argue that for most, these changes do represent fundamental shifts in the selection of texts, design of classroom activities, and ways in which we are asking students to read and write across content areas. These shifts may feel most radical to teachers of science, history, and math (particularly in addition to the ninety-three-page separate math standards). Remember that the standards and shifts outlined above are aimed equally at ELA teachers as they are at content-area teachers, and while the shifts may not seem tremendously daunting for an eighth-grade ELA teacher, they may feel overwhelming to a tenth-grade biology teacher. As leadership guru Robert Evans writes in his book *The Human Side of School Change*, we must remember that any large change may be experienced as a loss, or as a challenge to our competence, that creates confusion and often conflict.[5] School leaders and instructional coaches must not overestimate the degree of change in classroom practice that the Common Core State Standards may be asking of many secondary teachers. In addition to our own personal responses to the implementation of Common Core standards (whether wholehearted or skeptical), we must remember that improving the achievement of adolescents is not the task of a single teacher, but the task of teams, departments, and schools. The response of our colleagues is just as, if not more important than our own in many respects.

Thus, we spend the rest of this chapter drawing explicit connections between the Common Core standards, the six major shifts, and the six domains of literacy instruction outlined in this book. We hope that this discussion (and this book) will serve as one small antidote to the confusion teachers may experience when integrating the new standards with research and practice in adolescent literacy.

Overlapping Goals

There is clearly much overlap between the ideas the authors present in this book and the benchmarks outlined in the Common Core standards. Yet there is not always a one-to-one correspondence. Some of the domains outlined in this book are featured more prominently in the standards than others, and serve as learning goals in and of themselves. The use of multiple texts, particularly to analyze and understand ideas and themes across numerous text sources, is one such goal that is heavily emphasized in the standards (see Cynthia Shanahan's overview of these connections in chapter 10). Other skills, such as discussion, are positioned to act more as a means to achieve these goals. In our minds, the six domains we have presented function both as reasonable and evidence-based entry points into the world of adolescent literacy—if secondary teachers were to engage deeply in the six domains outlined in this book, they would be naturally addressing many of the same goals of the Common Core State Standards. We review the connections explicitly below, following the content and structure of the chapters in this book.

1. Disciplinary Literacy

While the fundamental assumptions of disciplinary literacy are not fully explained in the Common Core standards, the words *discipline* and *discipline-specific* appear repeatedly as an invitation for content-area teachers to teach the reading, writing, and presenting skills associated with their disciplines. On page 4 of the standards, the clearest statement of this shared responsibility is given: "The Standards insist that instruction in reading, writing, speaking, listening, and language be a shared responsibility within the school . . . recognizing that teachers in other areas [beyond ELA] must have a role in [developing students' literacy skills] as well."[6]

The emphasis on disciplinary literacy is also clear in the final section of the standards, with the focus on "Literacy in History/Social Studies, Science, and Technical Subjects." This final portion of the standards explicitly calls on content-area teachers to support students as they "Write arguments focused on discipline-specific content" and "Establish and maintain a formal style and objective tone [in writing] while attending to the norms and conventions of the discipline."[7] For history teachers working with eleventh- and twelfth-graders, the standards invite us to explicitly teach students how to "analyze in detail how a complex primary source is structured, including how key sentences, paragraphs, and larger portions of the text contribute to the whole."[8] In the sciences and technical subjects, students are asked to "cite specific textual evidence to support analysis of science and technical texts."[9] These standards prompt discipline-specific instruction in reading, writing, and presenting and reflect recent research and practices related to the field of disciplinary literacy.

As Galloway, Lawrence, Moje, and Messina write in chapters 2 and 3 of this book, the growing field of disciplinary literacy invites teachers to carefully consider the reading, writing, oral language, and presenting demands of the texts and tasks embedded in their discipline. Disciplinary literacy instruction at the secondary level is increasingly being trumpeted as a means to better prepare students for success in college and the workplace.[10] While researchers (such as Galloway, Lawrence, and Moje) and teachers and coaches (such as Messina) are just beginning to explore the exciting opportunities afforded by this way of thinking about instruction, the implicit focus on disciplinary literacy in the Common Core standards ensures that secondary teachers will be designing and implementing discipline-specific literacy lessons for years to come.

Resources for Teams Considering Connections to Disciplinary Literacy

Sullivan County Board of Cooperative Educational Services, Shift 2: Building Knowledge in the Disciplines: http://scboces.org/Page/684.

Video footage of teachers and students considering what it means to read like a historian: https://www.teachingchannel.org/videos/reading-like-a-historian-curriculum.

Wisconsin's approach to disciplinary literacy: http://standards.dpi.wi.gov/stn_disciplinaryliteracy.

Eastern Michigan Writing Project presentations about disciplinary literacy and the Common Core: http://emichwp.org/wp/professional-development/reading-and-writing-in-a-decade-of-standards/1125-2/dr-doug-bakers-introduction-to-disciplinary-literacy/.

Elizabeth Moje's speech at the National Writing Project Conference: "Disciplinary Literacy: Why It Matters and What We Should Do About It," http://www.nwp.org/cs/public/print/resource/3121.

2. Vocabulary

While very few educators would argue that teaching vocabulary and encouraging students to learn new words represents a radical shift in educational policy, the Common Core standards add a subtle but important distinction: "The vocabulary standards focus on understanding words and phrases, their relationships, and their nuances and on acquiring new vocabulary, *particularly general academic and domain-specific words and phrases*" (emphasis added).[11] Researchers, teachers, and coaches (such as Lawrence, Maher, Snow, and Dobbs in chapters 4 and 5) are increasingly noting the importance of emphasizing and teaching both *general academic* and *domain-specific* words to secondary students. Programs such as Word Generation (highlighted in chapters 4 and 6) demonstrate the power of introducing general academic words that students might encounter hundreds of times across content areas in all informational texts (and that might cause confusion without some small amount of explicit instruction). The shared responsibility of content-area teachers for introducing general academic words (suggested in the Common Core standards) is perhaps the most exciting and important part of programs such as Word Generation. Moreover, frameworks such as Flanigan and Greenwood's for choosing and teaching domain-specific words found in content-area texts (see chapter 5) give secondary teachers an idea of which words to teach explicitly, which to merely mention, or even which to skip during a particular lesson. General academic language instruction is also critical for ELLs.[12] For content-area teachers working within either sheltered English immersion (SEI) or transitional bilingual education (TBE) classroom settings, spending instructional time on academic language development can promote both language growth and acquisition of content. While the Common Core standards provide a few hints as to how teachers might spend instructional time focused on vocabulary (e.g., helping students use context clues to intuit word meanings; teaching Greek and Latin roots, prefixes, affixes, etc.), secondary teachers will surely benefit from more guidance. Chapters 4 and 5 in this book provide some suggestions for promoting word learning skills, each pointing toward abundant resources in press and online in this domain.

Resources for Teams Considering Connections to Vocabulary

Sullivan County Board of Cooperative Educational Services, Shift 6: Academic Vocabulary: http://scboces.org/Page/688.

Vocabulary strategies: http://www.adlit.org/strategy_library/; and http://www. readingeducator.com/strategies/vocabulary.htm.

Word Generation downloadable word lists, teacher and student guides: http://wg. serpmedia.org/.

Supporting academic language development for ELLs: http://www.colorincolorado.org/ web_resources/by_topic/academic_language/; and http://www.wida.us/.

3. Discussion

Under specific "Speaking and Listening" standards, the Common Core State Standards encourage teachers to engage students "in a range of conversations and collaborations with diverse partners" so that they might "[build] on others' ideas and [express] their own clearly and persuasively."[13] As part of classroom discussions, the standards suggest students should be able to "integrate and evaluate information presented in diverse media and formats," "evaluate a speaker's point of view, reasoning, and use of evidence and rhetoric," and present their own ideas using evidence, a range of media and visual displays, and with language appropriate to the task and audience.[14] Again, for seasoned secondary teachers, much of this may sound perfectly reasonable and much like discussions that have occurred in excellent secondary classrooms for years.

However, the real *shift* these standards encourage relates to the prominence discussion plays as an instructional tool, the range of discussion types indicated, and the evidence-based nature of those discussions. First, by providing anchor standards for speaking and listening that explicitly urge teachers across content areas to engage students in rich, authentic discussions about content (i.e., discussions about weighty topics in which authentic debate occurs and in which there are not always clear answers), the authors of the Common Core State Standards suggest that there should be far more language-rich, content-based discussions occurring in all secondary classrooms. While many readers may nod their heads at this statement, the inclusion of more discussion time in secondary classrooms does represent a shift from what researchers have historically found to be very little time spent on discussion in middle and high school classes (see statistics about time spent on discussion in Michener and Ford-Connors's chapter 6). Second, the nature of the discussions suggested by Common Core standards include teacher-led, student-led, pairs, small groups, etc., with "diverse partners." This wide range of discussion formats again represents a shift away from the predominantly teacher-led discussions found in traditional secondary classrooms (see chapter 6 and 7 for more about types of discussions).

Finally, Common Core standards encourage more attention to evidence-based discussions in which students identify and interpret arguments and claims in a text and in one another's speech. This represents a real shift away from traditional practices—students answering predominantly fact-based questions or engaging in lengthy opinion-based conversations not grounded in text. These are important and welcome changes in how secondary content-area teachers wield discussion as a strategic tool for increasing students' language, literacy, and content skills and knowledge. The Common Core does not always provide specific means to achieving the ends it suggests, and discussion is one domain in which many of our teaching colleagues have argued, "We need examples of how to have these conversations!" In response, Erdmann and Metzger's chapter 7 is a brief account of the journey many of us expect to take as we move from mostly teacher-led, whole-class discussions to more authentic, student-led classroom conversations. We believe that this is one domain in which more research and evidence of best practices is sorely needed.

Resources for Teams Considering Connections to Discussion

Sullivan County Board of Cooperative Educational Services, Shift 4: Text-Based Answers: http://scboces.org/Page/686.

Discussion and "thinking" routines for groups at all levels: http://www.pz.gse.harvard.edu/visible_thinking.php.

Protocols/structures for both teacher and student discussions: http://www.schoolreforminitiative.org/.

Leading discussions in English language arts: http://www.teachingliterature.org/teachingliterature/chapter5/activities.htm.

Strategies for student-led discussions: https://www.teachingchannel.org/videos/strategies-for-student-centered-discussion.

Sorting and classifying equations: Class discussion: https://www.teachingchannel.org/videos/sorting-classifying-equations-discussion.

Inquiry-based teaching: Discussing nonfiction (history): https://www.teachingchannel.org/videos/inquiry-based-teaching-discussing-non-fiction.

4. Digital Literacy

There are multiple references to students' reading and use of digital content throughout the Common Core standards, though not nearly as many (or explicit) references to students' *digital literacies* per se (i.e., students' multiple ways of reading, writing, and synthesizing nonprint, digital, and visual materials). Nor is there much mention of students' wide range of out-of-school literacies and how they may or may not connect with in-school literacies. The clearest connection in the standards comes from the constant inclusion of the phrase *digital sources* in nearly every line that talks about print (e.g., with regard to research writing, the standards ask students to "gather relevant information from multiple print and digital sources").[15] Taking this one step further, the researchers and teachers contributing to this volume (Lawrence, Warschauer, Zheng, and Mullins in chapter 8 and Ziergiebel in chapter 9) argue that secondary content-area teachers could be doing much more to incorporate and develop students' digital literacies in and out of school. Our authors argue that stronger digital literacy connections might increase students' overall motivation and engagement while simultaneously preparing them for digitally integrated college and workplace environments. Much like the oft-cited Common Core *shift* toward a better balance of literary and informational texts in the earliest grades, we see lots of room in the standards and in secondary classrooms to strike a better balance between traditional print and nontraditional digital materials.

The Common Core State Standards certainly suggest first steps in the domain of digital literacy—focusing on students' use of technology to conduct research, evaluate information, and consider the purposes of different text types. However, this represents only the beginning of what students have been and will be learning in digital environments. The authors of chapters 8 and 9 suggest multiple opportunities for teachers to make deeper connections between the content they are teaching and students' personal experiences with technology. Personalization of learning is perhaps the greatest opportunity technology affords, and in future revisions of the standards we would like to see this domain featured more prominently.

Resources for Teams Considering Connections to Digital Literacy

The New Literacies Reasearch Team at the University of Connecticut: http://www.newliteracies.uconn.edu/.

Educator Tools: http://www.digitalliteracy.gov/content/educator.

Kathy Schrock, *Literacy in the Digital Age*: http://www.schrockguide.net/literacy-in-the-digital-age.html.

YOUmedia Chicago's youth learning lab: http://youmediachicago.org/.

Some Cool Tools to Try: http://techinliteracy.files.wordpress.com/2011/07/some-cool-tools-to-try.pdf.

5. Multiple Texts

Cynthia Shanahan, in chapter 10, clearly reviews the connections between the Common Core standards and the notion that use of multiple texts must be a core instructional practice in secondary content-area classrooms. She outlines how students' use of multiple texts is "referred to more than eighty times across grade levels," is "evident in all major emphases (literature, informational texts, history/social studies, science/technical subjects and writing . . .)," and progresses "in expectations for reading . . . from general comparisons of texts . . . to comparisons of structure . . . to specific arguments in texts . . . to evaluations of credibility and usefulness" (see chapter 6). Shanahan goes so far as to include a table that provides examples of where the 6–12 portion of the Common Core standards highlights the use of multiple texts. Clearly, use of multiple texts is embedded in the new standards, and we could not agree more that strategic selection, use, and evaluation of multiple texts is of utmost importance across content areas—perhaps this goes without saying, given that it is one of the core domains highlighted in this volume! However, it is important to note that we as editors chose *multiple texts* as a core literacy domain over *text complexity*.

One of the most commonly cited shifts of the Common Core State Standards is the move toward encouraging close reading and evaluation of increasingly *complex texts* over time: "a grade-by-grade 'staircase' of increasing text complexity."[16] Debates over the language and intent behind instruction of complex texts in the standards have caused a great deal of controversy in the blogosphere, in articles, and in recently published books.[17] The standards' focus on students' close reading of challenging text seems like a direct contradiction of much of the wisdom in the field of reading for the past several decades, with an emphasis on finding students' instructional levels and encouraging students to read *just-right* books. In this debate, we adopt a moderate stance, much like the response from the International Reading Association (IRA).[18] The IRA clearly finds a middle ground here, and we agree: "The Common Core State Standards specify the levels of text that students need to be able to read effectively by the end of school years. However, this does not mean that all assigned reading should be at these levels. In order to help students to attain the necessary end-of-year levels, teachers need to establish an ambitious itinerary of rich and varied narrative and informational texts, including some texts that are easier than the Standards specify."[19]

In chapter 11, Lieberman and Looney strike a similar balance as they make concrete suggestions for secondary teachers wishing to create text sets and use multiple texts to teach particular content at different points throughout the school year. In their chapter, Lieberman and Looney suggest that text-leveling tools and frameworks should not be slavishly followed; instead, multiple measures of text complexity (as suggested in the Common Core standards) must be used to help a range of students acquire the skills and stamina needed to attack and comprehend complex texts across disciplines.[20]

Ultimately, our focus in this book on *multiple* texts is an intentional evasion of the text complexity debates, as we believe from our own experiences in schools that there is ample room for explicit instruction and consumption of complex texts as well as wide reading of texts that students find more comfortable and navigable (building stamina, fluency, and motivation). In other words, as long as a range of complexity is sought as part of the use of multiple texts, then we believe that the goals of the Common Core standards will be met.

Resources for Teams Considering Connections to Multiple Texts

Sullivan County Board of Cooperative Educational Services, Shift 3: Staircase of Complexity: http://scboces.org/Page/685.

Using multiple texts to teach content: http://www.learningpt.org/pdfs/literacy/shanahan. pdf.

Multiple Texts: Multiple Opportunities for Teaching and Learning: http://www.nwp.org/cs/public/print/resource/2809.

Literacy implementation guidance for the ELA Common Core State Standards: http://www.reading.org/Libraries/association-documents/ira_ccss_guidelines.pdf.

Education experts talk text complexity: http://www.ascd.org/Publications/newsletters/education-update/eu-apr12-qr-video.aspx.

Achieve the core, text complexity: http://www.achievethecore.org/ela-literacy-common-core/text-complexity.

6. Writing-to-Learn

Finally, many secondary content-area teachers (including ELA teachers) might be most apprehensive about the large focus on writing in the Common Core standards. Not only are a handful of anchor standards devoted specifically to writing, but most of the standards imply that writing is one of the ways that students will digest, analyze, and interpret what they've read. Accordingly, we have emphasized writing as a core skill in this book because it overlaps with aspects of the Common Core's writing standards and intentionally sidesteps the more traditional way that secondary teachers often think about writing instruction: writing to demonstrate knowledge. In our experience, secondary content-area classrooms are filled with writing projects that are assigned, collected, and graded without much instructional time spent modeling the writing process or teaching students how to write notes, outline, draft, or more generally use writing as a tool for understanding and learning content. The word *writing* appears hundreds of times in the Common Core standards, yet many of those appearances may confuse readers looking for guidance on how to engage students more thoughtfully in the writing process. Standards suggest that students "write narratives to develop real or imagined experiences or events using effective technique, relevant descriptive details, and well-structured event sequences," or "produce clear and coherent writing," or "conduct short research projects."[21] These standards are admirable goals for students to demonstrate mastery of a particular writing genre within a discipline. Much like the text complexity debate, however, we do not interpret the standards as solely focused on final products. We see the path toward sophisticated final written products as paved with a number of writing-to-learn strategies and skills.

Secondary content-area teachers may need to start by considering the most respected forms of writing in various disciplines: journal articles, poems, novels, proofs, critical analyses, etc. Then, through careful consideration and modeling of the processes leading to those polished products, teachers will be introducing skills that students can adopt and adapt for use in university and workplace settings. Final written products will arise not simply from teacher directions but as natural extensions of needing to share what has been learned. Again, as with our other core domains, we believe that a strong emphasis on writing-to-learn will in fact help teachers to better meet the demands of Common Core standards. The suggestions made by Jacobs in chapter 12, and Olson and D'Aoust in chapter 13, go a long way toward demonstrating how an emphasis on writing-to-learn is necessary and appropriate as teachers grapple with how to infuse writing into all aspects of secondary content-area instruction.

Resources for Teams Considering Connections to Writing

The National Writing Project: http://www.nwp.org/cs/public/print/doc/resources.csp.

New York Times lessons and prompts for addressing writing standards in Common Core: http://learning.blogs.nytimes.com/category/lesson-plans/common-core/.

National Council of Teachers of English, "Beliefs About the Teaching of Writing": http://www.ncte.org/positions/statements/writingbeliefs.

Adlit.org: http://www.adlit.org/media/mediatopics/writing/ and http://www.adlit.org/article/c139/.

Reference Guide to Writing Across the Curriculum: http://wac.colostate.edu/books/bazerman_wac/.

Gaps and Extensions

If we take a moment to read over the standards, it is easy to see that many aspects of content-area literacy lesson planning and instruction are left open to interpretation. How do seventh-grade science teachers encourage their students to "determine two or more central ideas in a text and analyze their development over the course of the text"?[22] Which literary nonfiction texts should a tenth-grade ELA teacher select to address the standards? How should an eighth-grade history teacher "engage [students] effectively in a range of collaborative discussions"?[23] More generally, how do teachers implement the standards among a student body with an increasingly wide range of learning needs and differences? What are the best practices for helping ELLs of varying language proficiency levels meet Common Core benchmarks? How can teachers provide accommodations for students with disabilities (SWDs) while still retaining the rigor and high expectations embedded in the standards? How can teachers challenge students with advanced knowledge in the content areas? The authors of the Common Core State Standards (the CCSSO and the NGA) recognized that the standards cannot and should not provide the answers to all pedagogical questions. They explicitly mention that, in the creation of the standards, they intentionally left multiple areas undefined. As written in the standards, "Teachers are thus free to provide students with whatever tools and knowledge their professional judgment and experience identify as most helpful for meeting the goals set out in the Standards."[24] Moreover, the Common Core standards only hint at the accommodations that might occur to truly meet all students' needs: "The Standards should also be read as allowing for the widest possible range of students to participate fully from the outset and as permitting appropriate accommodations to ensure maximum participation of students with special education needs."[25]

We see this openness and adaptability as a key strength of the document, a smart strategy to create a flexible and living set of guidelines that allow teachers to adapt and apply them according to the needs of their students. However, this room for interpretation may cause teachers to wonder how they are going to actually implement the standards in their day-to-day teaching, which ones (of the many) they should select to incorporate in their lesson plans, and why.

Like the Common Core State Standards, this book was not intended to be a comprehensive guide on literacy instruction in the content areas for all adolescents. We have strategically highlighted six core domains that we have found in our teaching and consulting to make the most sense to secondary content-area teachers and that have had the greatest impact in shifting teams' thinking about their work. We hope to have provided some concrete ideas, examples, and guidelines throughout this book, both from research studies and from the classrooms of veteran teachers.

For teachers wondering how to adjust their instruction within these core domains to meet the learning needs of their individual students, we provide an abbreviated listing of key resources below, resources that we have used in our consulting work and that we have identified for teams of teachers considering special topics and populations.

Fluency Instruction

The Ohio Literacy Alliance's quick and easy high school reading assessments (http://www.ohioliteracyalliance.org/fluency/fluency.htm) were designed to help teams of high school teachers assess students' fluency at the high school level. These freely available online reading passages provide a starting point for secondary content-area teachers thinking about measuring fluency.

Adlit.org's repository of fluency resources (http://www.adlit.org/article/c122/) provides a handful of short, free articles by respected educators on the topic of fluency instruction in secondary classrooms.

Timothy Rasinski's professional website (http://www.timrasinski.com/?page=presentations) offers a number of presentations, resources, and publications on the topic of fluency instruction across grade levels. One of the most respected researchers and authors writing about fluency instruction today, Rasinski offers a good starting place for those interested in thinking more about fluency instruction.

The International Reading Association (http://www.reading.org/) has published scores of articles and books related to the topic of fluency instruction across all grade levels. Not all of the resources available here are free to nonmembers; however, previews of materials are often offered.

Motivation and Engagement

Adlit.org's repository of motivation and engagement resources (http://www.adlit.org/article/c128/) provides a dozen short, free articles by respected educators related to adolescents' motivation and engagement in reading, writing, and content-area learning.

Adolescents' Engagement in Academic Literacy (http://www.cori.umd.edu/research-publications/2012_adolescents_engagement_ebook.pdf) is a 2012 online book by John T. Guthrie, Allan Wigfield, and Susan Lutz Klauda from the University of Maryland, College Park. In this freely available online volume, the contributors provide hundreds of pages of background information and research related to adolescents' motivation and engagement in reading processes.

Contexts for Engagement and Motivation in Reading (http://www.readingonline.org/articles/handbook/guthrie/index.html) is an online version of John T. Guthrie's chapter on engagement and motivation published in the *Handbook of Reading Research: Volume III* (2000). While there are subsequent editions of the handbook in print (including a volume specifically focusing on adolescent learners), this freely available online chapter provides a neat overview of the field for those seeking an introduction.

Students with particular instructional needs (ELLs, SWDs, and gifted students)

The Center for Applied Linguistics (www.cal.org/topics/ell/preK12.html and www.cal.org/create/) houses a large collection of online resources and downloadable research briefs and publications centering around instruction in language, literacy, and culture. These resources include intervention descriptions (such as the SIOP model) and instructional approaches across classroom settings, and specialized publications for learning about various ELL populations. In addition to this free information, multimedia resources can be purchased in the CAL store.

The What Works Clearinghouse (http://ies.ed.gov/ncee/wwc/), a division of the Institute of Education Sciences (IES), provides reviews and reports on the efficacy of various interventions for ELL and SWD instruction as well as practice guides to support their implementation in the classroom.

The Center on Instruction (http://centeroninstruction.org) provides a wealth of information on best instructional practices for ELL and SWD populations in the form of reader-friendly practice guides, research summaries, tools, and training materials.

The Center for Research on Education, Diversity, and Excellence Hawai'i Project (CREDE) (http://manoa.hawaii.edu/coe/crede/?p=79) offers a variety of tools to enable educators to better reach out to diverse populations of students. These tools include research briefs, practitioner reports, and multimedia resources.

The WIDA standards, which provide guidance for the instruction of ELLs K–12 and across content areas, have been adopted by thirty-one states and territories at the end of 2012. The website (www.wida.us) collects a range of information and instructional tools and resources for understanding and applying the standards and accompanying assessments in the classroom.

¡Colorín Colorado! (www.colorincolorado.org) is a Spanish/English bilingual website that provides insightful and practical guides and toolkits for teachers and other educators of Spanish-speaking ELLs. Sister sites (www.ldonline.org and www.adlit. org) provide similarly useful resources for SWD populations and adolescent literacy more broadly.

The National Association for Gifted Children (http://www.nagc.org/) provides a number of resources for teachers and teams looking to better support students at the highest end of the learning spectrum. Recently, resources specifically related to Common Core have been added (http://www.nagc.org/CommonCoreStateStandards. aspx).

The National Research Center on the Gifted and Talented (NRC/GT) (http://www.gifted. uconn.edu/nrcgt/) also provides a number of research-based articles and resources for supporting gifted and talented students.

Conclusion

In this chapter, we have provided explicit connections between the Common Core standards and the contents of this book; moreover, we have provided a few jumping-off points for readers interested in topics beyond our six core domains. Having extended our thinking a bit beyond the six core domains at the heart of this book, we now end with a brief reiteration of the main argument we outlined in chapter 1.

There are many fruitful avenues to explore when bridging content-area and literacy instruction. In this era of information overload, however, teachers are perhaps more likely to be overwhelmed by the glut of information related to adolescent literacy. Rather than present yet another list of strategies or detail all the possible ways teachers can effectively integrate content-area and literacy instruction, we have carefully identified six core areas of research and classroom practice that we believe provide a foothold for real change. We urge middle and high school teachers, instructional coaches, and leaders to consider the six domains reviewed in these pages and track their development and implementation among teams of teachers and groups of students. Through iterative cycles of collaborative teacher inquiry, we have seen these domains blossom and change the nature of teaching and learning in schools. Fueled and supported by the Common Core State Standards, we hope the same will be true for the teachers and leaders reading this book.

Notes

Chapter 1

1. Vicki A. Jacobs, "Adolescent Literacy: Putting the Crisis in Context," *Harvard Educational Review* 78, no. 1 (2008): 7–39.

2. Jacy Ippolito, Jennifer L. Steele, and Jennifer F. Samson, "Preface: Continuing the Conversation on Adolescent Literacy," in *Adolescent Literacy*, ed. Jacy Ippolito, Jennifer L. Steele, and Jennifer F. Samson (Cambridge, MA: Harvard Education Press, 2012), vii–xvii.

3. *Common Core State Standards for English Language Arts and Literacy in History/Social Studies, Science, and Technical Subjects* (Washington, DC: National Governors Association Center for Best Practices and the Council of Chief State School Officers, 2010).

4. Marilyn Jager Adams, *Beginning to Read: Thinking and Learning about Print* (Cambridge, MA: MIT Press, 1990); Catherine E. Snow, Susan M. Burns, and Peg Griffin, eds., *Preventing Reading Difficulties in Young Children* (Washington, DC: National Academy Press, 1998).

5. Stephen Provasnik, Patrick Gonzales, and David Miller, *U.S. Performance Across International Assessments of Student Achievement: Special Supplement to the Condition of Education 2009. NCES 2009-083* (Washington, DC: National Center for Education Statistics, 2009); Irwin Kirsch, Henry Braun, Kentaro Yamamoto, and Andrew Sum., *America's Perfect Storm: Three Forces Changing Our Nation's Future* (Princeton, NJ: Educational Testing Service, 2007), http://www.ets.org/Media/Education_Topics/pdf/AmericasPerfectStorm.pdf; Richard J. Murnane, John B. Willett, and Frank Levy, "The Growing Importance of Cognitive Skills in Wage Determination," *Review of Economics and Statistics* 77, no. 2 (1995): 251–266; U.S. Department of Education, *National Assessment of Educational Progress (NAEP), 1992, 1994, 1998, 2002, 2003, 2005, 2007 and 2009 Reading Assessments* (Washington, DC: Institute of Education Sciences, National Center for Education Statistics, 2011) http://nces.ed.gov/nationsreportcard/naepdata/dataset.aspx.

6. Gina Biancarosa and Catherine E. Snow, *Reading Next—A Vision for Action and Research in Middle and High School Literacy: A Report from Carnegie Corporation of New York* (Washington, DC: Alliance for Excellent Education, 2004), http://www.carnegie.org/literacy/pdf/ReadingNext.pdf; Carnegie Council on Advancing Adolescent Literacy, *Time to Act: An Agenda for Advancing Adolescent Literacy for College and Career Success* (New York: Carnegie Corporation of New York, 2010).

7. Pseudonyms have been used here and throughout this volume to protect students' and teachers' privacy.

8. Jacobs, "Adolescent Literacy."

9. Biancarosa and Snow, *Reading Next*, 7; Provasnik, Gonzales, and Miller, *U.S. Performance Across International Assessments*; U.S. Department of Education, "National Assessment of Educational Progress (NAEP)."

10. Timothy Shanahan and Cynthia Shanahan, "Teaching Disciplinary Literacy to Adolescents: Rethinking Content-Area Literacy," *Harvard Educational Review* 78, no. 1 (2008): 40–59.

11. Ibid.

12. Mark W. Conley, "Cognitive Strategy Instruction for Adolescents: What We Know about the Promise, What We Don't Know about the Potential," *Harvard Educational Review* 78, no. 1 (2008): 84–106.

13. SERP Institute, "What Do We Mean by Collective Efficacy?" http://ic.serpmedia.org/key_collective.html.

14. RAND Reading Study Group, *Reading for Understanding: Toward a Research and Development Program in Reading Comprehension* (Santa Monica, CA: Office of Education Research and Improvement, 2002).

Chapter 2

1. The authors of this chapter would like to thank those who have contributed to the intellectual process: Paola Uccelli and members of the Academic Language Study Group at Harvard University.

2. Zhihui Fang and Mary J. Schleppegrell, "Disciplinary Literacies Across Content Areas: Supporting Secondary Reading Through Functional Language Analysis," *Journal of Adolescent & Adult Literacy* 53, no. 7 (2010): 587–597.

3. Ibid; Jay L. Lemke, *Talking Science: Language, Learning, and Values* (Norwood, NJ: Ablex Pub, 1990); Jay L. Lemke, "Articulating Communities: Sociocultural Perspectives on Science Education," *Journal of Research in Science Teaching* 38, no. 3 (2001): 296–316; Catherine E. Snow and Paola Uccelli, "The Challenge of Academic Language," in *Cambridge Handbook of Literacy*, ed. David R. Olson and Nancy Torrance (New York: Cambridge University Press, 2009).

4. Carol Berkencotter and Thomas N. Huckin, *Genre Knowledge in Disciplinary Communication: Cognition/Culture/Power* (Hillsdale, NJ: Lawrence Erlbaum, 1995); Charles Bazerman, *Shaping Written Knowledge: The Genre and Activity of the Experimental Article in Science* (Madison, WI: University of Wisconsin Press, 1988).

5. *Common Core State Standards for English Language Arts and Literacy in History/Social Studies, Science, and Technical Subjects.* (Washington, DC: National Governors Association Center for Best Practices and the Council of Chief State School Officers, 2010); Gina Biancarosa, and Catherine E. Snow, *Reading Next: A Vision for Action and Research in Middle and High School Literacy—A Report to Carnegie Corporation of New York* (Washington, DC: Alliance for Excellent Education, 2004); Mary J. Schleppegrell, *The Language of Schooling: A Functional Linguistics Approach* (Mahwah, NJ: Erlbaum, 2004)..

6. Jacy Ippolito, Jennifer L. Steele, and Jennifer F. Samson. "Introduction: Why Adolescent Literacy Matters Now," *Harvard Educational Review* 78, no. 1 (2008): 1–6.

7. Snow and Uccelli, "The Challenge of Academic Language"; Alison L. Bailey and Francis A. Butler, "A Conceptual Framework of Academic English Language for Broad Application to Education," in *The Language Demands of School: Putting Academic English to the Test*, ed. Alison L. Bailey (New Haven, CT: Yale University Press, 2004), 68–102). Paola Uccelli, Christopher D. Barr, Christina L. Dobbs, Emily C.Phillips Galloway, Alejandra Meneses, and Emilio Sanchez, "Cross-Disciplinary Academic Language Skills: Developmental Trends and Individual Variability During the Adolescent Years," (under review).

8. Paola Uccelli et al., "Cross-Disciplinary Academic Language Skills: Developmental Trends and Individual Variability during the Adolescent Years," under review.

9. Schleppegrell, *The Language of Schooling*.

10. Lily Wong Fillmore and Catherine E. Snow, *What Teachers Need to Know About Language* (Washington, DC: US Department of Education, Office of Educational Research and Improvement, Educational Resources Information Center, 2000); Uccelli et al., "Cross-Disciplinary Academic Language Skills."

11. Uccelli et al., "Cross-Disciplinary Academic Language Skills"; Fillmore and Catherine E. Snow, *What Teachers Need to Know About Language*.

12. Fang and Schleppegrell, "Disciplinary Literacies Across Content Areas"

13. Lemke, "Articulating Communities." Thomas S. Kuhn, *The Structure of Scientific Revolutions* (Chicago: University of Chicago Press, 1962).

14. Donna E. Alvermann and Elizabeth B. Moje, "Adolescent Literacy Instruction and the Discourse of 'Every Teacher a Teacher of Reading,'" in *Theoretical Models and Processes of Reading*, 6th edition, ed. N. Unrau, R. Ruddell, and Donna E. Alvermann (Newark, DE: International Reading Association, 2013, in press), 1072-1104; Schleppegrell, *The Language of Schooling*.

15. CCSS, "Common Core State Standards for English Language Arts & Literacy in History/Social Studies, Science, and Technical Subjects."

16. Schleppegrell, *The Language of Schooling*; Timothy Shanahan and Cynthia Shanahan, "Teaching Disciplinary Literacy to Adolescents: Rethinking Content-Area Literacy," *Harvard Educational Review* 78, no. 1 (2008): 40–59.

17. Snow and Uccelli, "The Challenge of Academic Language"; Schleppegrell, *The Language of Schooling*.

18. Ken Hyland, *Academic Discourse: English in a Global Context* (London, Continuum International Publishing Group, 2009).

19. Ivar Bråten et al., "The Role of Epistemic Beliefs in the Comprehension of Multiple Expository Texts: Towards an Integrated Model," *Educational Psychologist* 46, no. 1 (2011): 48–70; M. Anne Britt and Jean-Francois Rouet, "Research Challenges in the Use of Multiple Documents," *Information Design Journal* 19, no. 1 (2011): 62–67.

20. Sam. S. Wineburg, "Historical Problem Solving: A Study of the Cognitive Processes Used in the Evaluation of Documentary and Pictorial Evidence," *Journal of Educational Psychology* 83, no. 1 (1991): 73–87.

21. Bråten et al., "The Role of Epistemic Beliefs"; William A. Sandoval, "Conceptual and Epistemic Aspects of Students' Scientific Explanations," *Journal of the Learning Sciences* 12, no. 1 (2003): 5–51; William A. Sandoval and Brian J. Reiser, "Explanation-Driven Inquiry: Integrating Conceptual and Epistemic Scaffolds for Scientific Inquiry," *Science Education* 88, no. 3 (2004): 345–372.

22. Y. Debbie Liu and Tina A. Grotzer, "Looking Forward: Teaching the Nature of the Science of Today and Tomorrow," in *Fostering Scientific Habits of Mind: Pedagogical Knowledge and Best Practices in Science Education*, ed. I.M. Saleh and M.S. Khine (Rotterdam: Sense Publishers, 2009): 9-36; Marcia C. Linn and Nancy Butler Songer, "How Do Students Make Sense?" *Merrill Palmer Quarterly* 39, no. 1 (1993); Nancy Butler Songer and Marcia C. Linn. "How Do Children's Views of Science Influence Knowledge Integration?" *Journal of Research in Science Teaching* 28, no. 9 (1991): 761–784.

23. Susan Carey and Carol Smith, "On Understanding the Nature of Scientific Knowledge," *Educational Psychologist* 28, no. 3 (1993): 235–251; Joseph Schwab, "Education and the Structure of the Disciplines," in *Science, Curriculum, and Liberal Education*, ed. Joseph Westbury and Neil J. Wilkof (Chicago: University of Chicago Press, 1978), 229–274.

24. Alvermann and Moje, "Adolescent Literacy Instruction."

25. Elizabeth B. Moje, "Everyday Funds of Knowledge and School Discourses," in *Encyclopedia of Language and Education*, vol. 3, ed. Marilyn Martin-Jones and Anne-Maroe De Mejia (Berlin, Germany: Springer, 2008), 341–355; Schwab, "Education and the Structure of the Disciplines."

26. John D. Bransford, Ann L. Brown, and Rodney R. Cocking, *How People Learn: Mind, Brain, Experience and School: Expanded Edition* (Washington, DC: National Academy Press, Washington, 2000), 143.

27. Liu and Grotzer, "Looking Forward"; Lee S. Shulman, "Knowledge and Teaching: Foundations of the New Reform," *Harvard Educational Review* 57, no. 1 (1987): 1–22.

28. Ibid.

29. Berkencotter and Huckin, *Genre Knowledge in Disciplinary Communication.*

30. Jerome S. Bruner, "The Importance of Structure," in *The Process of Education,* ed. Jerome S. Bruner (Cambridge, MA: Harvard University Press, 1960), 16–32.

31. Schwab, Education and the Structure of the Disciplines; Shulman, Knowledge and Teaching.

32. Schwab, Education and the Structure of the Disciplines.

33. Liping Ma, *Knowing and Teaching Elementary Mathematics: Teachers' Understanding of Fundamental Mathematics in China and the United States* (Mahwah, NJ: Lawrence Erlbaum, 1999).

34. Bruner, "The Importance of Structure."

35. Richard C. Anderson, "Role of the Reader's Schema in Comprehension, Learning, and Memory," in *Learning to Read in American Schools: Basal Readers and Content Texts,* ed. Richard C. Anderson, Jean Osborn, and Robert J. Tierney (Hillsdale, NJ: Erlbaum, 1984): 243–257; Richard C. Anderson and P. David Pearson, "A Schema-Theoretic View of Basic Processes in Reading Comprehension," in *Handbook of Reading Research,* ed. P. David Pearson (New York: Longman, 1984): 255-291.

36. Martin Nystrand, Adam Gamoran, Robert Kachur, and Catherine Prendergast, *Opening Dialogue* (New York: Teachers College Press, 1997).

37. Bruner, "The Importance of Structure," 12.

38. Moje, "Everyday Funds of Knowledge."

39. Elizabeth B. Moje, "Developing Socially Just Subject-Matter Instruction: A Review of the Literature on Disciplinary Literacy," in *Review of Research in Education,* ed. Laurence Parker (Washington, DC: American Educational Research Association, 2007), 1–44.

40. Donna E. Alvermann, Stephen F. Phelps, and Victoria R. Gillis, *Content Area Reading and Literacy: Succeeding in Today's Diverse Classroom, 6th ed.* (Boston, MA: Allyn & Bacon, 2010); Donna E. Alvermann and Leslie S. Rush, "Literacy Intervention Programs at the Middle and High School Levels," in *Adolescent Literacy Research and Practice,* ed. T. L. Jetton and J. A. Dole (New York: Guilford, 2004), 210–227; Fang and Schleppegrell, "Disciplinary Literacies across Content Areas"; Moje, "Developing Socially Just Subject-Matter Instruction."

41. Marianne Perie, Wendy S. Grigg, and Patricia L. Donahue, "National Assessment of Educational Progress: The Nation's Report Card," *Reading* (2005).

42. Paola Uccelli and Emily Phillips Galloway, *Supporting Deep Reading Comprehension of Academic Texts through Text Dependent Questions: A Guide for Practitioners* (Report to the New York City Department of Education) (New York: NYC-DOE, 2012).

43. Moje and Speyer, "The Reality of Challenging Texts."

44. M. Anne Britt and Cindy Aglinskas, "Improving Students' Ability to Identify and Use Source Information," *Cognition and Instruction* 20, no. 4 (2002): 485–522; Bruce VanSledright, *In Search of America's Past: Learning to Read History in Elementary School* (New York: Teachers College Press, 2002); Ralph P. Ferretti, Charles D. MacArthur, and Cynthia M. Okolo, "Teaching for Historical Understanding in Inclusive Classrooms," *Learning Disability Quarterly* 24 (2001): 59–71.

45. Carol D. Lee and Anika Spratley, *Reading in the Disciplines: The Challenges of Adolescent Literacy* (New York: Carnegie Corporation of New York, 2010).

46. Alvermann, Phelps, and Gillis, *Content Area Reading and Literacy*; William G. Brozo and Michele L. Simpson. *Content Literacy for Today's Adolescents: Honoring Diversity and Building Competence* (Columbus, OH: Merrill Prentice Hall, 2006).

47. Moje, "Developing Socially Just Subject-Matter Instruction."

48. Snow and Uccelli, "The Challenge of Academic Language."

49. Lee and Spratley, *Reading in the Disciplines.*

50. Clark A. Chinn and Betina A. Malhotra, "Epistemologically Authentic Reasoning in Schools: A Theoretical Framework for Evaluating Inquiry Tasks," *Science Education* 86 (2002): 175–218; Richard A. Duschl, Heidi A. Schweingruber, and Andrew W. Shouse, eds., *Taking Science to School: Learning and Teaching Science in Grades K–8* (Washington, DC: National Academies Press, 2007).

51. Liu and Grotzer, "Looking Forward."

52. Ibid

53. Richard J. Paxton, "A Deafening Silence: History Textbooks and the Students Who Read Them," *Review of Educational Research* 69, no. 3 (1999): 315–339.

54. Wineburg, "Historical Problem Solving."

55. Jennifer Wiley et al., "Source Evaluation, Comprehension, and Learning in Internet Science Inquiry Tasks," *American Educational Research Journal* 46, no. 4 (2009): 1060–1106; Phillip H. Winnie, "Self-Regulated Learning Viewed from Models of Information Processing," in *Self-Regulated Learning and Academic Achievement: Theoretical Perspectives*, ed. Barry J. Zimmerman and Dale H. Schunk (Mahwah, NJ: Lawrence Erlbaum, 2001).

56. Chinn and Malhotra, "Epistemologically Authentic Reasoning in Schools"; Marc Stadtler and Rainer Bromme, "Dealing with Multiple Documents on the WWW: The Role of Meta-Cognition in the Formation of Documents Models," *International Journal of Computer-Supported Collaborative Learning* 2 (2007): 191–210; Anat Yarden, Gilat Brill, and Hedda Falk, "Primary Literature as a Basis for a High-School Biology Curriculum," *Journal of Biological Education* 35, no. 4 (2001): 190–195.

57. Fang and Schleppegrell, "Disciplinary Literacies Across Content Areas."

58. Schleppegrell, *The Language of Schooling.*

59. Lemke, *Talking Science*, 129–130.

60. Elizabeth B. Moje and Jennifer Speyer, "The Reality of Challenging Texts in High School Science and Social Studies: How Teachers Can Mediate Comprehension," in *Best Practices in Adolescent Literacy Instruction*, ed. K. Hinchman and H. Sheridan-Thomas (New York: The Guilford Press, 2008), 185–211.

61. Britt and Aglinskas, "Improving Students' Ability to Identify Information"; Wineburg, "Historical Problem Solving"; Sam. S. Wineburg, "Reading Abraham Lincoln: An Expert-Expert Study in the Interpretation of Historical Texts," *Cognitive Science* 22, no. 3 (1998): 319–346.

62. Schleppegrell, *The Language of Schooling.*

63. Wineburg, "Historical Problem Solving."

64. Schleppegrell, *The Language of Schooling.*

65. Michael A. K. Halliday and Christian Matthiessen, *An Introduction to Functional Grammar* (New York, Oxford University Press, 2004).

66. Schleppegrell, *The Language of Schooling.*

67. Renee Schwartz and Norman Lederman, "What Scientists Say: Scientists' Views of Nature of Science and Relation to Science Context," *International Journal of Science Education* 30, no. 6 (2008): 727–771.

68. Schleppegrell, *The Language of Schooling.*

69. Halliday and Matthiessen, *An Introduction to Functional Grammar.*

70. Ibid.

71. Allen F. Repko, ed., *Interdisciplinary Research: Process and Theory* (Thousand Oaks, CA: Sage Publications, Incorporated, 2008).

72. Robert Scholes, *Textual Power: Literary Theory and the Teaching of English* (New Haven, CT: Yale University Press, 1986).

73. Repko, ed., *Interdisciplinary Research*, 77.

74. Schleppegrell, *The Language of Schooling*.

75. Scholes, *Textual Power*.

76. Dan Bialostosky, "What Should College English Be? Should College English Be Close Reading?" *College English* 69, no. 2 (2006): 111–116.

77. Robert E. Probst, *Response and Analysis: Teaching Literature in Secondary School* (Heinemann Educational Books, 2004), 320.

78. Mary Lee Barton and Clare Heidema, *Teaching Reading in Mathematics* (Aurora, CO: McREL [Mid-continent Research for Education and Learning], 2002).

79. Ibid.

80. Joshua Fahey Lawrence, "English Vocabulary Learning Trajectories of Students Whose Parents Speak a Language Other Than English: Steep Learning and Deep Summer Setback," *Reading & Writing: An Interdisciplinary Journal*, in press; Lawrence, "Summer Reading: Predicting Adolescent Word Learning from Aptitude, Time Spent Reading, and Text Type," *Reading Psychology* 30, no. 5 (2009): 445–465, doi: 10.1080/02702710802412008; Elizabeth B. Moje, Melanie Overby, Nicole Tysvaer, and Karen Morris, "The Complex World of Adolescent Literacy: Myths, Motivations, and Mysteries," *Harvard Educational Review* 78, no. 1 (2008): 107–154.

81. Elizabeth B. Moje et al., *Carnegie Content Area Student Literacy Survey* (Washington, DC: Strategic Education Research Partnership, 2011).

82. Nell K. Duke, "The Case for Informational Text," *Educational Leadership* 61, no. 6 (2004): 40–45.

83. Jacy Ippolito, Jennifer L. Steele, and Jennifer F. Samson, "Introduction: Why Sdolescent Literacy Matters Now," *Harvard Educational Review* 78, no. 1 (2008); Perie, Grigg, and Donahue, "National Assessment of Educational Progress."

84. Halliday and Matthiessen, *An Introduction to Functional Grammar*; Lemke, *Talking Science*.

85. Gordon Wells, "The Centrality of Talk in Education" in *Thinking voices: The Work of the National Oracy Project*, ed. Kate Norman (London: Hodder & Stoughton for the National Curriculum Council, 1992), 283–310.

86. Ian A.G. Wilkinson and Eun Hye Son, "16: A Dialogic Turn in Research on Learning and Teaching to Comprehend." *Handbook of Reading Research* 4 (2010): 359–387.

87. Moje and Speyer, "The Reality of Challenging Texts."

88. Alvermann and Moje, "Adolescent Literacy Instruction."

Chapter 3

1. Doug Buehl, *Developing Readers in the Academic Disciplines* (Newark, DE: International Reading Association, 2011).

2. Ruth Schoenbach, *Reading for Understanding: A Guide to Improving Reading in Middle and High School Classrooms* (San Francisco: Jossey-Bass Publishers, 1999).

3. See support website www.adlitpd.org/book.

4. Timothy Shanahan and Cynthia Shanahan, "Teaching Disciplinary Literacy to Adolescents: Rethinking Content-Area Literacy," *Harvard Educational Review* 78, no. 1 (2008).

5. See support website www.adlitpd.org/book.

6. See ibid.

7. Buehl, *Developing Readers in the Academic Disciplines*, 268.

8. Gay S. Pinnell and Irene Fountas, *The Continuum of Literacy Learning: A Guide to Teaching, K–8* (Portsmouth, NH: Heinemann, 2010).

9. Elizabeth B. Moje, "Foregrounding the Disciplines in Secondary Literacy Teaching and Learning: A Call for Change," *Journal of Adolescent and Adult Literacy* 52, no. 2 (2008): 96–107.

Chapter 4

1. Isabel L.Beck, Margaret G. McKeown, and Linda Kucan, *Bringing Words to Life: Robust Vocabulary Instruction* (New York: Guilford, 2002).

2. Martin A.Conway, Gillian Cohen, and Nicola Stanhope, "On the Very Long-Term Retention of Knowledge Acquired through Formal Education: Twelve Years of Cognitive Psychology," *Journal of Experimental Psychology* 120, no. 4 (1991): 395–409.

3. Serafima Gettys, Lorens Imhof, and Joseph D. Kautz, "Computer-Assisted Reading: The Effect of Glossing Format on Comprehension and Vocabulary Retention," *Foreign Language Annals* 34, no. 2 (2001): 91–99; T. Sima Paribakht and Marjorie Wesche, "Vocabulary Enhancement Activities and Reading for Meaning in Second Langauge Vocabulary Acquisition," in *Second Language Vocabulary Acquisition: A Rationale for Pedagogy*, ed. James Coady and Thomas Huckin (New York: Cambridge University Press, 1997).

4. William E. Nagy, Georgia Earnest García, Aydin Y. Durgunoglu, and Barbara Hancin-Bhatt, "Spanish-English Bilingual Students' Use of Cognates in English Reading," *Journal of Reading Behavior* 25, no. 3 (1993): 241–259.

5. Iñigo Yanguas, "Multimedia Glosses and Their Effect on L2 Text Comprehension and Vocabulary Learning," *Language Learning and Technology* 13, no. 2 (2009): 49-67.

6. Isabel L.Beck, Charles A. Perfetti, and Margaret G. McKeown, "Effects of Long-Term Vocabulary Instruction on Lexical Access and Reading Comprehension," *Journal of Educational Psychology* 74, no. 4 (1982): 506–521; Joseph R. Jenkins, Marcy L. Stein, and Katherine Wysocki, "Learning Vocabulary Through Reading," *American Educational Research Journal* 21, no. 4 (1984): 767–787; Margaret C. McKeown et al., Isabel L. Beck, Richard C. Omanson, and Martha T. Pople, "Some Effects of the Nature and Frequency of Vocabulary Instruction on the Knowledge and Use of Words," *Reading Research Quarterly* 20, no. 5 (1985): 522–535.

7. M. S. L. Swanborn and K. de Glopper, "Incidental Word Learning While Reading: A Meta-Analysis," *Review of Educational Research* 69, no. 3 (1999): 261–285.

8. Donald J. Bolger, Michal Balass, Eve Landen, and Charles A. Perfetti, "Context Variation and Definitions in Learning the Meanings of Words: An Instance-Based Learning Approach," *Discourse Processes* 45, no. 2 (2008): 122–159.

9. Dee Gardner, "Children's Immediate Understanding of Vocabulary: Contexts and Dictionary Definitions," *Reading Psychology* 28, no. 4 (2007): 331–373.

10. Bolger et al., "Context Variation and Definitions in Learning the Meanings of Words."

11. Gardner, "Children's Immediate Understanding of Vocabulary."

12. Judith A.Scott and William E. Nagy, "Understanding the Definitions of Unfamiliar Verbs," *Reading Research Quarterly* 32, no. 2 (1997): 184–200.

13. Barbara Heyns, *Summer Learning and the Effects of Schooling* (New York: Academic Press, 1978).

14. Joshua Lawrence, "English Vocabulary Learning Trajectories of Students Whose Parents Speak a Language Other Than English: Steep Learning and Deep Summer Setback," *Reading & Writing: An Interdisciplinary Journal* 25, no. 5 (2011): 1113–1141.

15. Joshua Lawrence et al., "Content-Area Notebook Writing: Supports and Demands Across Purpose, Genre and Discipline," *Journal of Adolescent and Adult Literacy*, in press.

16. Pseudonyms have been used to protect students' and teachers' privacy.

17. Catherine E. Snow, Joshua Lawrence, and Claire White, "Generating Knowledge of Academic Language Among Urban Middle School Students," *Journal of Research on Educational Effectiveness* 2, no. 4 (2009): 325–344

18. Joshua Lawrence et al., "Language Proficiency, Home-Language Status, and English Vocabulary Development: A Longitudinal Follow-Up of the Word Generation Program," *Bilingualism: Language and Cognition* 15, no. 3 (2012): 437–451.

Chapter 5

1. Richard C. Anderson and William E. Nagy, "The Vocabulary Conundrum," *American Educator* 16, no. 4 (1992): 14–18, 44–47.

2. Michael F. Graves and Susan Watts-Taffe, "For the Love of Words: Fostering Word Consciousness in Young Readers," *The Reading Teacher* 62, no. 3 (2008): 185–193; Holly B. Lane and Stephanie Arriaza Allen, "The Vocabulary-Rich Classroom: Modeling Sophisticated Word Use to Promote Word Consciousness and Vocabulary Growth," *The Reading Teacher* 63, no. 5 (2010): 362–370.

3. Perla B. Gámez and Nonie K. Lesaux, "The Relation between Exposure to Sophisticated and Complex Language and Early Adolescent English-Only and Language Minority Learners' Vocabulary," *Child Development* 83, no. 4 (2012): 1316–1331.

4. A. E. Cunningham and Ryan O'Donnell, "Reading and Vocabulary Growth," in *Vocabulary Instruction: Research to Practice,* 2nd edition, ed. James F Baumann and Edward J. Kame'enui (New York: Guilford, 2012), 256–279.

5. Michael F. Graves and Susan Watts-Taffe, "The Place of Word Consciousness in a Research-Based Vocabulary Program," in *What Research Has to Say about Reading Instruction, 3rd ed,* ed. A. E. Farstrup and S. J. Samuels (Newark, DE: International Reading Association, 2002), 140–165.

6. Wiley Blevins, *Teaching Phonics and Word Study in the Intermediate Grades: A Complete Source Book* (New York: Scholastic, 2001).

7. Michel J. Kieffer and Nonie Lesaux, "Breaking Down Words to Build Meaning: Morphology, Vocabulary, and Reading Comprehension in the Urban Classroom," *The Reading Teacher* 61, no. 2 (2007: 134-144.

8. Edgar Dale and Joseph O'Rourke, *Vocabulary Building* (Columbus, OH: Zaner-Bloser, 1986).

9. Steven A. Stahl and William E. Nagy, *Teaching Word Meanings* (Mahwah, NJ: Lawrence Erlbaum, 2006).

10. Kevin Flanigan and Scott C. Greenwood, "Effective Content Vocabulary Instruction in the Middle: Matching Students, Purposes, Words, and Strategies," *Journal of Adolescent and Adult Literacy* 51, no. 3 (2007): 228–238.

Chapter 6

1. See, for example, Judith A. Langer, "Beating the Odds: Teaching Middle and High School Students to Read and Write Well," *American Educational Research Journal* 38, no. 4 (2001): 837–880.

2. See, for example, Arthur Applebee, Judith A. Langer, Martin Nystrand, and Adam Gamoran, "Discussion-Based Approaches to Developing Understanding: Classroom Instruction and Student Performance in Middle and High School English," *American Educational Research Journal* 40, no. 3 (2003): 685–730; P. Karen Murphy et al., "Examining the Effects of Classroom Discussion on Students' Comprehension of Text: A Meta-Analysis," *Journal of Educational Psychology* 101, no. 3 (2009): 740–764.

3. Arthur Applebee, *Curriculum as Conversation: Transforming Traditions of Teaching and Learning* (University of Chicago Press, 1996); Martin Nystrand et al., *Opening Dialogue: Understanding the Dynamics of Language and Learning in the English Classroom* (New York: Teachers College Press, 1997).

4. Martin Nystrand and Adam Gamoran, "Instructional Discourse, Student Engagement, and Literature Achievement," *Research in the Teaching of English* 25, no. 3 (1991): 261–290; Nystrand et al., *Opening Dialogue.*

5. Clark A. Chinn, Richard C. Anderson, and Martha A. Waggoner, "Patterns of Discourse in Two Kinds of Literature Discussion," *Reading Research Quarterly* 36, no. 4 (2001): 378–411.

6. James T. Dillon, *Using Discussion in Classrooms* (Buckingham, UK: Open University Press, 1994), 13.

7. Courtney B. Cazden, *Classroom Discourse: The Language of Teaching and Learning.* (Portsmouth, NH: Heinemann Educational Books, Inc, 1998); Hugh Mehan, *Learning Lessons: Social Organization in the Classroom* (Cambridge, MA: Harvard University Press, 1979).

8. Noreen M. Webb, "Task-Related Verbal Interaction and Mathematics Learning in Small Groups," *Journal for Research in Mathematics Education* 22, no. 5 (1991): 366–389; Rupert Wegerif, "A Dialogic Understanding of the Relationship between CSCL and Teaching Thinking Skills," *International Journal of Computer-Supported Collaborative Learning* 1, no. 1 (2006): 143–157.

9. David K. Dickinson and Palton O. Tabors, eds., *Beginning Literacy with Language: Young Children Learning at Home and School* (Baltimore: Paul H. Brookes Publishing Co, 2001); Catherine E. Snow, M. Susan Burns, and Peg Griffin, *Preventing Reading Difficulties in Young Children* (Washington, DC: National Academy Press, 1998).

10. William E. Nagy and Judith A. Scott, "Vocabulary Processes," in *Theoretical Models and Processes of Reading*, 5th ed, ed. Robert B. Ruddell and Norman J. Unrau (Newark, DE: International Reading Association, 2004), 269–284; Mary J. Schleppegrell, "The Challenges of Academic Language in School Subjects," in *Spraket och kunskapen: att lara pa sitt andrasprak i skola och hogskola*, ed. Inger Lindberg and Karin Sandwall (Sweden: Goteborgs Universitet, 2006), 47–69; for a detailed look at the characteristics of secondary texts in all four content areas, we recommend reading: Z. Fang and M. Schleppegrell, *Reading in the Secondary Content Areas: A Language-Based Pedagogy* (Ann Arbor, MI: University of Michigan Press, 2008).

11. Patricia A. Alexander and Tamara L. Jetton, "Learning from Text: A Multidimensional and Developmental Perspective," in *Handbook of Reading Research*, vol. III, ed. Michael L. Kamil, Peter B. Mosenthal, P. David Pearson, and Rebecca Barr (Mahwah, NJ: Erlbaum, 2000), 285–310.

12. Joshua Lawrence and Catherine E. Snow, "Oral Discourse and Reading," in *Handbook of Reading Research*, vol. IV, ed. Michael L. Kamil, P. David Pearson, Elizabeth Birr Moje, and Peter Afflerback (New York: Routledge, 2010), 320–337.

13. Ibid.

14. Urie Bronfenbrenner and Pamela A. Morris, "The Ecology of Developmental Processes," in *The Handbook of Child Psychology: Theoretical Models of Human Development*, 5th ed. (New York: John Wiley & Sons, Inc, 1998), 993–1028.

15. Martin Nystrand, "Research on the Role of Classroom Discourse as it Affects Reading Comprehension," *Research in the Teaching of English* 40, no. 4 (2006): 392–412.

16. Chinn, Anderson, and Waggoner, "Patterns of Discourse."

17. Murphy et al., "Examining the Effects of Classroom Discussion."

18. Anna O. Soter et al., "What the Discourse Tells Us: Talk and Indicators of High-Level Comprehension," *International Journal of Educational Research* 47, no. 6 (2008): 372–391.

19. Applebee et al., "Discussion-Based Approaches"; Katherine L. McNeill and Diane Silva Pimentel, "Scientific Discourse in Three Urban Classrooms: The Role of the Teacher in Engaging High School Students in Argumentation," *Science Education* 94, no. 2 (2009): 203–229; Gordon E. Samson, Bernadette Strykowski, Thomas Weinstein, and Herbert J. Walberg, "The Effects of Teacher Questioning Levels on Student Achievement: A Quantitative Synthesis," *Journal of Educational Research* 80, no. 5 (1987): 290-295.

20. Applebee et al., "Discussion-Based Approaches"; Martin Nystrand et al., "Questions in Time: Investigating the Structure and Dynamics of Unfolding Classroom Discourse," *Discourse Processes* 35, no. 2 (2003): 135–198.

21. Christine Chin, "Teacher Questioning in Science Classrooms: Approaches that Stimulate Productive Thinking," *Journal of Research in Science Teaching* 44, no. 6 (2007): 815–843; McNeill and Pimentel, "Scientific Discourse in Three Urban Classrooms"; Mikyung J. Wolf, Amy C. Crosson, and Lauren B. Resnick, "Classroom Talk for Rigorous Reading Comprehension Instruction," *Reading Psychology* 26, no. 1 (2005): 27–53; Emily van Zee and Jim Minstrell, "Using Questioning to Guide Student Thinking," *Journal of the Learning Sciences* 6, no. 2 (1997): 227—269.

22. Wolf, Crosson, and Resnick, "Classroom Talk."

23. Nystrand and Gamoran, "Instructional Discourse"; Nystrand et al., *Opening Dialogue.*

24. Julie Nelson Christoph and Martin Nystrand, "Taking Risks, Negotiating Relationships: One Teacher's Transition toward a Dialogic Classroom," *Research in the Teaching of English* 36, no. 2 (2001): 249–286.

25. Chin, "Teacher Questioning in Science Classrooms"; van Zee and Minstrell, "Using Questioning."

26. Christine Chin and Jonathon Osborne, "Supporting Argumentation through Students' Questions: Case Studies in Science Classrooms," *Journal of the Learning Sciences* 19, no. 2 (2010): 230–284.

27. Hossein Nassaji and Gordon Wells, "What's the Use of Triadic Dialogue? An Investigation of Student-Teacher Interaction," *Applied Linguistics* 21, no. 3 (2000): 376–406.

28. Ibid.

29. Mary Catherine O'Connor and Sarah Michaels, "Aligning Academic Task and Participation Status Through Revoicing: Analysis of a Classroom Discourse Strategy," *Anthropology and Education Quarterly* 24, no. 4 (1993): 318–335.

30. Tina Sharpe, "How Can Teacher Talk Support Learning?" *Linguistics and Education* 19, no. 2 (2008): 132–148.

31. Dot McElhone, "Tell Us More: Reading Comprehension, Engagement, and Conceptual Press Discourse," *Reading Psychology* 33, no. 6 (2012): 525–561.

32. Applebee et al., "Discussion-Based Approaches"; Nystrand et al., *Opening Dialogue.*

33. Salika A. Lawrence, Roasanne Rabinowitz, and Heather Pern, "Reading Instruction in Secondary English Language Arts Classrooms," *Literacy Research and Instruction* 48, no. 1 (2008): 39–64.

34. Patricia L. Donahue, Kristin E. Voelkl, Jay R. Campbell, and John Mazzeo, *NAEP 1998 Reading Report Card for the Nation and the States (NCES 1999-500)* (Washington, DC: National Center for Educational Statistics, Office of Educational Research and Improvement, U.S. Department of Education, 1999).

35. Donna E. Alvermann et al., "Middle and High School Students' Perceptions of How They Experience Text-Based Discussions: A Multicase Study," *Reading Research Quarterly* 31, no. 3 (1996): 244–267.

36. Murphy et al., "Examining the Effects of Classroom Discussion."

37. Erin Marie Furtak, Tina Seidel, Heidi Iverson and Derek C. Briggs, "Experimental and Quasi-Experimental Studies of Inquiry-Based Science Teaching: A Meta-Analysis," *Review of Educational Research* 82, no. 3 (2012): 300–329..

38. Joshua Lawrence et al., "Word Generation Randomized Trial: Discussion Mediates the Impact of Program Treatment on Academic Word Learning" (under review); Webb, "Task-Related Verbal Interaction and Mathematics Learning."

39. The research reported here was funded by a grant from the Institute of Education Sciences, U.S. Department of Education, to the University of Maryland (No. R305A090152; Silverman (PI), Proctor (co-PI), and Harring (co-PI). The opinions expressed are those of the authors and do not represent views of the Institute or the U.S. Department of Education.

40. See Strategic Education Research Partnership (SERP), "Word Generation: A Middle School Academic Language Program," http://www.serpinstitute.org.

41. Laura Billings and Jill Fitzgerald, "Dialogic Discussion and the Paideia Seminar," *American Educational Research Journal* 39, no. 4 (2002): 907-941; Christoph and Nystrand, "Taking Risks, Negotiating Relationships."

42. Tracy Elizabeth et al., "Academic Discussions: An Analysis of Instructional Discourse and an Argument for an Integrative Assessment Framework," *American Educational Research Journal* 49, no. 6 (2012): 1214–1250, doi: 10.3102/0002831212456066.

43. Annemarie Sullivan Palincsar and Ann L. Brown, "Reciprocal Reaching of Comprehension-Fostering and Comprehension-Monitoring Activities," *Cognition and Instruction* 1, no. 2 (1984): 117–175; Annemarie Sullivan Palincsar, "Collaborative Approaches to Comprehension Instruction," in *Rethinking Reading Comprehension*, ed. Anne Polselli Sweet and Catherine E. Snow (New York: The Guilford Press, 2003), 99–114.

44. Isabel L. Beck et al., "Questioning the Author: A Yearlong Classroom Implementation to Engage Students with Text," *Elementary School Journal* 96, no. 4 (1996): 385–414; Cheryl Sandora, Isabel Beck, and Margaret McKeown, "A Comparison of Two Discussion Strategies on Students' Comprehension and Interpretation of Complex Literature," *Journal of Reading Psychology* 20 (1999): 177–212.

45. William M. Saunders and Claude Goldenberg, "Effects of Instructional Conversations and Literature Logs on Limited- and Fluent-English-Proficient Students' Story Comprehension and Thematic Understanding," *Elementary School Journal* 99, no. 4 (1999): 277–301.

46. Chinn, Anderson, and Waggoner, "Patterns of Discourse"; Alina Reznitskaya et al., "Influence of Oral Discussion on Written Argumentation," *Discourse Processes* 32, no. 2–3 (2001): 155–175.

47. John T. Guthrie, Emily Anderson, Solomon Alao, and Jennifer Rinehart, "Influences of Concept Oriented Reading Instruction on Strategy Use and Conceptual Learning from Text," *Elementary School Journal* 99, no. 4 (1999): 343–366; John T. Guthrie, Allan Wigfield, and Clare VonSecker, "Effects of Integrated Instruction on Motivation and Strategy Use in Reading," *Journal of Educational Psychology* 92, no. 2 (2000): 331–341.

48. Billings and Fitzgerald, "Dialogic Discussion."

49. Catherine E. Snow, Joshua Lawrence, and Claire White, "Generating Knowledge of Academic Language Among Urban Middle School Students," *Journal of Research on Educational Effectiveness* 2, no. 4 (2009): 325–344.

50. Joshua Lawrence et al., "Word Generation Randomized Trial."

51. Russell Gersten, Lynn S. Fuchs, Joanna P. Williams, and Scott Baker, , "Teaching Reading Comprehension Strategies to Students with Learning Disabilities: A Review of Research," *Review of Educational Research* 71, no. 2 (2001): 279–320.

52. Maureen P. Boyd and Don Rubin, "How Contingent Questioning Promotes Extended Student Talk: A Function of Display Questions," *Journal of Literacy Research* 38, no. 2 (2006): 141–169.

53. Esther Geva, "Second-Language Oral Proficiency and Second-Language Literacy," in *Developing Literacy in Second-Language Learners: Report of the National Literacy Panel on Language-Minority Children and Youth*, ed. Diane August and Timothy Shanahan (Mahwah, NJ: Lawrence Erlbaum Associates, 2006), 123–139.

54. Esther Geva and Fred Genesee, "First-Language Oral Proficiency and Second-Language Literacy," in *Developing Literacy in Second-Language Learners* (see note 52), 185–195.

Chapter 7

1. *Common Core State Standards for English Language Arts and Literacy in History/Social Studies, Science, and Technical Subjects* (Washington, DC: National Governors Association Center for Best Practices and the Council of Chief State School Officers, 2010).

2. Grant Wiggins and Jay McTighe, *Understanding by Design* (Alexandria, VA: ASCD, 2005).

Chapter 8

1. Plato, "Phaedrus," in *Complete Works*, ed. John M. Cooper and D. S. Hutchinson (Indianapolis. IN: Hacket, 1997), 552.

2. Joshua Lawrence, "Summer Reading: Predicting Adolescent Word Learning from Aptitude, Time Spent Reading, and Text Type," *Reading Psychology* 30, no. 5 (2009): 445–465, doi: 10.1080/02702710802412008.

3. P. Lee Reynolds and Sonya Symons, "Motivational Variables and Children's Text Search," *Journal of Educational Psychology* 93, no. 1 (2001): 14-23.

4. Randall McClure, "Googlepedia: Turning Information Behaviors into Research Skills," in *Writing Spaces: Readings on Writing*, vol. 2, ed. C. Lowe and P. Zemliansky (Anderson, SC: Parlor Press, 2011), http://wac.colostate.edu/books/writingspaces2/mcclure--googlepedia.pdf.

5. Raymond H. Clines and Elizabeth R. Cobb, *Research Writing Simplified: A Documentation Guide*, 6th ed. (New York: Pearson, 2010).

6. Shenglan Zhang, Nell K. Duke, and Laura M. Jiménez, "The WWWDOT Approach to Improving Students' Critical Evaluation of Websites," *The Reading Teacher* 65, no. 2 (2011): 150–158; Shenglan Zhang and Nell K. Duke, "Strategies for Internet Reading with Different Reading Purposes: A Descriptive Study of Twelve Good Internet Readers," *Journal of Literacy Research* 40, no. 1 (2008): 128–162.

7. Mark Warschauer, "Information Literacy in the Laptop Classroom," *Teachers College Record* 109, no. 11 (2007): 2511–2540.

8. Jim Cummins, Kristin Brown, and Dennis Sayers, *Literacy, Technology, and Diversity: Teaching for Success in Changing Times* (Boston: Pearson Allyn and Bacon, 2007).

9. Mark Warschauer, *Laptops and Literacy: Learning in the Wireless Classroom* (New York: Teachers College Press, 2006).

10. Cliff E. Konold, Robert Coulter, and Alan Feldman, "Engaging Students with Data," *Learning & Leading with Technology* 28, no. 3 (2000): 50–55.

11. P. Davis Pearson and Margaret C. Gallagher, "The Instruction of Reading Comprehension," *Contemporary Educational Psychology* 8, no. 3 (1983): 317–344.

12. Warschauer, *Learning in the Wireless Classroom*, 119.

13. Ibid.

14. Warschauer, *Learning in the Wireless Classroom*; Mark Warschauer, *Learning in the Cloud: How (and Why) to Transform Schools with Digital Media* (New York: Teachers College Press, 2011).

15. Pearson and Gallagher, "Instruction of Reading Comprehension."

16. Reynolds and Symons, "Motivational Variables."

17. John T.Guthrie et al., "Increasing Reading Comprehension and Engagement through Concept-Oriented Reading Instruction," *Journal of Educational Psychology* 96, no. 3 (2004): 403–423.

18. Mark Warschauer, Youngmin Park, and Randall Walker, "Transforming Digital Reading with Visual-Syntactic Text Formatting," *JALT CALL Journal* 7, no. 3 (2011): 255–270.

19. Warschauer, *Learning in the Wireless Classroom*; Warschauer, *Learning in the Cloud*.

20. Warschauer, *Learning in the Wireless Classroom*.

21. Rafael A. Calvo et al., "Collaborative Writing Support Tools on the Cloud," *Transactions on Learning Technologies* 4, no. 1 (2011): 88–97.

22. Lisa Ede andAndrea Lunsford, *Singular Texts/Plural Authors: Perspectives on Collaborative Writing* (Carbondale, IL: Southern Illinois University Press, 1992).

23. Neomy Storch, "Collaborative Writing: Product, Process, and Students' Reflections," *Journal of Second Language Writing* 14, no. 3 (2005): 153–173.

24. Folkert Kuiken and Ineke Vedder, "Collaborative Writing in L2: The effect of group interaction on text quality," in *New Directions for Research in L2 Writing*, vol. 11, ed. S. Ransdell and M.-L. Barbier (Dordrecht, Netherlands: Springer, 2002), 169–188.

25. Lorraine Higgins, Linda Flower, Joseph Petraglia, "Planning Text Together: The Role of Critical Reflection in Student Collaboration," *Written Communication* 9, no. 1 (1992): 48–84.

26. Joan K. Gallini and Neal Helman, "Audience Awareness in Technology-Mediated Environments," *Journal of Educational Computing Research* 13 (1995): 245–261.

27. Merrill Swain, "Three Functions of Output in Second Language Learning," in *Principle and Practice in Applied Linguistics: Studies in Honor of H. G. Widdowson*, ed. G. Cook and B. Seidlhofer (Oxford: Oxford University Press, 1995), 125–144.

28. Calvo et al., "Collaborative Writing."

29. Amie Goldberg, Michael Russell, M., Abigail Cook, "The Effects Of Computers On Student Writing: A Meta-Analysis Of Studies From 1992 To 2002," *Journal of Technology, Learning, and Assessment* 2, no.1 (2003).

30. Will Richardson, *Blogs, Wikis, Podcasts, and Other Powerful Web Tools for Classrooms*, 3rd ed. (Thousand Oaks, CA: Corwin Press, 2010).

31. Mark Warschauer and Paige Ware, "Automated Writing Evaluation: Defining the Classroom Research Agenda," *Language Teaching Research* (2006): 157–180.

32. Douglas Grimes and Mark Warschauer, "Utility in a Fallible Tool: A Multi-Site Case Study of Automated Writing Evaluation," *Journal of Technology, Language, and Assessment* 8, no. 6 (2010): 1–43.

33. Arthur Applebee, "A Study of Writing in the Secondary School," Final Report, NIE-G-79-0174 (Urbana, IL: National Council of Teachers of English, 1981); James Britton et al., *The Development of Writing Abilities (11–18)* (Basingstoke, UK: Macmillan Education, Ltd, 1975).

34. David Huffaker, "The Educated Blogger: Using Weblogs to Promote Literacy in the Classroom," *Association for the Advancement of Computing in Education Journal* 9, no. 6 (2004): 91–98; Kathleen C. West, "Weblogs and Literary Response: Socially Situated Identities and Hybrid Social Languages in English Class Blogs," *Journal of Adolescent & Adult Literacy* 51, no. 7 (2008): 588–598; Shelbie Witte, "'That's Online Writing, Not Boring School Writing': Writing with Blogs and the Talkback Project," *Journal of Adolescent & Adult Literacy* 51, no. 2 (2007): 92–96; Sigrun Biesenbach-Lucas and Donald Weasenforth, "E-mail and Word Processing in the ESL Classroom: How the Medium Affects the Message," *Language, Learning & Technology* 5, no.1 (2001): 135–165; Jennifer M. Heisler and Scott L. Crabill, "Who Are 'stinkybug' and 'Packerfan4'? Email Pseudonyms and Participants' Perceptions of Demography, Productivity, and Personality," *Journal of Computer-Mediated Communication* 12, no. 1 (2006): 114–135; Kevin Fahey, Joshua Lawrence, and Jeanne R. Paratore, "Using Electronic Portfolios to Make Learning Public," *Journal of Adolescent & Adult Literacy* 50, no. 6 (2007): 460–471.

35. Mark Warschauer and Douglas Grimes, "Audience, Authorship, and Artifact: The Emergent Semiotics of Web 2.0," *Annual Review of Applied Linguistics* 27 (2007): 1–23, doi: 10.1017/S0267190508070013.

36. Murat Gunel, Brian Hand, and Mark Andrew McDermott, "Writing for Different Audiences: Effects on High-School Students' Conceptual Understanding of Biology," *Learning and Instruction* 19, no. 4 (2009): 354–367.

37. Gert Rijlaarsdam et al., "Writing Experiment Manuals in Science Education: The Impact of Writing, Genre, and Audience," *International Journal of Science Education* 28, no. 2 (2006): 230–234; Ekaterina Midgette, Priti Haria, and Charles MacArthur, "The Effects of Content and

Audience Awareness Goals for Revision on the Persuasive Essays of Fifth- and Eighth-Grade Students," *Reading and Writing* 21, no. 1 (2008): 131–151.

38. Robert Nye and Alan E. Cober, *Beowulf; A New Telling* (New York: Hill and Wang, 1968).

39. Warschauer, *Learning in the Wireless Classroom* , 62.

40. Warschauer, "Information Literacy"; Mark Warschauer, Michele Knobel, and Leeann Stone, "Technology and Equity in Schooling: Deconstructing the Digital Divide," *Educational Policy* 18, no. 4 (2004): 562–588, doi: 10.1177/0895904804266469.

Chapter 9

1. David T. Hansen, *The Teacher and the World* (New York: Routledge, 2011).

2. Ibid.

3. Ibid.

4. Mizuko Ito et al., *Living and Learning with New Media* (Cambridge, MA: MIT Press, 2007).

5. Ibid.

6. All district content/guidance section citations are from Massachusetts Department of Elementary and Secondary Education, *Massachusetts Framework for English Language Arts and Literacy* (Malden, MA: Massachusetts Department of Elementary and Secondary Education, 2011).

7. Grant P. Wiggins and Jay McTighe, *Understanding by Design* (Alexandria, VA: ASCD, 2005).

8. Liz Robbins, "A Home for Sketchbooks of the World," *New York Times,* May 10, 2012, http://www.nytimes.com/2012/05/13/nyregion/at-the-brooklyn-art-library-a-home-for-personal-sketchbooks.html_r=0.

9. Hansen, *The Teacher and the World*, 9.

10. Laura Harrington, *Alice Bliss* (New York: Penguin Group, 2011), 163.

11. Timothy Shanahan and Cynthia Shanahan, "Teaching Disciplinary Literacy to Adolescents: Rethinking Content-Area Literacy," *Harvard Educational Review* 78, no. 1 (2008): 40–59.

12. Laura Harrington, *Alice Bliss* (New York: Penguin Group, 2011), 163.

13. Hansen, *The Teacher and the World*.

14. Jennifer M. Bogard and Mary C. McMackin, "Combining Traditional Literacies and New Literacies in a 21st-Century Writing Workshop," *The Reading Teacher* 65, no. 5 (2012): 313–323.

Chapter 10

1. *Common Core State Standards for English Language Arts and Literacy in History/Social Studies, Science, and Technical Subjects* (Washington, DC: National Governors Association Center for Best Practices and the Council of Chief State School Officers, 2010).

2. Samuel S. Wineburg, "On the Reading of Historical Texts: Notes on the Breach Between School and Academy," *American Educational Research Journal* 28, no. 3 (1991): 495–519.

3. Baruch Schwarz, "Collective Reading of Multiple Texts in Argumentative Activities," *International Journal of Educational Research* 39, no. 1–2 (2003): 133–151; Steven A. Stahl, et al., "What Happens When Students Read Multiple Source Documents in History?" *Reading Research Quarterly* 31, no. 4 (1996): 430–457; Charles A. Perfetti et al., "How Students Use Texts to Learn and Reason about Historical Uncertainty," in *Cognitive and Instructional Processes in History and the Social Sciences,* ed. Mario Carretero and James F. Voss (Hillsdale, NJ: Lawrence Erlbaum Associates, 1994), 257–283.

4. Charles Bazerman, "Physicists Reading Physics: Schema-Laden Purposes and Purpose Laden Schema," *Written Communication* 2, no. 1 (1985): 3–23; Timothy Shanahan and Cynthia Shanahan, "Teaching Disciplinary Literacy to Adolescents: Rethinking Content-Area Literacy," *Harvard Educational Review* 78, no. 1 (2008): 40–59.

5. Shanahan and Shanahan, "Teaching Disciplinary Literacy to Adolescents."

6. Mary Anne Britt and Cindy Aglinskas, "Improving Students' Ability to Identify and Use Source Information," *Cognition and Instruction* 20, no. 4 (2002): 485–522; Jeffrey D. Nokes, Janice A. Dole, and Douglas J. Hacker, "Teaching High School Students to Use Heuristics while Reading Historical Texts," *Journal of Educational Psychology* 99, no. 30 (2007): 492–504; Steven A. Stahl, et al., "When Students Read Multiple Source Documents"; Jennifer Wiley and James F. Voss, "Constructing Arguments from Multiple Sources: Tasks That Promote Understanding and Not Just Memory for Text," *Journal of Educational Psychology* 91, no. 2 (1999): 301–331; Michael B. W. Wolfe and Susan R. Goldman, "Relations Between Adolescents' Text Processing and Reasoning," *Cognition & Instruction* 23, no. 4 (2005): 467–502.

7. Rand J. Spiro and Jihn-Chang Jehng, "Cognitive Flexibility and Hypertext: Theory and Technology for the Non-Linear and Multidimensional Traversal of Complex Subject Matter," in *Cognition, Education, and Multimedia*, ed. Don Nix and Rand Spiro (Hillsdale, NJ: Erlbaum, 1990), 163–205.

8. Douglas K. Hartmann, "Eight Readers Reading: The Intertextual Links of Proficient Readers Reading Multiple Passages," *Reading Research Quarterly* 30, no. 3 (1995): 520–571.

9. Deborah Wells Rowe, "Literacy Learning as an Intertextual Process," in *Research in Literacy: Merging Perspectives,* Thirty-sixth Yearbook of the National Reading Conference, ed. John E. Readence and R Scott Baldwin (Rochester, NY: National Reading Conference, 1987), 101–112; Michael Worton and Judith Still, *Intertextuality: Theory and Practices* (Manchester, UK: Manchester University Press, 1990).

10. Walter Kintsch, *Comprehension: A Paradigm for Cognition* (New York: Cambridge University Press, 1998); Walter Kintsch, "Meaning in Context," in *Latent Semantic Analysis*, ed. Thomas K. Landauer, Danielle S. McNamara, Simon Dennis and Walter Kintsch (Mahwah, NJ: Erlbaum, 2007), 89–105.

11. Mary Anne Britt et al., "Content Integration and Source Separation in Learning from Multiple Texts," in *Narrative Comprehension, Causality, and Coherence*, ed. Susan R. Goldman, Arthur C. Graesser, and Paulus van den Broek (Mahwah, NJ: Erlbaum, 1999), 209–233; Mary Anne Britt and Jean-François Rouet, "Learning with Multiple Documents: Component Skills and Their Acquisition," in *Enhancing the Quality of Learning: Dispositions, Instruction, and Learning Processes*, ed. John R. Kirby and Michael J. Lawson (New York: Cambridge University Press, 2012), 276–314.

12. Jean-François Rouet, *The Skills of Document Use: From Text Comprehension to Web-Based Learning* (Mahwah, NJ: Lawrence Erlbaum Associates, 2006), 68.

13. Cynthia Shanahan, Timothy Shanahan, and Cynthia Misischia, "Analysis of Expert Readers in Three Disciplines: History, Mathematics, and Chemistry," *Journal of Literacy Research* 43, no. 4 (2011): 393–429.

14. Shanahan and Shanahan, "Teaching Disciplinary Literacy to Adolescents."

15. Shanahan, Shanahan, and Misischia, "Analysis of Expert Readers."

16. Bazerman, "Physicists Reading Physics."

17. Zhihui Fang and Mary J. Schleppegrell, "Disciplinary Literacies across Content Areas: Supporting Reading through Functional Language Analysis," *Journal of Adolescent and Adult Literacy* 53, no. 7 (2010): 587–597; Mary J. Schleppegrell and Zhihui Fang, *Reading in Secondary Content Areas: A Language-Based Pedagogy* (Ann Arbor, MI: University of Michigan Press, 2008).

18. Ivar Bråten and Helge I. Strømsø, "Effects of Personal Epistemology on the Understanding of Multiple Texts," *Reading Psychology* 27, no. 5 (2006): 457–484.

19. Michael J. Jacobson and Rand J. Spiro, "Hypertext Learning Environments, Cognitive Flexibility, and the Transfer of Complex Knowledge: An Empirical Investigation," *Journal of Educational Computing Research* 12, no. 5 (1995): 301–333.

20. Irene Rukavina and Meredyth Daneman, "Integration and Its Effect on Acquiring Knowledge about Competing Scientific Theories for Text," *Journal of Educational Psychology* 88, no. 2 (1996).

21. Ivar Braten, Helge I. Strømsø, and Marit S. Samuelstuen, "Are Sophisticated Students Always Better? The Role of Topic-Specific Personal Epistemology in the Understanding of Multiple Expository Texts," *Contemporary Educational Psychology* 33, no. 4 (2008): 814–840.

22. Lev S. Vygotsky, *Thought and Language* (Cambridge: MIT Press, 1962); James V. Wertsch, *Voices of the Mind: Sociocultural Approach to Mediated Action* (Boston: Harvard University Press, 1991); James V. Wertsch, *Mind as Action* (New York: Oxford University Press, 1998).

23. Cynthia Hynd, J. Yevette McWhorter, Virginia L. Phares, and C. William Suttles, "The Role of Instructional Variables in Conceptual Change in High School Physics Topics," *Journal of Research in Science Teaching* 31, no. 9 (1994): 933–946.

24. Cynthia Hynd, Jodi Patrick Holschuh, and Betty P. Hubbard, "Thinking Like a Historian: College Students' Reading of Multiple Historical Documents," *Journal of Literacy Research* 36, no. 2 (2004): 141–176.

25. Timothy Shanahan, B. Robinson, and Mary Schneider, "Integration of Curriculum or Interaction of People?" *Reading Teacher* 47, no. 2 (1993): 158–161; Bruce VanSledright, *In Search of America's Past: Learning to Read History in Elementary School* (New York: Teachers College Press, 2002); Bruce VanSledright, "Confronting History's Interpretive Paradox While Teaching Fifth Graders to Investigate the Past," *American Educational Research Journal* 39, no. 4 (2002): 1089–1115; Wolfe and Goldman, "Adolescents' Text Processing and Reasoning."

26. Hynd, Holschuh, and Hubbard, "Thinking Like A Historian."

27. Ibid.

28. Nokes, Dole, and Hacker, "Teaching High School Students to Use Heuristics."

29. Avishag Reisman, "Reading Like a Historian: Document-Based History Curriculum Intervention in Urban High Schools," *Cognition and Instruction* 30, no. 1 (2012): 86–112.

30. Reisman, "Reading Like a Historian."

31. Ivar Braten, Helge I. Strømsø, and Ladislao Salmerón, "Trust and Mistrust When ´Students Read Multiple Information Sources about Climate Change," *Learning and Instruction* 21, no. 2 (2011): 180–192; Helge Strømsø, Ivar Bråten, and Mary Anne Britt, "Reading Multiple Texts about Climate Change," *Learning and Instruction* 20, no. 3 (2009): 1–13; Laura Gil et al., "Summary Versus Argument Tasks When Working with Multiple Documents: Which Is Better for Whom?" *Contemporary Educational Psychology* 35, no. 3 (2010): 157–173; Helge Strømsø, Ivar Bråten and Marit S. Samuelsten, "Students' Strategic Use of Multiple Sources During Expository Text Reading: A Longitudinal Think-Aloud Study," *Cognition and Instruction* 21, no. 2 (2003): 113–147.

32. Strømsø, Bråten and. Samuelsten, "Students' Strategic Use of Multiple Sources."

33. Wiley and Voss, "Constructing Arguments from Multiple Sources"; Ludovic Le Bigot and Jean-François Rouet, "The Impact of Presentation Format, Task Assignment, and Prior Knowledge on Students' Comprehension of Multiple Online Documents," *Journal of Literacy Research* 39, no. 4 (2007): 445–470.

34. Laura Gil et al., "Summary Versus Argument Tasks When Working with Multiple Documents: Which Is Better for Whom?" *Contemporary Educational Psychology* 35, no. 3 (2010): 157–173.

35. Textual Tools Study Group, "Developing Scientific Literacy Through the Use of Literacy Teaching Strategies," in *Linking Science & Literacy in the K-8 Classroom,* ed. Douglas, R., Klentschy, M., & Worth, K., (Arlington, VA: NSTA Press, 2006) 261-285.

36. Greenleaf, Hanson, Herman, Litman, Madden, Rosen, Boscardin, Schneider, and Silver, "Integrating Literacy and Science Instruction in High School Biology; Impact on Teacher Practice,

Student Engagement, and Student Achievement" (Final Report to the National Science Foundation, Grant #0440379, 2009); Moje, E. B., Sutherland, L. M., Solomon, T. C., & Van Der Kerkhof, M. H., "Integrating Literacy Instruction into Secondary School Science Inquiry: The Challenges of Disciplinary Literacy Teaching and Professional Development" (unpublished manuscript, 2010).

Chapter 11

1. *Common Core State Standards for English Language Arts and Literacy in History/Social Studies, Science, and Technical Subjects* (Washington, DC: National Governors Association Center for Best Practices and the Council of Chief State School Officers, 2010), 3.
2. Cynthia Shanahan, *Using Multiple Texts to Teach Content* (Napervile, IL: North Central Regional Educational Laboratory, 2003).
3. NGA Center and CCSSO, *Common Core State Standards*, 36.
4. International Reading Association (IRA), "Literacy Implementation Guidance for the ELA Common Core State Standards," 2012, http://www.reading.org/Libraries/association-documents/ira_ccss_guidelines.pdf.
5. Irene Fountas and Gay Su Pinnell, *Teaching for Comprehending and Fluency: Thinking, Talking, and Writing about Reading, K–8* (Portsmouth, NH: Heinemann, 2006).
6. Ibid.
7. Lucy Calkins, Mary Ehrenworth, and Christopher Lehman, *Pathways to the Common Core: Accelerating Achievement* (Portsmouth, NH: Heinemann, 2012), 71.
8. Douglas Fisher and Nancy Frey, "Motivating Boys to Read: Inquiry, Modeling, and Choice Matter," *Journal of Adolescent & Adult Literacy* 55, no. 7 (2012): 587–596; National Institute for Literacy, "What Content Area Teachers Should Know About Adolescent Literacy," 2007, http://lincs.ed.gov/publications/pdf/adolescent_literacy07.pdf; Jeffrey D. Wilhelm, *You Gotta BE the Book: Teaching Engaged and Reflective Reading with Adolescents* (New York: Teachers College Press, 1997).
9. Nancie Atwell, *In the Middle: Writing, Reading, and Learning with Adolescents* (Portsmouth, NH: Heinemann, 1998).
10. Nancie Atwell, *The Reading Zone: How to Help Kids Become Skilled, Passionate, Habitual, Critical Readers* (New York: Scholastic, 2007), 12.
11. Elizabeth Birr Moje, Melanie Overby, Nicole Tysvaer, and Karen Morris, "The Complex World of Adolescent Literacy: Myths, Motivations, and Mysteries," *Harvard Educational Review* 78, no. 1 (2008): 107–154.
12. Spinelli novels include: *Crash, Loser, Maniac Magee, Stargirl,* and *Wringer.*
13. Sarah Foleno, Katie Gribben, and Pamela Shwartz, "Wide Reading in the Disciplines," presentation at the Disciplinary Literacy Network, Cambridge Public Schools, Cambridge, MA, 2012.
14. Fountas and Pinnell, *Teaching for Comprehending and Fluency.*
15. Gina Biancarosa, and Catherine E. Snow, *Reading Next: A Vision for Action and Research in Middle and High School Literacy*, report to Carnegie Corporation of New York (Washington, DC: Alliance for Excellent Education, 2006).
16. Calkins, Ehrenworth, and Lehman, *Pathways to the Common Core*, 29.
17. NGA Center and CCSSO, *Common Core State Standards*, 47, 73.

Chapter 12

1. Personal communications with high school teachers, May 2012.
2. Vicki Jacobs, "Adolescent Literacy: Putting the Crisis in Context," *Harvard Educational Review* 78, no. 1 (2008): 7–39; Arthur N. Applebee and Judith A. Langer, "EJ Extra: What Is Hap-

pening in the Teaching of Writing?" *English Journal* 98, no. 5 (2009): 18–28; Steven Graham and Michael Hebert, "Writing to Read: A Meta-Analysis of the Impact of Writing and Writing Instruction on Reading," *Harvard Educational Review* 81, no. 4 (2011): 710–744; National Assessment of Educational Progress, *The Nation's Report Card: Writing 2011 (National Assessment of Educational Progress at Grades 8 and 12),* October 8, 2012, http://nces.ed.gov/nationsreportcard/pdf/main2011/2012470.pdf; National Commission on Writing in America's Schools and Colleges, *The Neglected "R": The Need for a Writing Revolution,* April 2003, http://www.writing commission.org/report.html;

3. The National Commission on Writing in America's Schools and Colleges, *Writing: Powerful Message from State Government,* July 2005, http://www.collegeboard.com/prod_downloads/writingcom/powerful-message-from-state.pdf. National Institute for Literacy, *What Content Area Teachers Should Know About Adolescent Literacy* (Washington, DC: National Institute for Literacy, 2007).

4. Frank O'Hare, *Sentence-Combining: Improved Student Writing Without Formal Grammar Instruction,* Research Report no. 15 (Urbana, IL: National Council of Teachers of English, 1973); Helmer R. Myklebust, *Development and Disorders of Written Language: Vol. 1. Picture Story Language Test* (New York: Grune & Stratton, 1965); Samuel Torrey Orton, *Reading, Writing, and Speech Problems in Children* (New York: Norton, 1937); Kellogg W. Hunt, *Grammatical Structures Written at Three Grade Levels,* Research Report No. 3 (Urbana, IL: National Council of Teachers of English, 1965); Walter Loban, *Language Development: Kindergarten through Grade Twelve,* Research Report No. 18 (Urbana, IL: National Council of Teachers of English, 1976).

5. James N. Britton, Tony Burgess, Nancy Martin, Alex McLeod, and Harold Rosen, *The Development of Writing Abilities (11–18)* (Basingstoke, UK: Macmillan Education, Ltd, 1975); Arthur N. Applebee, *Writing in the Secondary School: English and the Content Areas,* Research Report No. 21 (Urbana, IL: National Council of Teachers of English, 1981).

6. Donald R. Bateman and Frank J. Zidonis, *The Effect of a Study of Transformational Grammar on the Writing of Ninth and Tenth Graders,* Research Report No. 6 (Urbana, IL: National Council of Teachers of English, 1966).

7. Hunt, *Grammatical Structures.*

8. Lev S. Vygotsky, *Thought and Language* (Cambridge, MA: MIT Press, 1962), 100.

9. Janet A. Emig, *The Composing Process of Twelfth Graders,* Research Report No. 13 (Urbana, IL: National Council of Teachers of English, 1971); Donald Graves, *Balance the Basics: Let Them Write* (New York: Ford Foundation, 1978); Sondra Perl, "The Composing Processes of Unskilled College Writers," *Research in the Teaching of English* 13, no. 4 (1979): 317–336.

10. Britton et al., *The Development of Writing Abilities;* Linda Flower, "Writer-Based Prose: A Cognitive Basis for Problems in Writing," *College English* 41, no. 1 (1979): 19–37; Graves, *Balance the Basics.*

11. The notion of writer-based prose builds on Vygotsky's (*Thought and Language*) notion of inner speech and Piaget's [1974] conception of egocentric language (Jean Piaget, *The Language and Thought of the Child.* [New York: New American Library, 1974]); the purposes of writer-based prose are very similar to those of Britton et al.'s (*The Development of Writing Abilities*) "expressive mode" and Graves's (*Balance the Basics*) "reactive mode" of writing.

12. Flower, "Writer-Based Prose"; Emig, *The Composing Process of Twelfth Graders.*

13. Flower, "Writer-Based Prose."

14. Compare with earlier arguments for using journals to support both the writing process and content learning such as Macrorie (see Ken Macrorie, *Writing to Be Read* (New York: Hayden Book Co., 1968); Toby Fulwiler, "Why We Teach Writing in the First Place," in *Forum: Essays*

on Theory and Practice in the Teaching of Writing, ed. Patricia L. Stock (Upper Montclair, NJ: Boynton/Cook, 1983): 273–286.

15. Macrorie, *Writing to Be Read*; Peter Elbow, *Writing with Power* (New York: Oxford University Press, 1981); Britton et al., *The Development of Writing Abilities (11–18)*.

16. Randall R. Freisinger, "Cross-Disciplinary Writing Workshops: Theory and Practice," *College English* 42, no. 2 (1980): 154–166.

17. Emig, *The Composing Process of Twelfth Graders*, 99–100.

18. The purposes of reader-based prose are very similar to those of Britton et al.'s (*The Development of Writing Abilities*) "transactional mode" and Graves's (*Balance the Basics*) "reflective mode" of writing; see also Flower, "Writer-Based Prose."

19. Ibid.

20. Toby Fulwiler, "Why We Teach Writing in the First Place"; C. H. Knoblauch and Lil Brannon, "Writing as Learning Through the Curriculum," *College English* 45, no. 5 (1983): 465–474; Elaine Maimon, *Writing in the Arts and Sciences* (Englewood Cliffs, NJ: Winthrop/Prentice Hall, 1981).

21. Applebee, *Writing in the Secondary School*; Nancie Atwell, *In the Middle: Writing, Reading, and Learning with Adolescents* (Portsmouth, NH: Boynton/Cook and Heinemann, 1987); Peter Elbow and Pat Belanoff, *A Community of Writers: A Workshop Course in Writing* (New York: McGraw-Hill, 1989); Donald Graves, *Writing: Teachers and Children at Work* (Exeter, NH: Heinemann, 1983).

22. Graham and Hebert, "Writing to Read"

23. Adapted from P. Connolly et al., "Informal Writing: Uses and Kinds," handout, Bard Institute for Writing and Thinking, 2012.

24. Ibid., 1.

25. Bloom's taxonomy categorizes learning (from the most concrete to the most abstract) as: knowledge, understanding, application, analysis, synthesis, and evaluation (Benjamin Bloom and David R. Krathwohl, *Taxonomy of Educational Objectives: The Classification of Educational Goals, by a Committee of College and University Examiners, Handbook 1: Cognitive Domain* [New York: Longman, 1956]). A revision of Bloom's taxonomy describes learning (from the most concrete to the most abstract) as: knowledge, understanding, application, analysis, evaluation, and creation (see Lorin W. Anderson and David R. Krathwohl, eds., *A Taxonomy for Learning, Teaching and Assessing: A Revision of Bloom's Taxonomy of Educational Objectives: Complete Edition* [New York: Longman, 2001]).

26. David Perkins and Tina Blythe, "Putting Understanding Up Front," *Educational Leadership* 51, no. 5 (1994): 4–7; Vito Perrone, "Toward a Pedagogy of Understanding," in *Lessons for New Teachers* (Boston: McGraw-Hill, 2000).

27. Judith A. Langer and Arthur N. Applebee, *How Writing Shapes Thinking: A Study of Teaching and Learning*, Research Report No. 22 (Urbana, IL: National Council of Teachers of English, 1987).

28. Norman Geschwind, "Brain of a Learning Disabled Individual," *Annals of Dyslexia* 32 (1984): 13–30; Richard C. Anderson and David P. Pearson, "A Schema-Theoretic View of Basic Processes in Reading Comprehension," in *Handbook of Reading Research*, ed. David P. Pearson (New York: Longman, 1984), 255–291; David E. Rumelhart, "Schemata: The Building Blocks of Cognition," in *Theoretical Issues in Reading Comprehension*, ed. R.J. Spiro, B.C. Bruce, and W.F. Brewer (Hillsdale, NJ: Erlbaum, 1980), 38–58.

29. Vicki Jacobs, "The Landscape of Adolescent Literacy," in *Adolescent Literacy, Field Tested: Effective Solutions for Every Classroom*, ed. Sheri R. Parris, Douglas Fisher, and Kathy Headley (Newark, DE: International Reading Association, 2009), 5–20.

30. P. Connolly et al., "Informal Writing: Uses and Kinds," 2.

31. Ann E. Berthoff, "Dialectical Notebooks and the Audit of Meaning," in *The Journal Book*, ed. Toby Fulwiler (Montclair, NJ: Boynton/Cook, 1987): 11–18.

32. "Believing and Doubting," handout, Bard Institute for Writing and Thinking, 2012.

33. Graham and Hebert, "Writing to Read"; National Institute for Literacy, *What Content Area Teachers Should Know About Adolescent Literacy*.

34. Douglas Fisher, Nancy Frey, and Diane Lapp, *In a Reading State of Mind: Brain Research, Teacher Modeling, and Comprehension Instruction* (Newark, DE: International Reading Association, 2009).

35. Donna M. Ogle, "K-W-L: A Teaching Model That Develops Active Reading of Informational Text," *The Reading Teacher* 39, no. 6 (1986): 564–570.

36. Paul Allison et al., "Strategies," handout, Bard Institute for Writing and Thinking, 2009), 1.

37. George Hillocks, Jr., *Teaching Writing as Reflective Practice* (New York: Teachers College Press, 1995); Langer and Applebee, *How Writing Shapes Thinking*; The National Council of Teachers of English, *NCTE Beliefs About the Teaching of Writing* (Urbana, IL: National Council of Teachers of English, 2004), http://www.ncte.org/positions/statements/writingbeliefs.

38. The traditional teaching of grammar was negatively correlated with improvement in composition. Of those strategies that did have positive correlations with improvement in composition, all but one (the use of written models) involved students' in constructing meaning: freewriting, sentence-combining, the definition and use of scales (or rubrics), and inquiry.

39. George Hillocks, Jr., *Research on Written Composition: New Directions for Teaching* (Urbana, IL: ERIC Clearinghouse on Reading and Communication Skills and the National Conference on Research in English, 1986), 249.

40. Steven Graham and Dolores Perin, *Writing Next: Effective Strategies to Improve Writing of Adolescents in Middle and High Schools*, and Alliance for Excellent Education report to the Carnegie Corporation of New York, http://carnegie.org/publications/search-publications/pub/225/.

41. Graham and Perin, *Writing Next*, 445.

42. Robert Jones and Joseph Comprone, "Where Do We Go Next in Writing Across the Curriculum?" *College Composition and Communication* 44, no. 1 (1993): 59–68.

43. *Common Core State Standards for English Language Arts and Literacy in History/Social Studies, Science, and Technical Subjects* (Washington, DC: National Governors Association Center for Best Practices and the Council of Chief State School Officers, 2010), 41.

44. *Common Core State Standards*, 4.

45. Ibid.

46. New London Group, "A Pedagogy of Multiliteracies: Designing Social Futures," *Harvard Educational Review* 66, no. 1 (1996): 1–18; Jack R. Sublette, "The Dartmouth Conference: Its Reports and Results," *English Journal* 35, no. 3 (1973): 348–357.

47. Timothy Shanahan and Cynthia Shanahan, "Teaching Disciplinary Literacy to Adolescents: Rethinking Content-Area Literacy," *Harvard Educational Review* 78, no. 1 (2008): 40–83

48. This chapter did not address a number of issues that are central to the teaching of writing, in general (e.g., the socio-cultural contexts of writing, the role of audience, the importance of collaboration, the role of new media and technology, the habits-of-mind characteristic of specific academic disciplines, the impact of teaching diverse students who have a range of learning needs, the notion of multiple literacies, and the generalizable writing skills that might be the particular purview of English teachers).

49. Jacobs, "Putting the Crisis in Context."

Chapter 13

1. *Common Core State Standards for English Language Arts and Literacy in History/Social Studies, Science, and Technical Subjects* (Washington, DC: National Governors Association Center for Best Practices and the Council of Chief State School Officers, 2010).

2. No Child Left Behind (NCLB) Act of 2001, Pub. L. No. 107–110, 115, Stat. 1425 (2001).

3. Arthur Applebee and Judith A. Langer, "A Snapshot of Writing Instruction in Middle Schools and High Schools," *English Journal* 100, no. 6 (2011): 14–27.

4. Ibid.

5. Steve Graham and Michael A. Hebert, *Writing to Read: Evidence for How Writing Can Improve Reading*, a Carnegie Corporation Time to Act Report (Washington, DC: Alliance for Excellent Education, 2010).

6. Thomas Newkirk, *Holding on to Good Ideas in a Time of Bad Ones: Six Literacy Strategies Worth Fighting For* (Portsmouth, NH: Heinemann, 2009), 69.

7. Carol Booth Olson, *The Reading/Writing Connection: Strategies for Teaching and Learning in the Secondary Classroom*, 3rd ed. (New York: Pearson, 2011), 21.

8. Marie Filardo, "The Laws of Probability," in *Thinking/Writing: Fostering Critical Thinking through Writing*, ed. Carol Booth Olson (New York: Harper Collins, 1992), 351–365.

9. *Common Core State Standards*, 4.

10. Justin Ewers, "Rewriting the Legend of Paul Revere: Every Schoolchild Knows the Story, but Most of It Is Wrong," U.S. News and World Report. July 27, 2008, http://www.usnews.com/news/national/articles/2008/06/27/rewriting-the-legend-of-paul-revere.

11. Donna Ogle, "K-W-L: A Teaching Model that Develops Active Reading of Expository Text," *The Reading Teacher* 39, no. 6 (1986): 564–570.

12. Hal Holbrook (reader), "Paul Revere's Ride," *The Poetry of Henry Wadsworth Longfellow* (Saland Publishing, 2009).

13. Ewers, "Rewriting the Legend of Paul Revere," http://www.usnews.com/news/national/articles/2008/06/27/rewriting-the-legend-of-paul-revere.

14. Tom Romano, *Blending Genre, Blending Style: Writing Multigenre Papers* (Portsmouth, NH: Heinemann, 2000).

15. Michael Ondaatje *The Collected Works of Billy the Kid* (Harmondsworth, England/New York: Penguin Books, 1984).

16. Romano, *Blending Genre, Blending Style*, 20, 24.

17. Ibid., 45.

Chapter 14

1. Angela Breidenstein, Kevin Fahey, Carl Glickman, and Frances Hensley, *Leadership for Powerful Learning: A Guide for Instructional Leaders* (New York: Teachers College Press, 2012); Thomas R. Guskey, "Professional Development and Teacher Change," *Teachers and Teaching: Theory and Practice* 8, no. 3–4 (2002); Susan Moore Johnson, "Having It Both Ways: Building the Capacity of Individual Teachers and their Schools," *Harvard Educational Review* 82, no. 1 (2012): 107–122.

2. Breidenstein et al., *Leadership for Powerful Learning*; Nancy Fichtman Dana and Diane Yendol-Hoppey, *The Reflective Educator's Guide to Professional Development: Coaching Inquiry-Oriented Learning Communities* (Thousand Oaks, CA: Corwin Press, 2008); ReLeah Cossett Lent, "Creating a Literacy Learning Community," in *Literacy Learning Communities: A Guide for Creating Sustainable Change in Secondary Schools* (Portsmouth, NH: Heinemann, 2007), 60–80; Johnson, "Having It Both Ways."

3. Ronald A. Heifetz, *Leadership Without Easy Answers* (Cambridge, MA: Harvard University Press, 1994); Ronald A. Heifetz and Martin Linsky, *Leadership on the Line: Staying Alive Through the Dangers of Leading* (Boston: Harvard Business School Press, 2002); Ronald A. Heifetz, Alexander Grashow, and Martin Linsky, *The Practice of Adaptive Leadership: Tools and Tactics for Changing Your Organization and the World* (Boston: Harvard Business Press, 2009).

4. Heifetz, Grashow, and Linsky, *Adaptive Leadership*, 71.

5. Ibid., 71–72.

6. http://www.spellingcity.com/high-school-science-vocabulary.html or http://dynamo.dictionary.com/high-school-science-vocabulary

7. To learn more about the Frayer Model, see http://www.adlit.org/strategies/22369/.

8. Heifetz, Grashow, and Linsky, *Adaptive Leadership*, 72.

9. Gina Biancarosa and Catherine E. Snow, *Reading Next—A Vision for Action and Research in Middle and High School Literacy: A Report from Carnegie Corporation of New York* (Washington, DC: Alliance for Excellent Education, 2004), http://www.carnegie.org/fileadmin/Media/Publications/PDF/ReadingNext.pdf.

10. Heifetz, Grashow, and Linsky, *Adaptive Leadership*, 19–23.

11. Dana and Yendol-Hoppey, *The Reflective Educator's Guide*; Lent, "Creating a Literacy Learning Community"; Karen S. Louis and Sharon D. Kruse, *Professionalism and Community: Perspectives on Reforming Urban Schools* (Thousand Oaks, CA: Corwin Press, 1995); Richard DuFour, Robert Eaker, and Rebecca DuFour, *On Common Ground: The Power of Professional Learning Communities* (Bloomington: Solution Tree, 2005).

12. Richard DuFour, "What Is a 'Professional Learning Community'?" *Educational Leadership* 61, no. 8 (2004): 6–11.

13. Anthony S. Bryk, Penny Bender Sebring, Elaine Allensworth, Stuart Luppescu, and John Q. Easton, *Organizing Schools for Improvement: Lessons from Chicago* (Chicago: University of Chicago Press, 2010); Dana and Diane Yendol-Hoppey, *The Reflective Educator's Guide*; Richard F. Elmore, *School Reform from the Inside Out: Policy, Practice, and Performance* (Cambridge, MA: Harvard Education Press, 2004); Louis and Kruse, *Professionalism and Community*; Kruse, Sharon, Karen Seashore Louis, and Anthony Bryk. "Building Professional Community in Schools." *Issues in Restructuring Schools* 6 (1994): 4–5, http://www.wcer.wisc.edu/archive/cors/Issues_in_Restructuring_Schools/ISSUES_NO_6_SPRING_1994.pdf.

14. Lent, "Creating a Literacy Learning Community."

15. Michael Huberman, "Networks That Alter Teaching: Conceptualizations, Exchanges, and Experiments," *Teachers and Teaching: Theory and Practice* 1, no. 2 (1995): 193–211.

16. Jacy Ippolito and Joanna Lieberman, "Literacy Leaders: Reading Specialists and Literacy Coaches in the Secondary School," in *Best Practices of Literacy Leaders*, ed. Rita M. Bean and Allison Swan Dagen (New York: Guilford Press, 2012), 61–85.

17. Michael C. McKenna and Sharon Walpole, *The Literacy Coaching Challenge: Models and Methods for Grades K–8* (New York: Guilford Press, 2008), 1–15.

18. Jacy Ippolito, "Investigating How Literacy Coaches Understand and Balance Responsive and Directive Relationships with Teachers," in *Literacy Coaching: Research & Practice: 2009 CEDER yearbook,* ed. J. Cassidy, S. D. Garrett, and M. Sailors (Corpus Christi, TX: Center for Educational Development, Evaluation, and Research, 2010); Jacy Ippolito, "Three Ways That Literacy Coaches Balance Responsive and Directive Relationships with Teachers," *Elementary School Journal* 111, no. 1 (2010): 164–190.

19. Ippolito, "How Literacy Coaches Understand and Balance Relationships with Teachers"; Ippolito, "Three Ways that Literacy Coaches Balance Relationships with Teachers."

20. Mary Catherine Moran, *Differentiated Literacy Coaching: Scaffolding for Student and Teacher Success* (Alexandria, VA: ASCD, 2007), 13–17.

21. Elizabeth A. City, "Is Coaching the Best Use of Resources? For Some Schools, Other Investments Should Come First," *Harvard Education Letter* 23, no. 5 (2007): 8, 6–7.

22. International Reading Association (IRA), *Standards for Middle and High School Literacy Coaches*, http://www.reading.org/downloads/resources/597coaching_standards.pdf

23. To view the self-assessment, visit: http://www.literacycoachingonline.org/library/resources/self-assessmentformshsliteracycoaches.html

24. Diane C. Brown, Rebecca J. Reumann-Moore, Roseann Liu, Jolley Bruce Christmas, Morgan Riffer, Pierre L. duPlessis, and Holly Plastaras Maluk, "Making a Difference: Year Two Report of the Pennsylvania High School Coaching Initiative," http://www.researchforaction.org/publication-listing/?id=24; Marsh et al., *Supporting Literacy Across the Sunshine State: A Study of Florida Middle School Reading Coaches* (Santa Monica, CA: The RAND Corporation, 2008).

25. Lent, "Creating a Literacy Learning Community."

26. Roland S. Barth, "Improving Relationships Within the Schoolhouse," *Educational Leadership* 63, no. 6 (2006): 8–13.

27. David Allen and Tina Blythe, *The Facilitator's Book of Questions: Tools for Looking Together at Student and Teacher Work* (New York: Teachers College Press, 2004); Ippolito, "Three Ways that Literacy Coaches Balance Relationships with Teachers"; Joseph P. McDonald et al., *The Power of Protocols: An Educator's Guide to Better Practice* (New York: Teachers College Press, 2003); Peterson et al., "Reflective Coaching Conversations: A Missing Piece," *The Reading Teacher* 62, no. 6 (2009): 500–509.

28. Ippolito and Lieberman, "Literacy Leaders," 79.

29. See Project Zero's Visible Thinking Routines: http://pzweb.harvard.edu/vt

30. Jacy Ippolito and Francesca Pomerantz, "Improving Teacher Professional Development with Literacy-Focused Discussion Protocols" (unpublished manuscript).

31. For more information about Critical Friends Groups, see http://www.schoolreforminitiative.org/core-practices/.

32. http://www.nsrfharmony.org/; www.schoolreforminitiative.org; and http://www.literacycoachingonline.org/tools.html.

33. http://cals.serpmedia.org/.

34. Unless otherwise noted, protocols can be found on the School Reform Initiative's website: http://www.schoolreforminitiative.org/.

35. Guskey, "Professional Development and Teacher Change."

36. Ippolito and Lieberman, "Literacy Leaders," 63–85.

37. Ippolito, "How Literacy Coaches Understand and Balance Relationships with Teachers"; Ippolito, "Three Ways that Literacy Coaches Balance Relationships with Teachers."

Chapter 15

1. *Common Core State Standards for English Language Arts and Literacy in History/Social Studies, Science, and Technical Subjects* (Washington, DC: National Governors Association Center for Best Practices and the Council of Chief State School Officers, 2010).

2. EngageNY, "Pedagogical Shifts demanded by the Common Core State Standards." http://engageny.org/sites/default/files/resource/attachments/common-core-shifts.pdf.

3. Vicki A. Jacobs, "Adolescent Literacy: Putting the Crisis in Context." *Harvard Educational Review* 78, no. 1 (2008): 7–39.

4. New Mexico Public Education Department (NMPED), "Common Core State Standards Shifts in ELA/Literacy," http://newmexicocommoncore.org/pages/view/85/common-core-state-standards-shifts-in-elaliteracy/10/.

5. Robert Evans, *The Human Side of School Change: Reform, Resistance, and the Real-Life Problems of Innovation* (San Francisco: Jossey-Bass, 1996).

6. *Common Core State Standards*, 4.

7. Ibid., 64.

8. Ibid., 61.

9. Ibid., 62.

10. Timothy Shanahan and Cynthia Shanahan, "Teaching Disciplinary Literacy to Adolescents: Rethinking Content-Area Literacy," *Harvard Educational Review* 78, no. 1 (2008): 40–59; Doug Buehl, *Developing Readers in the Academic Disciplines* (Newark, DE: International Reading Association, 2011); Cynthia Shanahan, Timothy Shanahan, and Cynthia Misischia, "Analysis of Expert Readers in Three Disciplines: History, Mathematics, and Chemistry," *Journal of Literacy Research* 43, no. 4 (2011): 393–429.

11. *Common Core State Standards*, 8.

12. David J.Francis et al., *Practical Guidelines for the Education of English Language Learners: Research-Based Recommendations for Instruction and Academic Interventions* (Portsmouth, NH: RMC Research Corporation, Center on Instruction, 2006), http://www.centeroninstruction.org/files/ELL1-Interventions.pdf.

13. *Common Core State Standards*, 48.

14. Ibid., 48–50.

15. Ibid., 41.

16. Ibid., 8.

17. Timothy Shanahan, "Common Core Standards versus Guided Reading, Part 1," *Shanahan on Literacy* (blog), June 29, 2011, http://www.shanahanonliteracy.com/2011/06/common-core-standards-versus-guided.html; Timothy Shanahan, "More Evidence Supporting Hard Text," *Shanahan on Literacy* (blog), July 11, 2011, http://www.shanahanonliteracy.com/2011/07/more-evidence-supporting-hard-text.html; Timothy Shanahan, Douglas Fisher, and Nancy Frey, "The Challenge of Challenging Text," *Reading: The Core Skill* 69, no. 6 (2012): 58–62, http://www.ascd.org/publications/educational-leadership/mar12/vol69/num06/The-Challenge-of-Challenging-Text.aspx; Douglas Fisher, Nancy Frey, and Diane Lapp. *Text Complexity: Raising Rigor in Reading* (Newark, DE: International Reading Association, 2012).

18. International Reading Association (IRA), "Literacy Implementation Guidance for the ELA: Common Core State Standards," http://www.reading.org/Libraries/association-documents/ira_ccss_guidelines.pdf.

19. Ibid., 1.

20. *Common Core State Standards*, 57.

21. Ibid., 43–44.

22. Ibid., 39.

23. Ibid., 49.

24. Ibid., 4.

25. Ibid., 6.

Acknowledgments

This book has been a highly collaborative effort, and we would like to specifically thank some of the people who contributed greatly to its form and substance.

Thank you to:

The members of AdLit PD and Consulting, who have helped us refine our work to better support middle and high school educators. (See www.adlitpd.org.)

Our colleagues working in middle and high schools across New England and beyond who have influenced our writing, teaching, and research. Thank you particularly to Jenee Ramos of Brookline Public Schools and Todd Wallingford of Hudson Public Schools.

Dr. Kevin Fahey, professor of Adolescent Education and Leadership at Salem State Uni versity, Salem, Massachusetts.

Peter Butcavage, for his graphic design work . (See www.studioheavylead.com/graphicdesign.)

The School Reform Initiative (SRI), which creates transformational learning communities fiercely committed to educational equity and excellence. The work of SRI, including protocols and tools, has greatly shaped our thinking and is referenced across multiple chapters. (See http://schoolreforminitiative.org.)

Our colleagues and collaborators at the Massachusetts Department of Elementary and Secondary Education, especially Dorothy Earle, David Parker, and Susan Wheltle, for continued support across the many phases of this work.

Our collaborators at the Strategic Education Research Partnership, especially Suzanne Donovan, Matt Elinger, Patrick Hurley, and Juliana Pare-Blagoev. (See http://www.serpinstitute.org/.)

Special thanks to Claire White, Director, Word Generation Program.

All our collaborators who have informed or vetted this work at Boston University (Cathy O'Connor, Jeanne Paratore); Harvard Graduate School of Education (Nonie Leseaux, Pamela Mason); Boston College (Patrick Proctor); University of California, Irvine (Anny Jin Kyong Hwang, Judy Chin-Hsi Lin, Alex Lin, Judy Kuan-Ying Liu, Viet Vu, Soo-bin Yim, and all the students in EDU 346).

This work is a product that had many, many influences; too many to list completely. If there are any omissions, the fault is completely our own.

About the Editors

Jacy Ippolito is an Assistant Professor in the School of Education at Salem State University, Salem, Massachusetts. His research and teaching focus on the intersection of adolescent literacy, literacy coaching, school reform, and teacher leadership. Since completing his doctorate in education at the Harvard Graduate School of Education (HGSE), Ippolito has taught courses at Salem State and HGSE, and he continues to consult in Boston-area K–12 schools as a licensed reading specialist and literacy coach. Ippolito's writing has appeared most recently in the books *Adolescent Literacy* (2012), *Best Practices of Literacy Leaders* (2012), and *Essential Questions in Adolescent* Literacy (2009), as well as in journals and online publications such as *The Elementary School Journal* (2010), Texas A&M Corpus Christi's *CEDER Yearbook* (2010), the Literacy Coaching Clearinghouse (2009), the Massachusetts Reading Association's *Primer* (2009; 2005), the *Harvard Educational Review*'s Special Issue on Adolescent Literacy (2008), and the International Reading Association's *Standards for Middle and High School Literacy Coaches* (2006). After earning his master's degree in education from HGSE, Ippolito taught in the Cambridge Public Schools for over seven years. He also holds a bachelor's degree in English and psychology from the University of Delaware's Honors Program.

Joshua Fahey Lawrence is an Assistant Professor of Language, Literacy and Technology in the Department of Education, University of California, Irvine. His research focuses on creating and testing interventions and teaching methods to improve adolescent literacy outcomes and understanding L1 and L2 language and literacy development. Lawrence's experience as a Boston Public School teacher has motivated his interest in children's language and literacy development. After receiving his doctorate at Boston University, Lawrence completed a postdoctoral fellowship at the Harvard Graduate School of Education under the advisement of Catherine Snow. During that time, he worked on a quasi-experimental study of the Word Generation program in Boston schools. The first paper from this study demonstrated that language-minority learners benefited more from program participation than English monolinguals did (published in the *Journal of Research on Educational Effectiveness*). A follow-up study suggested differential impacts for proficient and limited-proficiency language-minority students, and that improvement from program participation was sustained a year after the end of the program (in *Bilingualism: Language and Cognition*). More recently, Lawrence has been working on a randomized trial of the Word Generation program funded by the Institute of Educational Sciences (Catherine Snow, Principal Investigator). Lawrence is a research associate with the Strategic Educational Research Partnership and committed to leveraging the results of research to build literacy knowledge and improve instruction for struggling students.

Colleen Zaller has a master's degree in applied linguistics, with a focus on adolescent literacy and language development among English language learners. Over the past four years, she was a Research and Evaluation Associate at Brown University. She has led evaluations of the written, taught, and tested curriculum for English language learners in New York and Connecticut and has conducted implementation research of adolescent literacy interventions funded under the Striving Readers program. In addition to her work in evaluation, Zaller has delivered professional development workshops on school improvement for diverse learners and instructional approaches to enhance learning for English learners. Prior to her work at Brown University, Zaller coordinated intervention services and taught English language arts and ESL to adolescents and adults in urban settings in Baltimore, Boston, and Providence and abroad in Mexico and China.

About the Contributors

Catherine D'Aoust is the Codirector of the University of California, Irvine, Writing Project, where she coordinates professional development activities and provides English language arts in-service workshops in reading and writing instruction. A former high school English teacher, D'Aoust also was the K–12 coordinator of English language arts in Mission Viejo, California, for twenty-five years. She is a contributing author to *Practical Ideas for Teaching Writing*, *Portfolios in the Writing Classroom: An Introduction*, *Thinking Writing*, and most recently the What Works Clearinghouse publication *Teaching Elementary School Students to Be Effective Writers*.

Christina L. Dobbs is a clinical assistant professor of English Education at Boston University, where she teaches courses in adolescent literacy and works in training new teachers. Her research interests include academic language development, the argumentative writing of students, and writing instruction. She has served as an adjunct instructor at the Harvard Graduate School of Education, Lesley University, Simmons College, and Salem State University and as a consultant for several New England school districts focused on improving adolescent literacy instruction. Dobbs served as the manuscripts editor for the *Harvard Educational Review* and edited a volume titled *Humanizing Education: Critical Alternatives to Reform*. She is a former high school teacher, literacy coach, and reading specialist.

Abigail Erdmann has been a teacher of English since 1973 in Brookline, Massachusetts, primarily in School-Within-a-School (SWS), Brookline High School's democratic alternative school. She has written articles for *Education Weekly*, the *Harvard Educational Review*, and the *Smith Alumnae Quarterly*. In 2011, she was awarded the Olmsted Prize from Williams College for excellence in high school teaching. Funds from the award enabled her to establish Race Reels, a documentary series about race and racism. Erdmann has developed over thirty English courses, most recently a course called Identity, Race and Literature, which seeks to teach students concepts and ways of speaking to each other that will improve hard conversations about race.

Evelyn Ford-Connors is a lecturer at the Boston University School of Education, where she teaches courses in literacy development, instruction, and assessment. She is also the Associate Director of the Donald D. Durrell Reading & Writing Clinic. Her primary research interests focus on the literacy needs of struggling readers and writers, with particular attention to adolescent learners. Ford-Connors has created a literacy-based after-school intervention for high school students and is currently studying teachers' instructional talk. She also works with classroom teachers in the study and improvement of instructional practices that promote students' literacy growth.

Emily Phillips Galloway is currently pursuing doctoral studies in the Language and Literacy concentration at the Harvard Graduate School of Education. Before beginning her doctoral studies, she was a Michael Pressley Memorial Fellow at the Benchmark School in Media, Pennsylvania, where she taught adolescent struggling readers in grades 6, 7, and 8. While at Benchmark under the direction of Dr. Irene Gaskins, Galloway conducted research in the area of academic language development and on the impact of learner differences on adolescent reading development. Currently, she supports teachers seeking reading specialist licensure to develop pedagogies that foster students' literacy growth and conducts research in the area of academic language proficiency assessment.

Vicki A. Jacobs is a lecturer on education, Director of the Field Experience Program, and Director of Fieldwork for the Teacher Education Program at the Harvard Graduate School of Education where she has taught courses on adolescent literacy, literacy and learning, curriculum development, and the teaching of English. Her published works focus on adolescent literacy development and instruction and on teacher education. Jacobs is Senior Series Consultant for *Vocabulary Workshop* (William H. Sadlier, Inc., 2012). She is also an associate of the Bard College Institute for Writing and Thinking and has served as a member of the National Faculty, President of the Massachusetts Association of College and University Reading Educators, President of the Massachusetts Association of Teacher Education, and member of the executive board of the Massachusetts Reading Association.

Joanna Lieberman is a district literacy coach for the Cambridge Public Schools in Cambridge, Massachusetts. Her primary professional interests and expertise focus on adolescent literacy and literacy coaching. Her most recent publication includes a coauthored book chapter titled "Reading Specialists and Literacy Coaches in Secondary Schools." She has worked as a teacher, literacy specialist, and literacy consultant in New York City, Westchester County (New York), and Massachusetts. Lieberman completed her master's degree in education at the Harvard Graduate School of Education.

Janet Looney is a literacy consultant in Massachusetts, following her thirty-five-year career in the Cambridge Public Schools as a reading specialist, elementary classroom teacher, and middle school English language arts and social studies teacher, literacy coach, and literacy coordinator. She holds a master's degree in reading, and her interests and expertise focus on adolescent literacy.

Bridget Maher is currently a middle and high school history and English teacher at an independent school in Ann Arbor, Michigan. She has served on various curriculum development teams at the school. Prior to teaching, Maher earned her master's degree in Language and Literacy at the Harvard Graduate School of Education. During her undergraduate work at the University of Michigan, she triple-majored in history, English, and social studies. The experience of multiple content-area instruction has informed her philosophy of classroom instruction and cross-content-area literacy. Currently, Maher and her fellow seventh-grade teaching colleagues are publishing a paper focusing on cross-content area literacy instruction using a debate model for analytical writing structures across science, English, history, and public speaking.

Lisa Messina is a district literacy/instructional coach for the Cambridge Public Schools, in Cambridge, Massachusetts. In this role, she is responsible for professional development for school-based literacy coaches and ELA/humanities teachers, training staff in the use of one-on-one developmental reading assessment and district writing assessments, collecting and monitoring student data, assisting school-based literacy teams with the implementation of the school-wide literacy program, and working with administrators concerning curriculum, instruction and interventions for struggling readers. Messina spent the first eleven years of her career teaching English and reading at a diverse, urban high school in California, where she also served as English Department Chair and Title I Coordinator/Professional Developer for seven years. Messina earned her reading specialist certification and EdM in Language and Literacy from Harvard University in 2007.

Margaret Metzger is an educational consultant in Massachusetts. She devoted over thirty years as an English teacher at Brookline High School in Brookline, Massachusetts. She was the codirector of a mentoring program called Teachers Mentoring Teachers. Metzger has written articles for the *English Journal, Phi Delta Kappan, Harvard Educational Review, Teacher Magazine,* and others. Two of her most recent articles include "Teaching How Language Reveals Character" (2007) and "Learning to Discipline" (2002). She also has taught courses in the graduate education programs at Simmons College, the Harvard Graduate School of Education, and Brown University. In 2005 she won the Caverly Award for most outstanding teacher at Brookline High School.

Catherine J. Michener is an advanced doctoral candidate in Curriculum and Instruction at Boston College. Her research interests include second language and literacy development, literacy instruction, language policy, and institutional supports for immigrant students in multicultural and multilingual schooling contexts. Her dissertation is an analysis of the features of classroom discussion that relate to student reading and vocabulary achievement. Michener is a former middle and high school bilingual and sheltered instruction teacher in Massachusetts. She has taught courses in second language acquisition and pedagogy to pre- and in-service teachers as adjunct faculty at Salem State University, Boston College, and the University of California, Irvine.

Elizabeth Birr Moje is Associate Dean for Research and an Arthur F. Thurnau Professor in the School of Education at the University of Michigan, Ann Arbor, Michigan. She also serves as a Faculty Associate in the University's Institute for Social Research, and a Faculty Affiliate in Latino/a Studies. Moje teaches undergraduate and graduate courses in secondary and adolescent literacy, literacy and cultural theory, and qualitative and mixed research methods. Her research interests revolve around the intersection between the literacies and texts youth are asked to learn in the disciplines (particularly in science and social studies) and the literacies and texts they experience outside of school. In addition, Moje studies how youth make culture and enact identities from their home and community literacies, and from ethnic cultures, popular cultures, and school cultures. These research interests stem from the start of her career, when she taught history, biology, and drama at high schools in Colorado and Michigan. Her current research focuses on communities and schools in Detroit. Moje has authored or edited four books and numerous book chapters, as well as articles in journals such as the *Harvard Educational Review, Review of Research in Education, Reading Research Quarterly, Teachers College Record, Journal of Literacy Research, Journal of Adolescent & Adult Literacy, Research in the Teaching of English, Urban Review, Journal of Research in Science Teaching,* and *Science Education.*

Diana Mullins is a doctoral student in Language, Literacy, and Technology at the University of California, Irvine. She has been a part of the Maine Learning Technology Initiative since 2001 as a teacher and coach. The public schools in Maine provide one-to-one computing for all middle school students and teachers, so technology integration has informed all aspects of her teaching and learning. Mullins specializes in interdisciplinary learning and reading/writing workshops, and she has enjoyed coaching middle level students in the performing arts. She attended Lesley University, where she earned a master's degree in Curriculum and Instruction: Literacy, Reading, and Writing. In addition to being a classroom teacher, Mullins has also been a literacy coach and a reading specialist in grades 6 through 8. She has developed and directed teacher in-service professional development, most recently in collaboration with Southern Maine Writing Project Fellows. She has worked with many teachers to create curriculum and assessments for reading and writing classes in secondary classrooms.

Carol Booth Olson is the Director of the UCI/National Writing Project and associate professor in the Department of Education at the University of California, Irvine. She received her PhD in American Literature from UCLA in 1977 and was honored as Outstanding Graduate Woman of the Year. Olson has edited three books: *Practical Ideas for Teaching Writing as Process* (1997), the best-selling publication of the California Department of Education (1986; 1987); *Thinking/Writing: Fostering Critical Thinking Through Writing* (Harper Collins, 1992); and *Reading, Thinking, and Writing About Multicultural Literature* (Scott Foresman Publishers, 1996). In addition, her single-author text, *The Reading/Writing Connection*, is now in its third edition (Allyn & Bacon/Pearson, 2007). Olson has also published over thirty journal articles on interactive strategies for teaching writing, fostering critical thinking through writing, applying multiple intelligences theory to language arts instruction, using multicultural literature with students of culturally diverse backgrounds, and other subjects.

Cynthia Shanahan is a professor in the Department of Curriculum and Instruction at the College of Education, University of Illinois at Chicago, Associate Dean for Academic Affairs, and Executive Director of the college's Council on Teacher Education. Her primary research focus is adolescent literacy, especially in the areas of disciplinary literacy, conceptual change, and the reading of multiple texts. As the Principal Investigator in a National Reading Research Center study, Shanahan examined the use of texts in learning science and history, culminating in her book, *Learning from Text across Conceptual Domains* (1998). Through a grant from the Carnegie Foundation, she and her colleagues extended this work to examine the reading processes of historians, chemists, and mathematicians. She has taught literacy to underprepared college students for more than twenty years.

Catherine E. Snow is the Patricia Albjerg Graham Professor of Education at the Harvard Graduate School of Education. Catherine is an expert on language and literacy development in children, focusing on how oral language skills are acquired and how they relate to literacy outcomes. Snow has chaired two national panels: the National Academy of Sciences committee that prepared the report *Preventing Reading Difficulties in Young Children*, and the RAND Reading Study Group that prepared *Reading for Understanding: Toward an R&D Program in Reading Comprehension*. She is currently co-Prinicipal Investigator of an *Institute of Education Sciences*–Funded Reading for Understanding study of the determinants of reading comprehension in grades 4 through 8. The study, called *Catalyzing Comprehension Through Discussion and Debate*, is testing the effectiveness of classroom interventions that focus on supporting student participation in discussion through the presentation of engaging moral and civic dilemmas and accessible curricular materials.

Mark Warschauer is a professor in the Department of Education and the Department of Informatics at the University of California, Irvine, Director of UCI's PhD in Education program, and founding Director of UCI's Digital Learning Lab. He has previously taught and conducted research at the University of California, Berkeley; the University of Hawaii; Moscow Linguistics University; and Charles University in Prague. Warschauer's research focuses on the integration of information and communication technologies (ICT) in schools and community centers; the impact of ICT on language and literacy practices; and the relationship of ICT to institutional reform, democracy, and social development. His most recent book, *Learning in the Cloud: How (and Why) to Transform Schools with Digital Media*, was published by Teachers College Press in 2011. His previous books have focused on the development of new electronic literacies among culturally and linguistically diverse students; on technology, equity, and social inclusion; and on the role of ICT in second language learning and teaching. He is now engaged in research projects on the use of digital media for reading and writing.

Binbin Zheng is a PhD candidate in the School of Education at the University of California, Irvine, specializing in Language, Literacy, and Technology. Her research interests focus on educational evaluations and technology-supported new literacy studies.

Ann Mechem Ziergiebel is a visiting instructor in the Adolescent Education and Leadership Department at Salem State University, Salem, Massachusetts. She is pursuing her doctorate in Educational Studies at Lesley University, Cambridge, Massachusetts, focusing on equity of voice across academic disciplines. Ziergiebel devoted twenty-three years to teaching middle school social studies and humanities in the Gloucester Public Schools, Gloucester, Massachusetts.

Index

academic achievement
classroom discourse and, 87
knowledge building and, 100
lackluster, 5
at secondary level, 2
test results, 2, 6
academic discussion. *See* discussion(s)
academic texts. *See* disciplinary texts
academic vocabulary, 21, 63–69, 239
accessibility, 164–168
accountability, 1
adaptive dilemmas, 216–219, 221–222, 229–231
Adlit.org, 247
adolescent literacy
"crisis" of, 6, 181
increased attention to, 2
research on, 1–3
Adolescents' Engagement in Academic Literacy, 247
American Dream, 137–140
apprenticeship model, 39–41
Aristotle, 13
attitudinal writing, 188
audience, for writing, 127
authentic questions, 90–91
automate writing evaluation (AWE) programs, 126
autonomous learning, 123–125

backward design, 133
balanced literacy approach, 2
basic literacy, 7
big ideas, 133–134, 138
book groups, 171

Carnegie Corporation, 2
Center for Applied Linguistics, 247–248
Center for Research on Education, Diversity, and Excellence (CREDE), 248
Center on Instruction, 248
change, adaptive vs. technical, 216–219, 229–231
claims, 156

classroom discussion. *See* discussion(s)
ClipRead, 123, 124
close reading, 30, 34, 156, 243
coaching models, 223–224
See also literacy coaches
code-breaking skills, 20
cognition, 183
cognitive coaching, 223–224
cognitive flexibility theory, 147
cognitive psychology, 150
collaborative learning, 41
collaborative reasoning (CR), 101
collaborative resource management, 224–225
collaborative writing, 125
collective efficacy, 11
¡Colorín Colorado!, 248
Common Core State Standards
adoption of, 235
for comprehension, 139, 174
for digital literacy, 242
disciplinary literacy and, 14, 38, 44, 45, 131, 141, 238–239
for discussion, 90, 240–241
goals of, 237–238
historical context for, 1–2
implementation of, 100, 245–246
for literary nonfiction, 174–175
meeting challenge of, 235–249
multiple texts and, 145–146, 148–149, 163, 165, 176, 237–238, 243–244
student engagement and, 172
for vocabulary, 239–240
for writing, 193–194, 197, 204, 244–245
communication technology, 117–118
See also digital literacy
communities of practice, 40–41
comparisons, 146
complex texts, 165, 243
composition, 192
comprehension. *See* reading comprehension
concept-oriented reading instruction (CORI), 101